SEX WORKERS UNITE

SEX
A History of the Movement
WORKERS
from Stonewall to SlutWalk
UNITE

Melinda Chateauvert

Beacon Press
Boston

BEACON PRESS
Boston, Massachusetts
www.beacon.org

Beacon Press books
are published under the auspices of
the Unitarian Universalist Association of Congregations.

16 15 14 13   8 7 6 5 4 3 2 1

This book is printed on acid-free paper that meets the uncoated paper
ANSI/NISO specifications for permanence as revised in 1992.

Text design and composition by Kim Arney
Illustrations by Gabi Anderson

Library of Congress Cataloging-in-Publication Data
Chateauvert, Melinda.
Sex workers unite : a history of the movement from Stonewall
to SlutWalk / Melinda Chateauvert.
pages   cm
Includes bibliographical references and index.
ISBN 978-0-8070-6139-8 (cloth) — ISBN 978-0-8070-6140-4 (ebook)
1. Prostitutes—Political activity—United States. 2. Prostitutes—Civil rights—United
States. 3. Prostitutes—Labor unions—United States. 4. Sex-oriented businesses—
Law and legislation—United States. 5. Prostitution—United States.
6. Social justice—United States. I. Title.

HQ144.C46 2013
306.740973—dc23   2013023148

Author's note: The illustrations preceding each chapter are recreations of buttons,
stickers, and promotional materials for sex-worker campaigns and advocacy groups.
Spanning five decades, they express some of the demands made by activists and their
allies for sexual freedom, health justice, workers' rights, and the end of whore stigma,
and capture the vibrant political and cultural history of the sex workers' movement.

For
Gail, Gayle, Sandy, Maluda, Sunny, Linda, Chris,
Anna, Dawn, Chrissy, Colette, Candy, Jeri, Kathy,
the girls of "GirlsGirlsGirls"

Don't stop fighting, don't stop living, and
goddammit, don't stop having fun.
—MARGO ST. JAMES

CONTENTS

INTRODUCTION

SEX WORKERS ARE FIGHTERS. They aren't young girls begging in a freezing Dickensian fog; they aren't "Pretty Women" looking for Prince Charming; they aren't victimized teenage runaways exploited by savage (read: black) pimps; they don't have golden hearts; and they aren't crack hos neglecting their babies to find a fix. They aren't American or Jamaican gigolos looking to fleece middle-aged women or gay hustlers cruising for sugar daddies. And some sex workers may look like these stereotypes, yet they are fighters too.

Sex workers have been fighting for their right to work, for respect and justice, for a very long time. It would be extraordinary if members of the oldest profession had never complained, had never organized, or had never fought back. They have a lot to fight. Many wonder, "Why do they hate us?" Reverend Howard Moody of New York's Judson Memorial Church heard a Times Square streetwalker complain about her confrontation with a passerby in the 1970s:

> We ain't doin' nothin' to them. Yesterday I'm just standin' on the corner, not doin' nothin,' and this bitch come by and says, "Get

"Be Nice to Sex Workers": Button, designed by Melinda Chateauvert for HIPS (Helping Individual Prostitutes Survive), Washington, DC, based on their t-shirt.

off the street, you dirty slut." If she hadn't been so fast I'd have kicked her ass. I wasn't hurtin' her. Where does she get off, callin' me names? You mean she ain't never fucked for favors? We just tryin' to make a livin' like everybody else.[1]

Moral judgments about prostitutes embolden people to throw stones and insults. Politicians pander to the "women's vote" by introducing legislation to punish sex workers and everyone near them. Police target street-based sex workers to show they're "cleaning up" the city; FBI and immigration officials arrest female sex workers as trafficked, and claim their associates held them in sexual slavery. In the face of such disempowerment, it's no wonder that sex workers fight. Their survival depends on it.

Sex workers must fight for their lives. Serial murderers and rapists target prostitutes, and police compound the violence with sloppy or scant investigations of their deaths. In 2001, Gary Leon Ridgway admitted to killing forty-nine street-based workers in the Green River area of Seattle because he knew they were vulnerable. For twenty years, police did not pay attention as his victims disappeared. Ridgway is only one of some five hundred serial murderers convicted since 1970 who have preyed on female sex workers and women perceived to be sex workers; more than three thousand women have died in the last four decades.

This pattern of violence, combined with police neglect, is why sex workers lobbied the US government for years to acknowledge that these crimes are human rights violations. In 2011, the Department of Justice acknowledged the pattern of crimes committed against "persons in prostitution," but has been slow to provide law enforcement officials with best practice guidelines for handling victims in the sex trades with respect.[2]

Sex workers are laborers who earn money to perform sexual services or who provide erotic entertainment to clients individually or collectively. Their participation in the sex industry may be the result of choice, circumstance, or coercion. Carol Leigh—the Scarlot Harlot—coined the gender-neutral term "sex work" in 1978 to describe the many diverse occupations of the sex industry. Sex workers are escorts, exotic dancers, porn stars, peep-show workers, professional dominants, rent boys, phone-sex operators, strippers, webcam performers, erotic priestesses, prostitutes, and providers of a vast array of niche adult services. Additionally, the sex sector employs tens of thousands of service workers—security personnel, film and technical crews, and behind-the-scenes workers—who are not sex workers.[3]

Reliable statistics on the number of people working in the sex industry at any given time are difficult to calculate because of the illegality of some occupations and the stigma associated with even legal forms of sex work. Most calculations are based on arrests, skewing estimates toward street-based populations, but failing to capture sex workers arrested on charges other than prostitution. In 1990, health researchers estimated that one in one hundred US women had done some form of sex work during her lifetime. Perhaps the public education campaign of St. James Infirmary says it best: "Someone you know is a sex worker."[4]

Many occupations in the US sex industry are legal, and the duties, skills, and responsibilities required to perform these jobs are described in international trade agreements and the *Occupational Outlook Handbook*, a federal guidebook for job seekers. Employment in legal commercial sex businesses, including the pornography industry, may account for half of all sex workers today. In California, there are over five hundred "escort" companies providing "all other personal services" in the state's Economic Development Department database. Because many are escorts and exotic dancers by choice and may have college degrees and possess other forms of human capital and privilege, many consider these workers the most empowered. Nonetheless, they too have reason to fear harassment and discrimination because of the work they do.[5]

Escorts are paid for spending time with clients as "dates," as "girlfriends" or "boyfriends," not for sexual services per se. Out of public view, independent sex workers are less likely to be arrested, in part because they tend to heavily screen prospective customers. The occasional newspaper headline about a high-profile bust, whether of New York Governor Elliot Spitzer or Deborah Jean Palfrey, "The DC Madam," does more to restore the reputation of a scandal-rife police department than to shut down the escort industry. When public pressure to do something about crime mounts, police sweep up street-based workers. Neighborhood residents take false comfort in the belief that empty sidewalks discourage crime.[6]

Some people engage in transactional sex casually or temporarily to supplement low-wage work, to cover extraordinary or emergency expenses, or to survive until the next meager social security check or food stamps arrive. "Girls do what they have to do to survive," as do homeless boys, undocumented immigrants, transgender people of color, and other marginalized and social undesirables. They hustle, using sex—the one form of labor capital they possess—to obtain food, shelter, clothing, medicine, physical protection, and other necessities. Such trades are survival strategies for a population shut out of other forms of work, in a nation that does not affirm a human right to shelter, food, or health care.[7]

Sex workers are fierce fighters because their jobs demand perspicacity, persistence, and a kind of emotional ruthlessness in order to succeed. These skills have also made them canny political activists, contrary to the stereotype of disempowered victims in need of moral rescue. *Sex Workers Unite!* tells stories about sex workers who have fought for dignity and human rights from the 1960s to today, documenting a global movement for self-determination that is as multifaceted as the sex industry and as diverse as human sexuality.

"No bad women, just bad laws" captures the movement's long-standing demand to abolish laws criminalizing erotic services and sexual labor. There are dozens of reasons for decriminalization, and sex workers don't all agree whether other laws prohibiting street solicitation, pandering, pimping, brothel-keeping, and moving across state borders should be repealed. Yet, based on the experiences of sex workers in other countries, US activists are skeptical that government regulation of the industry will enhance their rights as workers or as citizens.[8]

"Decriminalization is the beginning of the solution, it's not the solution itself," argued Robyn Few, founder of the Sex Workers Organizing Project-USA (SWOP-USA). Contemporary activists believe that criminalizing sex work and related activities perpetuates structural and interpersonal violence, and thus endangers the lives and limits the choices of people in the sex trades.[9]

Movement activists generally do not support legalization that allows state oversight and licensing of sex workers. Regulation, they believe, would not benefit workers and could harshly punish those who refused to be "pimped" by the state. Historically, official supervision has imposed mandatory health inspections on workers (but not clients) and usually designated prostitution zones controlled by the police.

Registration as a prostitute becomes a public record, limiting the ability of sex workers to seek other forms of work when they want to leave the commercial sex industry.[10]

Contemporary "deregulation" in the commercial sex industry has led to too little oversight, some say, pointing out that owners don't comply with labor laws and health and safety regulations while workers are diligently policed. Activists think sex businesses should be regulated by the same government agencies that oversee non-sex businesses. If special rules are needed, then sex workers should participate in writing and enforcing them because, Carol Leigh suggests, self-regulation promotes human rights and political empowerment.[11]

The time has come to talk about sex work. The issues are critical and contemporary. The United States is one of the few industrialized nations to criminalize prostitution. Sex work is legal in fifty nations, including Canada, Mexico, Brazil, Macau, the Netherlands, Austria, New Zealand, Israel, Germany, France, and England; it is legal with limitations in another eleven nations, including Australia, India, Norway, Japan, and Spain. In 1949, the United States voted against a United Nations convention calling for the decriminalization of prostitution; forty-eight countries endorsed it.[12]

The uneven enforcement of prostitution laws across the United States, even within municipal boundaries, is the result of political pressure and police whims. This variation results in a suspect pattern of selective enforcement punishing women and transwomen of color on the street more than any other group. To activists and advocates, racism is blatantly apparent in the arrest and sentencing statistics. The disparate racial impact of prostitution laws on people of color, especially those who are gender-nonconforming, is one rationale for decriminalization.[13]

The growth of the multibillion-dollar international commercial sex industry has altered the meaning of decriminalization, particularly since many activists have legal jobs in the industry or pursue careers outside it. Although providing intimate, erotic *services* is a crime in most states and territories, it is not a crime to offer erotic *entertainment*, as long as community decency standards are observed. Working in the pornography industry, sex chat rooms, peep shows; serving beer at Hooters; and doing other sex work for commercial establishments (brick and mortar as well as virtual) are perfectly legitimate.

This form of legalization has not eliminated discrimination. Though legal commercial sex workers pay income taxes, state officials often dismiss complaints about labor, civil, and human rights violations. Lackadaisical enforcement shows that neither decriminalization nor legalization will bring rainbows and unicorns. People in the sex trades will continue to confront stigmas and public policies that penalize their work choices, their personal freedoms, and even their families, lovers, and friends.

Sex workers want to stop trafficking and end sexual coercion too, and they have assisted people trapped by criminals into unlawful labor contracts in the sex industry. Trafficking, they agree, is a human rights concern that exemplifies the ills of neoliberal globalization and anti-immigration policies. Trafficking occurs when labor contractors or smugglers exploit the undocumented immigrant's status: refusing to return a passport, forcing them to work without pay, threatening to report their "illegal" status to authorities. Coerced and undocumented workers labor in every low-wage industry in the United States, and are far more numerous in agriculture, food processing, and food service sectors than the sex industry. Though international conventions already prohibit forced labor, the United States categorizes trafficked sex workers as special victims, subjecting them to interrogation before (perhaps) issuing special-category visas. Lawyers with the Sex Workers Project of the Urban Justice Center (SWP), one of the first US programs to assist survivors of human trafficking, believe that decriminalizing prostitution would allow immigrants to more easily seek protection from criminals who have abused them.

"Stop shaming us to death!" sex workers chant. Activists believe decriminalizing prostitution would empower workers to organize on their terms. Sex workers want respect and human rights, the basic necessities for democratic participation. Activists want a voice in the political process; they believe that engaging in sexual commerce should not be grounds for disenfranchisement. Rescue, rehabilitation, and prostitution diversion programs reinforce stigma and victimization.

Around the world, sex workers have organized Red Umbrella campaigns to resist violence and discrimination, and to symbolize their collective strength. Activists want the human rights expressed in the landmark Declaration of the Rights of Sex Workers adopted in Brussels in 2005. Human rights for sex workers means recognizing them as people

fully capable of making decisions about their lives, to move freely in cities and to migrate to other nations, to defend themselves against violence
and threats to their health, to enjoy the respect of fellow citizens and the
public servants who are supposed to protect them. They want access to
public resources and meaningful participation in the body politic. Criminalization is a human rights issue because it disregards the fundamental
principles of self-determination, bodily integrity, and sexual freedom.[14]

This history of the sex workers' movement is a collection of stories
about activists and their allies who confronted moralistic politicians,
paternalistic feminists, and fraternizing business owners who sought to
make their careers and pimp their livelihoods off workers in the sex industry. People have fought back in many different ways, as this book at-
tests. Their stories are varied in time, intent, and locale; and the people in
them relied on different tactics, strategies, and goals. Some talked to me
about politics wearing hooker heels; other activists preferred their bunny
slippers or Doc Martens. In some stories, sex workers win, sometimes
they lose, and sometimes they just discover new movement allies.

Readers who are sex workers or activists—or both—may find the
stories here will help them become better activists. For readers who are
neither, I hope these stories lay to rest the old, tired stereotypes about
prostitutes, and recognize sex workers' long fight for rights, respect,
and justice.

CHAPTER 1

"THE REVOLUTION IS FINALLY HERE!"

Sex Work and Strategic Sex

"MY GOD, THE REVOLUTION IS HERE. The revolution is finally here!" Sylvia Rivera remembers thinking when she and other transgender sex workers and gay hustlers fought back against yet another rousting by the Morals Squad at New York City's Stonewall Inn in June 1969. Three years earlier, at Compton's Cafeteria in San Francisco's Tenderloin, where transgender sex workers and their friends gathered at the end of night, another routine arrest had led to a riotous confrontation with the police.[1]

Since the end of prohibition, vice squads all over the United States had raided bars and afterhours clubs rousting prostitutes, "B-girls," "notorious queers," "flagrant homosexuals," "screaming queens," and other "sex deviates" who patronized public establishments. The 1960s riots at Compton's Cafeteria and the Stonewall Inn mark the forgotten and fiery beginnings of the contemporary sex workers' movement.[2]

The routine rousting in San Francisco's Tenderloin in 1966 might have been just that, until the street queen under arrest threw a cup of coffee in the patrolman's face. Then the patrons at Compton's erupted.

"Sex Work Is Real Work": Button, designed by Carol Leigh, from the Whore Store.

Chairs flew, plates were thrown, and purses and high-heeled pumps pummeled the cops. The protest was over quickly and largely forgotten until transgender historian and activist Susan Stryker rediscovered the story in the late 1990s. The film *Screaming Queens: The Riot at Compton's Cafeteria* documents the presence and leadership of sex workers in that protest and also illustrates the intertwining of activism and identity, civil rights consciousness, and gendered respectability.[3]

The intransigent stigma of prostitution colors remembrances of those times. Rioter Felicia Elizondo felt the stigma of turning tricks, while Amanda St. Jaymes and Tamara Ching found a new sense of dignity after this riotous claim for civil rights. They also acted from a new sense of legitimacy. *The Transsexual Phenomenon*, published in 1966 by Kinsey Institute sexologist Harry Benjamin, gave a scientific identity to their outcast group, Ching recalled.[4]

Benjamin's book was a lifeline, yet its message was contextualized through contemporary civil rights activism and equal opportunity programs that offered a route to respectable work. Elizondo, St. Jaymes, and Ching situated their rights claims in their identity as transsexuals, and protested against the discrimination they faced as "he-shes" from the police, potential employers, landlords, and even the proprietors of Compton's. Hustling was a way to make a living, but they wanted real jobs, a decent place to live, and the freedom to congregate unmolested with their friends and lovers in a late-night cafeteria in the Tenderloin. They wanted to leave the streets, not decriminalize prostitution.[5]

The story of one June night in 1969 in Greenwich Village doesn't often mention how the outlaws and outcasts who patronized the Stonewall Inn made their living. Instead, the mainstream LGBT rights movement prefers a "politically correct" version that celebrates the defiance of "gays" and "lesbians" without mentioning that these queers were also sex workers, transgender people, hustlers, tricks, drug users, and drug sellers.[6]

Even more suppressed is the identity of eighteen-year-old Sylvia Ray Rivera and her transgender comrade and fellow sex worker, Marsha P. ("Pay it no mind!") Johnson, who took out their anger during the Stonewall riots. Rivera recalled, "I wanted to do every destructive thing I could think of to get back at those who had hurt us over the years. Letting loose, fighting back, was the only way to get across to straight society and the cops that we weren't going to take their fucking bullshit any more."[7]

Rivera's anger has often been reimagined by other storytellers. She was a "Queer Rican," a transgender heroine, a survivor of streets since the age of eleven, a homeless youth activist. In each of these constructions, her life and her work and her anger have been rendered in ways that are meaningful for a particular politicized identity. Her name is invoked to raise identity consciousness and to create specific versions of an origin myth for modern gay rights history.[8]

Only when Rivera tells her story do we realize that she often supported herself as a sex worker. She never hid her work life or her drug addiction. In 1970, Rivera asked Johnson to join Street Transvestite Action Revolutionaries (STAR), "a very revolutionary group." STAR offered a nightly refuge for adolescent street queens. Rivera, Johnson, and the adults hustled to keep it going. The project was a pioneering effort providing nonjudgmental welcome space for homeless transgender youth.[9] Despite her persistent activism, by 1973, Rivera had to fight to speak at the gay pride rally celebrating Stonewall because the crowd didn't want to hear from a transgender sex worker.[10]

Gay liberation groups were reluctant to support people like Rivera or to accept sex workers and transgender people in the movement. When sex work is mentioned, it is a source of shame that has been overcome, freeing queers (especially transwomen) from denigration. The movement's emphasis on sexual respectability is a form of *whorephobia*, which stigmatizes those who trade sex for money or support; it is a type of sex panic that reflects the deep-seated belief that identity politics and civil rights requires weeding out members for gender nonconformity, sexual deviancy, and drug dependency. Heroes must be noble and virtuous, worthy of acceptance by straight America. But LGBT and queer history *should* include sex workers because many sex-worker activists are queer and some queer activists support themselves through sex work.[11]

The Compton's and Stonewall riots reveal the complexities of documenting the history of sex-worker activism, the construction of identity, the concerns that motivated participants, and the ideologies that leaders drew on to articulate the movement's demands. The claim that sex workers led the riots complicates ideas about identity, rights, work, and freedom. Citizenship matters shaped the agendas of gay rights and women's groups in the 1960s and 1970s, obliging leaders to represent their members as "normal." The process led to shunning sex workers, gender nonconformists, and other "deviants," unless they could be rescued and reformed into useful members of society.[12]

The sex-workers' movement thus serves as a counter-narrative to identity-rights movements that drew their ideology from liberalism and middle-class respectability. The movements of the 1960s and 1970s did not distinguish between biological sex and gender roles, seeing these human characteristics as "natural" rather than cultural constructions. Gender propriety and sexual morality, tightly bound into racialist beliefs, were crucial in the African American civil rights movement. Those whose private lives weren't "normal" or "straight" stayed closeted to preserve the reputation of the movement. Only the wildest rebels and the most privileged class risked "outing" themselves as nonconformists; deviant sexuality, adultery, contraception, and prostitution destabilized the family, the foundation of civil society. "Dangerous radicals" were purged from the ranks of these movements, sometimes with pressure from the FBI. Only prostitutes, hustlers, and homosexuals who vowed to leave the streets (and promiscuous sex) behind could participate.[13]

Respectability, not flamboyance, is the central theme of the recent focus on marriage equality, full military service, and an end to employment discrimination against gay men and lesbians. The long exclusion of transgender people from the proposed federal Employment Non-Discrimination Act, ENDA, is just one example of the tenacious link between sex-gender conformity and civil rights. The women's movement of the 1960s challenged gender roles, but grounded its ideology in liberal citizenship; even today women cannot seem to free themselves from romantic ideas about monogamy and marriage. Sexual respectability and "straight" lives endowed the movement's leaders with moral authority, giving them the power to demand the rights and privileges of citizenship for their members.[14]

Strategic sex couldn't be kept in the bedroom. Coming out in the 1960s and 1970s meant organizing for freedom of sexual and gender expression. After Stonewall, Sylvia Rivera and other hustlers found a political home in the Gay Liberation Front (GLF), formed with activists from the pansexual Sexual Freedom League, the New Left, and a few lesbian feminists. Challenging the liberal framework, GLF called for both a sexual revolution and the overthrow of a corrupt capitalist system. Like other groups of the time, it was fundamentally identity-based, though its members rejected the bourgeois concerns of "straight" re-spectability that seemed so dear to the earlier homophile organiza-tions. GLF's radically utopian ideology was drawn from the feminist mantra that "the personal is political" yet rejected feminism's solipsism by considering *everyone's* experiences of oppression. It questioned the authority of civil society and academia to make moral judgments about lifestyles and sexual choices. During its brief heyday, GLF integrated sexual identity into liberation theory, laying the groundwork for hu-man rights thinking about sexual matters.[15]

GLF's identity politics emphasized self-expression to "let it all hang out." Members' transgressive cultural tactics, including "gender-fucking" and sexual experimentation, were forms of political self-determination and cultural protest. They made room for prostitutes and hustlers, in-cluding transwomen, straight and lesbian prostitutes, gay-for-pay hus-tlers, and stone-butch dyke pimps who joined the counterculture. But as anticapitalists, members couldn't agree whether people should continue to charge for sex after the revolution.[16]

Disagreements over sex confused the women's movement too, and prostitution was its "scarlet menace" before the porn wars began. In the 1960s and 1970s, feminists argued over whether sex work could poten-tially liberate women or would perpetuate sexual oppression. To fight the sexual double standard, sex workers and "straight" feminists agreed they needed to abolish laws that punished female carnality, including adul-tery, abortion, and prostitution. But others were discomfited about sexual matters. Patriarchy, sexual violence, and struggles to define a "feminist" sexuality made prostitution a difficult issue for the National Organiza-tion for Women (NOW) and more radical women's groups. Prominent voices in the women's movement clung to the traditional view that the abolition of prostitution would protect women, a position that informed later efforts to wipe out pornography. They agreed to decriminalization only because they saw it as an interim step toward shutting down the entire sex industry after the revolution.[17]

Radical feminists supported abolition because they wanted to end male control of women's sexuality. Prostitutes, they hypothesized, were the "most oppressed"—their sexuality determined by the pimps, cus-tomers, and police who controlled them. However, like the GLF, radical feminists didn't spend a lot of time trying to change prostitution laws (since straight men also controlled the legislatures and the courts). Instead, they chose consciousness-raising: prostitutes had to be rescued from their "false consciousness." Once they "understood" their oppression, they would leave prostitution to join the feminist revolution to overthrow patriarchy.

Sex workers wanted rights before the revolution, and they had their own feminist analysis. Sexual freedom and women's control over their own bodies were fundamental issues, they asserted, rejecting claims that prostitutes were oppressed and sexually victimized. Men were inferior because they had to pay women money for sex. As prostitutes, they chose their sexual partners and negotiated the acts to be performed and the price their customers would pay. If every woman required men to pay for sex, women would rule the world.

The refusal of "straight" feminists to accept the personal experiences of sex workers as legitimate grounds for analysis represented a critical moment in the history of feminist politics. It was a turning point for feminist prostitutes. They realized that "loose women" would not win rights as long as virtuous and private behavior remained prerequisites for rights. Putting restrictions on gender, number of encounters, and locations where a woman could "hook up" limited sexual self-determination to the privileged woman who could afford a room of her own. Moral respectability is embedded in liberal citizenship; even the demand for sexual privacy is a housebound concept that reinforces class differences by presuming people have access to private space.

Despite multiple efforts to forge alliances, no mainstream organization ever embraced sex workers as an identity group. Some liberal groups have taken up sexual privacy as an issue of mutual interest, though they use different rationales. No mainstream group can challenge the monogamous family ideal and remain politically viable. Bedroom-privacy arguments have overturned (some) laws prohibiting sodomy, birth control, and sex between unmarried persons. But sex work is commercial sex, and therefore public, and is unprotected by sexual privacy arguments. Public sex is at the heart of sex panics, sex wars, and gender wars, and in these highly charged contestations, sex work remains suspect.

The experiences of sex-worker activists in these movements shed light on several divisive moments in recent history. Disagreements over the proper place for sexual expression and debates over whether sex is a private matter or a means of (public) self-determination have split liberals and radicals since the 1960s. The messy tensions between these perspectives have made it practically impossible for sex to be discussed dispassionately. Among African American leaders, sexual behavior is still dirty laundry that cannot be mentioned in public; the feminist and gay rights movements have largely failed to integrate sex work issues into their agendas.

In the face of whorephobia, sex workers organized. The first and most recognized sex workers' group was COYOTE (an acronym for Call Off Your Old Tired Ethics), founded by Margo St. James in 1973 in San Francisco. Members struggled over questions of identity, condemning "whore stigma" and the "deviant" label, while lobbying for inclusion in the mainstream women's movement. In the early 1980s, activists confronted AIDS and the anti-porn movement, finding common cause with other sex criminals. By the 1990s, as the neoliberal economy and global trade developments worried North America, sex-worker activists took on working conditions in the growing commercial sex industry. The expansion of the prison-industrial complex, though long a concern of activists, took on new urgency after September 11, 2001. "See something, say something" citizen surveillance, computer-monitored crime tracking, and border-crossing vigilantes entrapped street trade workers and sexual outlaws. And throughout these decades, some sex workers have engaged in cultural activism, embracing the tactics of storytelling, public performance art, and filmmaking to raise awareness and fight stereotypes about sex work. This tremendous creativity, dedication, and energy have kept the movement alive.

Organizers have engaged in direct action, lobbied legislators, negotiated with public officials, brought lawsuits, mounted ballot initiatives, organized unions, provided health care, and thrown a lot of wild parties. Tracing these tactics as they evolved shows the transition from civil rights–oriented strategies to a human rights framework. Leaders understood that to address the needs and rights of US sex workers, they had to broaden the concept of citizenship to universal human rights principles. The shift realigned the movement's goals to support sex workers' struggles internationally.[18]

The AIDS crisis demonstrated that coalitions were necessary to effectively confront the government's quick-to-convict, slow-to-cure response. Through the AIDS Coalition to Unleash Power (ACT UP), sex workers of all genders organized politically to fight laws that singled them out for punishment as vectors of disease. When San Francisco's political establishment shuttered the bathhouses, sex workers and (some) gay male AIDS activists saw a sex panic. They believed spaces for public sex, including bathhouses, porn stores, X-rated movie theaters, and massage parlors, should become sites for educating adults about safer sex practices, disease prevention, and safe drug use. Yet they were also slammed by the anti-porn activists, who supported prohibitions on public sex in the belief that porn violated women's civil rights.

The California Prostitutes Education Project (CAL-PEP) began as a COYOTE project in 1985, intended to conduct research on the prevalence of AIDS among women. It also started the first sex-worker-run AIDS education and condom distribution program in the United States; ironically, outreach workers had to confront the stigma of condom use—that only prostitutes used condoms.[19]

CAL-PEP, like Women With A Vision in New Orleans and Danny Cockerline's "Men at Work" and "Happy Hooking" materials for the Prostitutes' Safe Sex Project in Toronto, marked the beginning of a harm reduction movement that would transform sex-worker activism. Their tactic of direct service built on human rights principles to fight AIDS and sexual ignorance. Distributing condoms without regard to age or sex defied the "just say no" political culture of the Reagan-Mulroney era.[20]

The gender-neutral term "sex worker" allowed movement organizers to separate the job from the person who performed it and, linguistically at least, allied sex workers with the labor movement. As workers, activists demanded rights as wage earners. In the moral construction of citizenship, unrepentant whores "ask for it": they can't be victims, so they cannot be ripped off or raped. But empowered sex workers can and do complain when the boss steals their wages or a customer refuses to pay for services provided. Unlike sexual behavior, work is honorable and represents an economic and social contribution. Relations between employee and employer, between laborer and contractor are governed by an established set of hard-won labor laws and contract rights. Those who suffer from wage theft, abysmal working conditions, and workplace violence have legal recourse; US labor laws apply to all workers regardless of their national citizenship or immigration status. Advocates and allies tend to show more respect to workers than to prostitutes; they are willing to discuss strategy rather than dictate it.

A third wave of feminist, queer, and questioning sex workers began labor organizing in the 1990s to address the problems they experienced as the commercial sex industry expanded. The Exotic Dancers Alliance (EDA), US PROStitutes Collective (US PROS), the Sex Workers' Outreach Project USA (SWOP-USA), Feminist Anti-Censorship Taskforce (FACT), the St. James Infirmary, *PONY X-press*, *Danzine*, *Hook*, and dozens of others used the information superhighway to discuss issues and network. Though women tended to lead most of these groups, membership began to include gay men and transwomen in conscious rejection of the woman-identified politics practiced by second-wave feminists.

San Francisco was the center of "Whore Power" in the 1990s, as sex workers came out of the closet—or rather their dressing rooms—to take on the political establishment. The Board of Supervisors chartered the Task Force on Prostitution in 1994; half its members were former or current sex workers. The EDA formed to fight wage exploitation and labor violations by strip club and adult-theater owners. The Lusty Lady peepshow workers won a collective-bargaining agreement in 1996. Margo St. James ran for supervisor, leveraging her voters against her old friend Willie Brown, then the mayor. And on June 2, 1999, the St. James Infirmary (SJI), the first occupational health clinic for sex workers, opened its doors.[21]

SJI offers nonjudgmental health services to all in the sex industry and sex trades, combining harm reduction with grassroots community organizing that has transformed sex-worker health. Like CAL-PEP, sex workers have researched and designed programs to meet their needs, far beyond "pussy health"—the usual legal-political concerns about sexually transmitted infections. For example, until SJI, no medical research had been done on the podiatric problems caused from working all night in "hooker heels." By embedding social justice into direct services and organizing, activists have placed human rights at the center for both policymaking and practice, even as funding may prohibit direct involvement in politics.

During the AIDS crisis, harm reduction activists challenged the (neo-Malthusian) practice of reserving lifesaving drugs and medical care for people who demonstrated morally correct behavior. Activists refused to accept a political economy that used bourgeois notions of respectability to bestow benefits only to the privileged. They did not believe sex lives or work choices rendered anyone unworthy of health care.

By meeting people where they are without judgment, harm reduction is the practice of human rights philosophy. Human rights activism empowers the disenfranchised to create the conditions in which marginalized people can speak their truths and craft their own solutions to the problems they identify. Sex workers believe they must decide their own liberation strategies. They have reframed the movement's goals to reflect their own experiences and participated in the postmodern project of turning social conventions upside down. Redefining "victimhood," they have begun to disengage sexual morality from citizenship through cultural interventions and critical legal studies. Human rights and harm reduction have reconfigured campaigns for decriminalization.

Sex workers and their allies are challenging the whorephobia of criminal sex laws. Historically, victims of sexualized crimes (including prostitution and trafficking) are expected to testify that they were led astray by the perpetrator, their innocence corrupted or misled by naivete. Linda Lovelace used this defense when she renounced her role in *Deep Throat* and the pornography industry in general.

Slut-shaming implies that victims of sex violence "asked for it" because they were sexually promiscuous or dressed provocatively. Victims are also expected to surrender their power, allowing others to determine their needs; "rescuers" compound the violation of human rights by dictating solutions without consulting the "rescued." "Save us from our saviours," say unionized sex workers in Kolkata, India, in protest of American evangelicals' and Anglo feminists' rescue schemes. In India, Bangladesh, Thailand, and elsewhere in Asia, women say they would rather be prostitutes than slave over factory sewing machines, making clothes for multinational conglomerates in firetrap workshops and buildings that can (and do) collapse at any moment.[22]

Human rights for sex workers reframes decriminalization. The goal is broader, requiring the reorientation of American society, redefining the meaning of "citizenship" to incorporate human rights, and putting an end to structural and interpersonal violence. Many in the sex workers' movement no longer seek or care to ally with second-wave feminist or mainstream gay rights leaders; they're not relevant even when the organization's name includes the words "human rights."

The growth of the commercial sex industry poses new organizing dilemmas and political challenges for sex workers. The legalized status of the industry provides workers (and customers) with some protection from stigma, one reason for its exponential growth. But de facto decriminalization or deregulation extracts huge concessions from its workers. State labor and health officials rarely protect workers' bona fide interests, and they have little bargaining power. Some sex workers think that the recent organizing successes of home health aides, domestic workers, and agricultural laborers suggest other approaches.[23]

Legalized and regulated commercial sex businesses, like other competitive industries, seek to corner the market by controlling or even eliminating the local independent sex trade. As urban space and the Internet become more commercialized, private companies with little government oversight determine who has the right to occupy public space or to patronize public accommodations. Banning independent sex workers from advertising on Craigslist or elsewhere is the online equivalent of banning prostitutes from bars, clubs, hotels, parks, or sidewalks.[24]

Women of color are the fastest-growing prison population; most have committed nonviolent crimes. Prostitution and HIV are status crimes. In thirty-four states, prostitution is a felony if the sex worker is HIV positive, without regard to the type of service performed or whether transmission to the client occurred. No HIV-positive client, it appears, has ever been prosecuted. The war on drugs has punished sex workers heavily, especially people in street-based trades.[25] Criminalization follows sex workers long after their sentences: barring access to jobs and public programs, including drug treatment, low-income housing, and scholarships; and restricting their ability to obtain professional licenses—including in the sex industry—a form of "civil death" that encourages recidivism.

Gentrification has pushed people in the sex trades and street economy out of city centers. Zoning laws and "move along" ordinances have forced sex workers into isolated areas, making the work even more dangerous. In deindustrialized areas like Hunts Point in the Bronx, sex workers, drug users, and other marginalized people are more vulnerable to abuse by police and violent criminals.[26]

New coalitions of activists are strategizing against police brutality, especially attacks on women of color and transgender people of color. INCITE! Women of Color Against Violence, which formed in 2000, is assisting people with participatory research surveys of their communities, documenting the help that is routinely denied "young women in the sex trades and street economy." It is collecting stories about institutionalized violence from social service agencies as well as developing innovative strategies to resist and organize.[27]

The human rights leadership demonstrated by other nations on the issues of sex work, harm reduction, drug policy, and incarceration inspires social justice advocates in the United States who want to change domestic policies. Retrograde laws give the lie to White House proclamations about its commitments to human rights. Though life isn't perfect for sex workers anywhere, there are examples of progress. In 2005, President Lula da Silva rejected $40 million from the United States to fight AIDS because it came with the stipulation that Brazil's government take a pledge against prostitution. On International Sex Workers' Rights Day in 2011, activists petitioned the UN Human Rights Council to investigate the US government's refusal to "address violence and other human rights abuses against sex workers."[28]

In "post-racial" America, social justice and human rights are not popular topics. Examining the accomplishments and failures of the sex workers' movement helps to explain why other economic and racial justice movements have stalled. The people in these movements share many goals: they all seek respect, rights, and power for marginalized groups. They are identifiable by their multiple campaigns and longevity and their reliance on nonviolent direct action tactics.

Sex workers sometimes say they'd rather be respected than legal, and focus their activism on challenging whorephobia and slut-shaming. They want safe spaces that respect all sex workers, no matter where or how they work, or their class, race, gender, or sexuality. The idea of a safe space was the goal of Rivera and Johnson when they organized STAR. Whore culture, webcam pioneer Melissa Gira blogged, turned the ladies' toilet into "the perfect think tank, where we can trade business cards & fix eyeliner both." The San Francisco Sex Worker Film and Arts Festival has reworked the traditional "whore's bath" (a quick sponge bath between customers) into a spa day that offers sex workers a "magical healing space" in which to care for themselves and others.[29]

Realpolitik remains critical. A ballot proposition on decriminalization won 45 percent of the vote in San Francisco in 2008, after long weeks of knocking on doors and savvy ad graphics like artist Sadie Lune's "I Want You to Stop Punishing Me" poster in the style of the classic Uncle Sam Army recruitment poster. The Sex Workers Project pushed New York State to expunge prostitution convictions from trafficking victims' criminal records.

It's a complex, ever-evolving movement. Almost fifty years on, activists have made progress, but social justice for sex workers remains elusive. It's time to survey the work and assess some of its successes and failures, and perhaps envision plans for future organizing.[30] The next chapter of the "revolution" Sylvia Rivera saw in Greenwich Village began a few blocks north, with a few gangbusting feminist prostitutes who stormed a conference in a Chelsea high school in 1971.

CHAPTER 2

"THOSE FEW CAME ON LIKE GANGBUSTERS"

Prostitution and Sisterhood

WOMEN AREN'T SUPPOSED TO LIKE PROSTITUTION. Women aren't supposed to like sex. Women are supposed to like monogamy and marriage. Women are supposed to love romance. Women are supposed to find fulfillment in a husband, children, and a house with a picket fence. And Cinderella was real. This was the romantic mystique that feminists in the 1960s challenged to free womankind from what Betty Friedan called "the problem that has no name."[1]

The problem *did* have a name, feminists concluded, and its name was *patriarchy*. Male-dominated society reduced women to a sexual identity, to "wife, spinster, lesbian, whore." The emancipation of women would require the transformation of society, creating public roles for women beyond their sexual utility. Adapting Lysistrata's strategy to modern times, radical feminists in the late 1960s believed that in the war against

---

"Someone I Love Is a Sex Worker": Button, designed by Carol Leigh, from the Whore Store. Original in author's possession, purchased at the Desiree Alliance Conference, Chicago 2008.

male chauvinism, women should stop serving men sexually. Prostitutes were their main target. In the logic of "straight" feminists and "political" lesbians, prostitutes were completely enslaved by men. They "were convinced that by performing as paid sex objects prostitutes perpetuate the ultimate insult on themselves and all women."[2]

Sex workers felt insulted by these feminists. How dare those "straight" women lecture them about their sexual oppression? They stormed a meeting of feminists in Westchester, New York, in 1970 to confront "the false piety with which 'proper' women and men stigmatize prostitutes." These "proper" feminists wanted to discuss "rehabilitation," but prostitutes announced "they neither needed nor wanted to be rehabilitated." "Calling the stunned feminists hypocrites and whores," they said all women were "taught to 'hustle' at an early age in order to sell themselves . . . and 'hustle' men in most sexual relationships."[3]

Women of all classes were expected to attract men. So why were women who traded sex for marriage respected, but women who traded sex for money shunned? In New York, as in most states, adultery and prostitution were women's crimes, grounds for divorce and imprisonment. Several states made a wife's "lewd and lascivious behavior" before and after marriage grounds for divorce; until 1975, Virginia allowed a man to divorce merely on the grounds his wife had been a prostitute before marriage. Prostitutes, married women, lesbians, and single women had many things in common, yet just as many reasons to distrust one another.[4]

Kate Millett acknowledged that "a dramatic shift in perspective in the world of 'straight' women" would have to occur for the feminist movement to accept prostitutes (if not prostitution), from whom they were "historically divided . . . by their respectability." And Millett knew that it would require real work on the part of "straight" women to earn the trust of sex workers. "The only image of 'straight' women they have, of nonprostitutes, is one of contemptuous, moralistic, jealous, or disapproving respectable women."[5]

Whores, Housewives and Others (WHO) organized in San Francisco in 1971 to "expose the hypocrisy in laws that controlled female sexuality, primarily prostitution." WHO (the "'Others' were the dykes, but you couldn't say the word out loud then," explained founder Margo St. James) sought to bring women together based on their commonalities.

Like many ad hoc feminist groups in those years, its few members engaged primarily in consciousness-raising, reading, and analyzing women's oppression.

Sexuality figured prominently but not exclusively in WHO's goals. St. James declared that WHO wanted "sexual freedom, freedom of the body, the recognition of the right to engage in consensual sex with whomever we please for whatever motive; the end to the myth that women who are seductive are evil." She believed those freedoms and rights were feminism's central goals. After WHO dissolved, these beliefs formed the core of COYOTE's howls against the oppressive sexual morality that trapped all women and challenged the women's movement throughout its peak years.[6]

WHO and COYOTE were part of the explosion of women's groups in the early 1970s as feminism fractured into factions that differed on the primary cause of female oppression and the correct strategy for liberation. COYOTE represented just one of dozens of organizations formed for working women, among them the Coalition of Labor Union Women; 9to5, the National Association of Working Women; National Women's Law Center; Black Women for Wages for Housework; the English Collective of Prostitutes; Black Women Organized for Action; and the National Black Feminist Organization. The National Organization for Women (NOW) represented the liberal mainstream, at least at the top, but was merely one of thousands of organizations, national and local, advocating for women. In Manhattan alone, there were several NOW chapters of varying radicalism, as well as dozens of groups, formal and informal, organizing women (and some men) in neighborhoods, workplaces, and, as the popular WITCH (Women's International Terrorist Conspiracy from Hell) T-shirt read, in a "sewing circle and ladies' terrorist society." From the far left to the solidly centrist, women explored ideas and protest tactics as diverse and as radical as any imagined in that era.[7]

Identity politics dominated these years, as defined by the belief that the personal is political. As feminists began to identify numerous female identities, new organizing opportunities and political fractures emerged. The "lavender menace" demanded recognition in the feminist movement and in the gay rights movement, forcing leaders to acknowledge issues specific to lesbian identity. Black women, who had participated in the movement from the start (if not before white women got it together),

challenged the racism and class-privileged assumptions of white feminists, drawing strength from Black Power politics.[8] At the end of the '70s,
the black lesbian Combahee River Collective formed to demand attention to the murders of twelve black women "universally described as runaways, prostitutes, or drug addicts who [society said] 'deserved' to die
because of how they had lived."[9]

Feminist prostitutes had their own analyses of personal politics.
They hoped to find sisterhood with other feminists who had demonstrated against the unjust treatment of women by police and the courts in
Manhattan. But radical "straight" feminists split over prostitution: some
saw revolutionary potential in requiring men to pay for wages for sexual
services and housework, though many more viewed it as sexual coercion. Working without a definition of sexual harassment, feminists did
not distinguish between unsolicited demands for sex and women who
bartered sexual favors at work or at home to advance their careers or to
obtain material goods: both were forms of sexual coercion, analogous, in
their view, to prostitution. Analyses centered on men's constant demands
for sex and women's lack of economic power. From a Marxist-feminist
perspective, neither complicity nor consent could be given freely when
women had only their sexual labor to sell.

In December 1971, at a conference in lower Manhattan, feminist sex
workers disrupted a panel of radical feminists debating the proposition
that the elimination of prostitution was essential to women's liberation.
Feminists of almost every persuasion agreed to support decriminalization rather than legalization, but their analyses of prostitution and their
visions of the future perfect differed radically. Having grown up in the
girdled fifties, most "straight" feminists were conflicted about sex, forced
into a femininity that expected sexual ignorance.

The available sexology books were hardly suitable for developing a
positive feminist sexuality. The texts ranged from Masters and Johnson's
best seller, *Human Sexual Response*, and Valerie Solanas's *SCUM Manifesto* ("SCUM" standing for the Society for Cutting Up Men) to Anne
Koedt's essay "The Myth of the Vaginal Orgasm," all of which were filtered through the lens of women's limited sexual experiences. It is hardly
surprising that tensions smoldered when the "loose women" and bad
girls tried to build coalitions with the "good girls" and "straight" feminists to decriminalize prostitution.[10]

The orthodoxy of radical feminist sexual politics did not develop without challenge: from the start, "gangbuster" sex workers and sexual outlaws shouted their opinions in conferences and loitered on sidewalks, refusing the stigmatizing label of "deviant" and caring little about "respectability." If no one ever actually uttered the phrase "sex is good" in these confrontations, that message was nonetheless delivered.

Bad-girl and good-girl feminists acknowledged they had been divided historically over false moral values, but sex workers offered an alternative vision for women's emancipation: when women could negotiate sex freely, without fear of arrest or violence, men would no longer have the power to determine women's lives.

"PROSTITUTES, PIMPS, AND PORNOGRAPHY"

It was perhaps not surprising that sex workers would have a difficult time making the cut during the rush for feminist sisterhood. In the 1950s, when many future feminists were in high school, good girls and bad girls didn't mix. The "fast girls" of the city's suburbs were shunned: they wore denim, skipped school to smoke cigarettes in the parking lot, led boys astray, and got pregnant. Their teenage rebellions seemed rather tame, however, compared with "the ugly superfluous [characters] of the underworld: whores, toughs, transvestites, losers all" on the waterfront who were captured in the era's transgressive fiction. Hubert Selby's *Last Exit to Brooklyn*, published in the United States in 1964, gave readers the enormous-breasted Tralala, for whom "success is to make it as a whore," and Georgette, "the transvestite faggot" brutally gang-raped out of her romantic ambition to walk hand in hand with Vinnie, the neighborhood tough. By 1970, feminists recognized these morality lessons were concocted to keep them in their "place." But it was hard to overcome their distrust of bad girls and not to pity the whores.[11]

Good girls, bad girls, and bad cops had become big problems for New York City Mayor John Lindsay by the spring of 1971. Times Square merchants, tourists, Broadway theater patrons, the police, and the press complained that "dangerous riffraff types" had taken over "Prostitutes' Promenade" along Eighth Avenue between Forty-Second and Fiftieth Streets. African American women migrated south to Times Square after the 1964 Harlem riots made their white customers afraid of the "ghetto." Muggings and the high-profile stabbing deaths of two European visitors raised concerns that crime was out of control; newly appointed New York City police commissioner Patrick Murphy beefed up patrols, blaming prostitutes for street crimes.[12]

Though he was considered a policy wonk by patrolmen because of his tenure at the liberal Brookings Institute in Washington, DC, Murphy did not distinguish between female street criminals and sex workers. The two women "who leaped from a yellow car" to steal the wallet of West German defense minister Franz Josef Strauss had prior convictions for prostitution, so it was assumed they were still prostitutes. Pickpocketing and mugging aren't part of an honest whore's job description, but once a woman is labeled a whore, she's always a whore.

Lawyers in favor of decriminalization noted in the leftist weekly the *Nation* in 1972 that policymakers needed to distinguish between prostitution and such offenses as public nuisance, mugging, rape, and murder, which may happen to be committed by persons who sell or solicit sex. Streetwalkers who annoyed men by their advances, or men who similarly annoyed women, should be liable to arrest on the ground of public nuisance. If prostitutes or pimps robbed or beat patrons, the victims should charge robbery or bodily harm, not prostitution.[13] Criminologists would puzzle over the social causes that led to a noticeable increase in the number of female offenders in the 1970s, because they had traditionally linked sexual promiscuity with women's criminality. To them, "prostitute" meant a female-gendered person who engaged in antisocial behavior.[14]

A noticeable change in the type and manner of women on the Times Square stroll concerned New York Police Department (NYPD) officers and the *New York Times*. Just a few years earlier, the area was known for "the numbers of well-dressed, well-groomed women who politely accosted prosperous-appearing tourists, convention visitors and [male] residents of the hotels and luxury apartment houses" in the area. Patrolmen saw them working, but the women were discreet and respectable-looking and their clients were men of wealth, well-heeled tourists, and on-the-town conventioneers.

In 1971, the "northward migration" of "riffraff" to Times Square brought "less attractive women who often cruise in cars and attack and rob men who spurn their trade," according to the police. Now the women "don't wait for night. They pick up businessmen at the lunch hour and they proposition construction workers—anyone, any time at all." Race and color also mattered: black and Hispanic women were crossing old racial borders to work where the money was.[15]

Street crimes by women reflected a "new desperation," speculated a reporter for the *New York Times*, that came with the economic downturn, along with "greater freedom in sexual mores" and increases in drug addiction (and a spike in the price of smack). Times Square in particular, this reporter argued, had become a major sex and drug market since 1967 when Governor Nelson Rockefeller focused drug policies on treatment rather than punishment. Two thousand women (and an uncounted number of gay hustlers and transwomen) openly solicited in Midtown, the reporter continued, and competition led to "threats of violence on street corners, police crackdowns, and the opening of new territories."[16]

Times Square, of course, had a long history as a sex district, but an increase in the number of streetwalkers was not the only reason for changes in its street culture. Changes in state law had reduced the penalties for soliciting and prostitution to misdemeanors, and these years also marked a great migration of (mostly white) teens and young adults to New York and other coastal cities. This new labor pool of young women and men, willingly or not, found work in the sex industry or turned tricks to survive. In addition, *Miller v. California*, the Supreme Court's overturning of obscenity laws, opened up new opportunities in the commercial sex industry for businessmen to openly produce, sell, and show pornographic films. In the years immediately following *Miller*, Manhattan was the nation's porn capital. Live sex shows, massage parlors, book and "adult novelty" stores, hotels that rented rooms by the hour, and other sexually oriented businesses also contributed to the atmosphere. New York State lowered the legal drinking age to eighteen, attracting suburban teenagers from nearby states. Civil rights lawyers and civil libertarians challenged enforcement of loitering and vagrancy laws that police used to harass blacks, hippies, and gay men. Times Square's fame as the "crossroads of America" contributed to its new notoriety.

For the women who had once strolled the sidewalks in relative safety, shifts in the street culture led to another migration. By the start of the 1970s, "high class" sex workers were as afraid of Times Square as "straight" women. In response, entrepreneurs such as Xaviera Hollander (the "Happy Hooker") and Sydney Biddle Barrows (the "Mayflower Madam") established call operations that carefully screened both workers and clients; many of these new shops moved to Central Park South, Yorkville, or the East Side along Lexington Avenue near the Waldorf Astoria Hotel. Luxury apartment dwellers complained, while City Council member Ed Koch opined that it was a plot by landlords: prostitutes drove out tenants with rent-controlled apartments so new tenants could be charged higher prices. The class divide between street-based workers and indoor sex workers grew.[17]

Mayor Lindsay let loose a new wave of repression against public sex in July 1971 by appointing a police task force "to eliminate the abuses that have tarnished [the] character" of midtown Manhattan. He intended to enforce the state's new law "against public display of pornography" in order to force commercial sex businesses to tone down their advertising and merchandising practices. Police arrested thousands for prostitution that summer, which was "about as effective as pacification programs in Vietnam," wrote New York Magazine journalist Gail Sheehy.[18]

Repression of prostitution focused on the public nuisances associated with the trade. The primary targets were the "sleazy hotels" in the area, much to the delight of the Hotel Association spokesman. "Pimps" were another concern, in part because the word was becoming racialized with the popularity of blaxploitation movies and pulp fiction. In operational terms, police began to arrest male friends of sex workers who loitered in the area, holding them responsible for street crime.

"Straight" women participated in the policing of streetwalkers, aggressively displaying their disapproval, at least when in the company of a man. Making deliberate eye contact, their faces expressed "contempt, rage, disgust, embarrassment, annoyance." Some intolerant women would comment loudly, "How disgusting" or "Dirty bitch" as they walked past. The working women called them out on their insecurities, replying, "At least I don't give it away!" and "Where do you think he goes after he takes you home?"[19]

Police took seriously the good girls' complaints about street harassment. Midtown office workers (including female employees of the New York Times) as well as theater and restaurant patrons complained that it had become "almost impossible to walk alone along Eighth Avenue during the lunch hour without being annoyed by a man at least once on every block." Commissioner Murphy said police would target "men who accost women who happen to be walking in the area." Notably, this directive was not intended to stop well-behaved (white) customers, but the men who harassed women in the belief that any female out in public was "selling it." John A. Hamilton, describing himself as a "sensuous man" in the *Times*, felt himself the object of "pursuit."[20]

A week after the mayor's press conference, Murphy went after patrons of adult bookstores and theaters by using state laws against johns, the customers. Soliciting became a gender-neutral offense only with the Rockefeller reforms. Whether these men, almost invariably described in the press as middle-aged white men in business suits, were engaged in illegal activity is questionable; they were not soliciting women for prostitution.

Police raided eight sex shows in one night, arresting twenty men and women on "charges of obscenity, public lewdness, consensual sodomy, obstructing governmental administration and, in one case, second-degree assault." But as a clerk at Filmland told the *Times*, "We're not breaking the law—it's all legal." Another manager said he ran a "class" burlesque theater. If people wanted to see nudity, they should buy tickets to *Oh! Calcutta!*, the popular Broadway musical featuring nude performers. Bess Myerson, the first Jewish Miss America and then commissioner of Consumer Affairs, stayed out of the controversy, reminding a reporter that her office could only inspect and license theaters; it could do nothing about their content.[21]

Commissioner Murphy was desperate to find a villain to justify his harsh campaign and to assist Manhattan District Attorney Frank Hogan with high-profile felony cases. Prostitution was "only" a misdemeanor, turning street sweeps into costly revolving-door displays of police power. Vice detectives were further frustrated when the courts abolished one of their favorite harassment methods. For years, whenever a woman was arrested on prostitution charges, the police would inform all of her neighbors, an effective means of forcing her to move along.[22] Attacking pornography and pimps was the solution to Commissioner Murphy's public relations dilemma.

To convince the public there was a new threat, Murphy allied with *Times* reporter Murray Schumach, who wrote many stories that summer about the link between "prostitutes, pimps and pornography," Schumach's favorite alliterative lead. Schumach and Murphy, like anti-pornography activists of the era, saw themselves as defending law and order; they thought porn represented the moral degeneration of

America. In their zeal, they charged performers in live sex shows with prostitution.[23] Pornography represented the nation's moral erosion, according to a contemporary sociological study. "Conporns" believed porn was a foreign plot, encouraged by conspiratorial efforts of Communists and/or organized crime, and "liberals" were the dupes of the conspiracy (87 percent of the Conporns felt that organized crime was somehow connected to pornography; 61 percent felt that Communism was somehow connected).[24]

Though these self-proclaimed "good citizens" were convinced there was a connection between porn, communists, and the Mafia, the 1970 report by President Nixon's Commission on Obscenity and Pornography had found little evidence to support these beliefs. Nor did the Commission's social scientists find that pornography had a "causal relation to juvenile delinquency, sex crimes, or sexual deviancy." But truth and social science couldn't stop the combined forces of the NYPD and the *New York Times*, even when anecdotes but no actual data existed.[25]

"The pimps are hardened criminals," Commissioner Murphy explained to Schumach, trying to connect the dots:

> The pimps and the people behind them put up the money for the clothes and the apartments for the prostitutes when they are set up here by organized crime. . . . When we meet a pimp, we find the criminal record for assault, hold-ups, for larceny. These pimps, with their new Cadillacs, are trying to move up in the world of organized crime.[26]

The commissioner admitted, however, that "a number of pimps in the Midtown area were apparently independent operators with only the most casual connection to organized crime." He swore that the major ones were "likely" connected, but Schumach never asked for his proof. He also suggested that, given the number of women arrested for prostitution who also used drugs, pimps were probably connected to the narcotics trade. "Over and over again it has become clear that organized crime has moved into prostitution here through the pimps."[27]

Murphy used ethnic and racial code words to identify pimps and organized crime members. Yet the alleged connection between black pimps and mobsters is spurious, unless Murphy believed Italian Americans (whom the media routinely associated with the Mafia) had voluntarily committed to an affirmative action plan.

"Prostitutes, pimps and pornography" was a good public relations strategy to distract New Yorkers from coinciding revelations of police corruption. Allegations of misconduct made by NYPD detectives Frank Serpico and David Durk had filled the *Times'* headlines the year before, forcing Mayor Lindsay to act. He appointed Whitman Knapp, a Wall Street attorney whose first Supreme Court appearance was in defense of the state's obscenity law, to head the investigation. The Knapp Commission revealed a pattern of shakedowns, payoffs, and official obliviousness "in precinct houses throughout the five boroughs. . . . No officer seemed to be immune from the scourge of a department found to be riddled with graft and unable to police itself." As Lindsay's new police commissioner, Murphy intended to demonstrate his commitment to cleaning up the ranks.[28]

Commissioner Murphy's strategy was so old it's a wonder that the good citizens of New York—or of any city—could be fooled by it. Yet if the public wasn't quite bamboozled, it was appreciably distracted. Other politicians were relieved as well, because focusing on sex crimes could be pitched so many ways: as a morals campaign; a Nixonian restoration of law and order, a clean streets crusade, or an effort to end street harassment and public nuisances, to "fix broken windows," or, more seriously, violence against women. And however they were sold, anti-prostitution campaigns brought out women voters, because women weren't supposed to like prostitutes or prostitution.

"Straight" feminists didn't like prostitution but they were not fooled by the police commissioner's strategy. Some were stereotypically "hysterical" when New York City Criminal Court judge Morris Schwalb denied bail to two women hauled in on misdemeanor prostitution charges. "'Streetwalking prostitutes contribute to disease,' the judge declared. 'They are responsible for serious crimes.'" After filing a writ of habeas corpus on behalf of the women, the New York Civil Liberties Union called the judge's action "an utterly outrageous exercise of judicial power." Joan Goldberg, "who is active in the women's liberation movement," won the release of one of the defendants. When even more women were rounded up on Commissioner Murphy's order, *Time* magazine reported that "50 militant Women's Liberationists picketed the criminal court" to protest prostitution as "MEN'S CRIME AGAINST WOMEN."[29]

"Militant feminists" stated their objections to the laws on prostitution when state assemblymen Stephen Solarz and Antonio Olivieri held a Manhattan hearing on victimless crimes, including homosexuality, prostitution, and gambling, in September 1971. For a two-year period starting in 1967, the maximum penalty for prostitution in New York State was fifteen days in jail. After loud protests from police and voters upstate and downstate, prostitution became a Class B misdemeanor with a maximum sentence of ninety-one days. The assemblymen had invited testimony from selected feminists but many more showed up, demanding to speak.[30]

As an official witness, New York Radical Feminists founder Susan Brownmiller testified that prostitution laws were unjust to women, noting, "It is foolish to prosecute a woman for a crime in which she is the victim, but it is reprehensible to let a man go free for the criminal act of purchasing another's body."[31]

Two years later, Brownmiller's best-selling *Against Our Will* radicalized women's attitudes toward rape. She argued in that book, as she did in her testimony, against prostitution and pornography—that all women were victims of men's routine sexual violence and gender subjugation, yet men were rarely disciplined for their crimes. Citing now-discredited psychiatric studies of imprisoned prostitutes, Brownmiller reiterated the claim that as young girls, most sex workers were sexually abused; the "shame and loss of self-esteem . . . careened into promiscuity" as they grew older.[32]

Solarz and Olivieri had intended to hear only from Brownmiller as the representative of women's opinion. But sixteen "'women's liberation' partisans, shrieking and shouting," broke into the room and demanded they be heard. The assemblymen abruptly dismissed the hearing and ran out of the building. They considered hiding in the Harvard Club (which excluded women) across the street, but thought better of evading angry women voters and eventually agreed to have lunch with a few of the militants to hear them out.

Representing a variety of mainstream and radical feminist organizations, the women agreed with Brownmiller that women should not be arrested for prostitution, but they disagreed on "how the law should deal with prostitutes' customers." Some thought "men should be imprisoned for soliciting women for prostitution while others said that men should not be prosecuted at all. And some said the men should merely be fined." Reporter Gail Sheehy suggested a three-pronged solution: decriminalization, a female morals commissioner appointed by the mayor, and rehabilitation centers for prostitutes as an alternative to incarceration. To back up her suggestions, Sheehy brought with her two former sex workers whom she'd interviewed for her July *New York Magazine* article, "Hustling."[33]

The good girls thought bad girls were a problem that needed solving. For Mayor Lindsay, bad girls were a political headache; for Commissioner Murphy—and the *Times*—prostitutes, pimps, and pornography were a means to divert readers' attention; for assemblymen Solarz and Olivieri, the good girls were a force to be feared. No one thought to ask the bad girls what they thought, although several hundred had been arrested in the four months since Murphy's Times Square sweeps had begun.

PROSTITUTION AND SISTERHOOD?

"Prostitution provokes gut-level feelings in women precisely because it reveals so starkly fundamental and tacit assumptions about women's relations in a patriarchal society. It reminds us that we are defined by our sexuality: i.e., wife, spinster, lesbian, whore; and it reminds us that most women are dependent on men . . . in one way or another [to] secure our survival in exchange for the commodity that men want most from us. Feminists see this sexual objectification as dehumanizing and degrading—with the ultimate degradation experienced by women who sell their bodies to earn a living."

—Kate Millett, *The Prostitution Papers*[34]

"The double standard is a bitch . . . [and] the hooker catches shit from all ends. She provides a service made necessary by the inbred hypocrisies and contradictions of the System, and then is condemned by that same System for her behavior."

—Ellen Strong, "The Hooker" in *Sisterhood Is Powerful*[35]

No wonder the feminist "Conference on Prostitution" that opened in Chelsea High School in December 1971 turned into a disaster. Sisterhood and prostitution, indeed! Thirty women belonging variously to the Radical Feminists, the New Democratic Coalition, the Feminists, the New

Women Lawyers, and the Redstockings, and perhaps a WITCH or two, decided to hold a conference on prostitution (conferencing was a popular organizing tactic among feminists). This one followed the standard template: an opening plenary, a dozen workshops, and a final discussion panel on "The Elimination of Prostitution." What at first seemed promising became, as *Village Voice* reporter Robin Reisig lamented, "a bewildering day for sisterhood."[36]

The 1971 conference was one of the earliest confrontations between sex workers and feminists who had never worked in the sex industry. It did not bode well for future alliances. In consciousness-raising sessions before the conference, "straight" women decided they had at times traded sex for career advancement or material gains. They now felt like prostitutes because it was sex for money and not "love." They felt their patronizing attitudes were proof of their "compassion."

Talking with each other, they spoke of their own experiences, a practice on which feminists relied to discover "universal" truths and develop feminist theory. "[Prostitution] was a difficult issue for feminists to get a clear-cut position on because I think a lot of women were middle-class—*straight* would be a better word—and thought of prostitutes as fallen women," said one of the organizers of the conference as she explained how some of the organizers' attitudes changed before the conference. They discovered the gap to be bridged was not as wide as they had imagined.[37] "Straight" feminists were angry because patriarchy turned "women as sex objects, women exploited by men." They wanted to believe prostitutes "were their sisters, the women who were the symbol of what the women's movement was about."

Feminists felt magnanimous. They reminded themselves that prostitutes were not fallen women, they were victims; sexual moralism was a tool of patriarchy. The prostitution conference, they believed, would "erase 'one of the lines that divide women'—good girl from bad." According to the *Village Voice*, "The feminists who organized the conference believe it is possible to achieve social change that would give women other opportunities and that would make it shameful for *men* who buy women's bodies. They wanted to communicate with the prostitutes."[38]

The Saturday morning plenary featured feminists who would become leading thinkers in the movement. It began "sedately enough with information: excellent papers on theory, definitions, statistics, history, the convolutions of the law, its arbitrary enforcement (as, for example, in the case of 'wayward minors' or 'massage parlors'), and with proposals for reform," reported Kate Millett.[39]

Artist-activist Ruth Leavitt spoke on "The Patriarchy of Prostitution," theologian Mary Daly on "How the Church Encourages Prostitution," psychologist Florence Rush on "The Myth of Sexual Delinquency—the Good Girl and the Bad," and attorney Ruth Seidenberg on prostitution and the law. Paula Conrad talked about prostitution's relationship to the military, detailing the exploitation, objectification, and murder of Vietnamese women and children by the United States' soldiers.[40] Feminists' member Pam Kearon spoke on "The Psychology of the John."

> She got many enthusiastic cheers for a speech that centered largely on ridiculing men's fears of impotence and was studded, so to speak, with cheap shots at the "enemy." When another speaker posited the need to understand male sexual psychology as well as female, the audience booed, and Kearon walked off the stage and out of the auditorium.[41]

Kearon would continue to upset feminists—and others—in a *Village Voice* article a few weeks later, in which she wrote "the distinction between prostitutes and other women who consort with men is that the latter are 'unpaid vaginas.'" It was a view that, at the time, struck more than one person "as puritanical in the extreme," though anti-trafficking activists adopted similar rhetoric in the 1990s.[42]

Organizers wanted to have "currently working prostitutes" speak, but they failed to find any woman willing to take the risk. They did however recruit Fran Christman, a thirty-two-year-old former prostitute and volunteer with the Fortune Society, a prison reform and support group for "ex-cons," including gay men. Christman, who had also participated in the demonstration at Solarz and Olivieri's hearing, spoke against prostitution with the fervor of the saved. "Filled with guilt as we all were after any amount of time in 'the life,'" as another feminist ex-hooker wrote, "we attempt to exorcise the guilt by shouldering the whole burden of blame, accepting the definition of 'sick' or 'deviant,' and striving to become proper."[43]

It was quite a plenary, and at first seemed to affirm Kate Millett's "absurd optimism" about the possibility that the conference would move feminism "forward, sped along with the strength of many women's energies." These themes were to be further discussed in the afternoon workshops. That was "where all hell broke loose—between the prostitute and the movement."[44]

"These few women came on like gangbusters," Millett recalled. Feminist prostitutes did come to the conference; organizers' outreach efforts had succeeded. "Not many. Not perhaps the most representative," Millett wrote (whatever that meant). "But a handful of women were there who were still in the life, rather than members of the movement who had turned a trick or nearly turned a trick under the pressure and exigencies of a past life."[45]

These sex workers were not the living tropes the organizers expected. They did not look like the women they sometimes harassed in "The Deuce" (Forty-Second Street):

> They did not fit the stereotype of prostitute. One ["Donna"] looked like an exotically dressed high-fashion type. The others looked like you and me. Most of them were middle-class prostitutes, high-priced prostitutes, white call girls with expensive habits. One had a master's degree. Another had an Ivy League education. And they were, they said, feminist prostitutes.[46]

And they utterly confused the "straights" who believed their politics were radical, left, and pure.

Throughout their rap sessions before the conference and during the plenary, "straight" feminists had dealt with "the prostitute" only as a trope, not as a human being. Indeed, literary critic Barbara Jacobs' workshop was not about prostitution, but the representation of prostitutes in culture. She planned to expose the media's "romantic myth of prostitute as sought, accepted, glamorous and wealthy." This was perhaps the metaphor the Feminists analyzed in their workshop, "Prostitution and the Ideology of Sexism," which offered:

A theoretical framework for understanding prostitution as an integral part of women's oppression, the ideology of sexism and the function/activity theory. As a group with a consistent theory and position on prostitution, the Feminists will discuss their various actions around prostitution and how they came to introduce the issue into the women's movement.[47]

"Straights" had the gall to tell prostitutes what their position was in the movement. It was as condescending as the apocryphal story about Stokely Carmichael telling the Student Nonviolent Coordinating Committee (SNCC) women that their position in the movement was prone. Even Millett, who claimed she "began to *listen*" earlier that summer while filming her documentary *Three Lives*, allowing the testimony of prostitutes to "affect me, shake me, haunt me, overcome me," failed to see beyond the cant of "straight" feminists' doctrine. Millett's own scribbled notes on the conference program reflected whore stigma: "Pros'n is nec evil or good prostitutes are the evil" and "Cops + shrinks wonder what was Boston Strangler's Mom was like" [*sic*]. Her notes also reveal the movement's commitment to abolishing patriarchal control: "legalization makes state a pimp"; "Let's get the pimp"; and a rather utopian misreading of anthropology texts by European colonialists, "In soc[ieties] where paternity is not rec[ognized] there are sex roles + sexism but no prostitution or concubinage."[48]

Metaphor, shame, and limited sexual experiences were not good materials from which to develop authentic political theory. Gathered in self-selecting, homogenous consciousness-raising groups, straight women and "political lesbians" struggled to analyze work that none admitted they had done. (No wonder the few women who had actually done sex work were afraid to come out to their feminist sisters.) Instead, they talked about times when they "felt" they had prostituted themselves, stories about having sex for reasons other than for pleasure or love. They may have consented to sex with their boss, they may have offered sex to their boyfriends, but upon reflection, they now believed that society forced them to trade sex for gain. The line was rather fuzzy: some may have been ashamed that they followed Helen Gurley Brown's advice to "sleep their way to the top." But it's also possible that some were subjected to sexual harassment, a form of illegal gender discrimination that had not been conceptualized in 1971:[49]

> "Some of us had turned some tricks," the woman told [Reisig]. "We felt in our careers as models, as actresses, we were hustling to get a job—blow a guy and go to summer stock. Several of us did it. I did, out of ambition. If I could do it out of ambition, I can understand how any woman could do it out of ambition. They aren't 'fallen women' or different. They are people we can reach."[50]

Feminists confused sexual coercion with sex work because they knew only the metaphor of prostitution. They drew on cultural messages about bad girls who used sex to get ahead, women who were stigmatized as wanton, wretched, and evil. One organizer told Reisig: "We got twelve women to talk about being raped. That was easy—you're pure victim. In this there is complicity." But in categorically rejecting the myth that women "asked" to be raped, they didn't know what to do about women who offered sexual pleasure honestly and with consent in exchange for cash.[51]

No wonder sex workers were hurt and reacted angrily to this self-righteous rhetoric. They thought the conference would welcome their input, let them talk about their lives, choices, and issues. They wanted the support of other women, but how dare these feminists presume "they could debate, decide, or even discuss" the situation of prostitutes? "The first thing they could tell us—the message coming through a burst of understandable indignation," Millett wrote, "was that we were judgmental, meddlesome, and ignorant."[52]

There was little trust on any side. Sex workers at the conference may not have fit the streetwalker or call girl stereotype, but to radical feminists they were "obviously" and "blatantly" heterosexual. The lesbian prostitute couldn't be imagined, even though femmes had been around for years, supporting their difficult-to-employ butch lovers. Nor did sex workers trust "straight" feminists, who they suspected could be as hypocritical in their condemnation as the loudest Bible-thumping preacher on a Saturday night. In their fervor for a "lesbian experience" and to validate their view that men were sexually unnecessary, some radical feminists hired—or tried to hire—prostitutes for sex.[53]

Yet there was hope for understanding on that December Saturday. Though many of the planned workshops fell apart, movement women stopped "defending themselves long enough to listen or vie with each other for approval from the prostitutes."[54] It was a conversation that "prolonged itself in doorways and staircases or over the post-mortem drinks in bars," Millett remembered; "We were at last becoming persons to each other." That is, until Sunday's summary panel, "an inadvertent masterpiece of tactless precipitance" entitled "Toward the Elimination of Prostitution." "Sunday's panel began, as panels often do, with theory," Reisig reported. Decriminalization was the main topic.

> Lyn Vincent of The Feminists spoke about decriminalizing pros-
> tituting for the prostitute and increasing the criminal penalty for
> the john "guilty of the crime of using women." Kate Millett men-
> tioned . . . at the Philadelphia Panthers' Constitutional Convention
> of Revolutionary People . . . black women tried but failed to get the
> Panthers to pass a resolution against pimping.

Then Millett turned "over the discussion to the real experts":

> "You cannot sit here, a panel of women not involved with it, and
> make decrees about how 50 to 100,000 women are going to change
> their lives," said Donna, the exotically dressed prostitute. (Names
> are changed.) "It's degrading and sexist, but so are a lot of things."

The demand to abolish prostitution was not problematic simply be-cause it threatened women's livelihoods, as Millett suggested. The prob-lem was that "straight" feminists condemned sexual freedom for women and for men, and instead sought to perpetuate sexual shame. In this cen-sorious atmosphere, sex workers distrusted "straight" women's support for decriminalization. How else but to interpret this as a first step toward abolition? Decriminalization wasn't enough for many of the feminists. They wanted to get rid of prostitution, not take it over. "We have to get rid of it because it oppresses and degrades all of us," said Lyn Vincent, drawing hisses from some prostitutes and some feminists as well. Dis-putes exploded all over the auditorium. Donna was furious. Over and over, she talked of the risks she took to attend the conference: "All of us—look at us—we feel destroyed. Why do you think we came here to-day if we didn't feel the need for other women? . . . I risked myself."

Reisig's report continued:

Minda Bikman of the Radical Feminists observed that we women took a risk giving the conference and that we risked ourselves starting the movement three years ago and . . . WHAM! Donna slugged Minda.

"She's telling me she took a chance," Donna screamed. "I want to kill her!"

Minda dissolved into tears. The conference dissolved into chaos.

It was one of those moments that would happen again (and again) in the feminist movement: a debate whether sex was good or bad for women with implicit or explicit agendas for controlling male sexuality.[55]

Conference organizers "felt much more compassion than was credited, and were left with a sense of perplexity about what had happened." Decriminalizing only prostitution, while maintaining penalties against solicitation, pimping, pornography, and auxiliary activities, was not enough. Sex workers argued that if "straights" really desired sisterhood with their (not) downtrodden sisters, their common goal should be sexual freedom, not the end of sex.[56]

In retrospect, it might be argued that the sex workers who attended the 1971 conference had made a tactical mistake. Unlike "straights," they had not caucused before meeting; they did not hammer out a "consistent theory and position on prostitution" before showing up. After all, as Millett patronizingly (and falsely) reminded her readers, "Outsiders did not organize." But in the praxis of street corners, the reception rooms of massage parlors, and the living rooms of brothels, consciousness-raising among sex workers about working conditions, tricks, cops, lovers, and families had been going on longer than the women's movement. "The actual life experienced by women" had *never* "been hidden from other women," Millett observed, or from those who hung out with sex workers. They knew how male society shamed women and priced sexuality; it was their "widely shared and eminently valid" experience that "straights" needed to hear.[57]

Feminist prostitutes rejected the "prestigious title" of "most oppressed" that radical feminists awarded them. They refused to wallow in their theoretical victimization and did not tolerate pity from their theoretically less oppressed sisters. Besides, "We make more money than you chicks!"[58]

They made more money *and* they were cool. Prostitutes didn't have the sexual hang-ups of "straight" women. They felt sexually liberated and rejected society's stigmatization of female sexuality. They believed sexual freedom was central to women's liberation. Sex workers flipped the much-despised sexual double standard on its head. Liberation would come when society did not expect women to be chaste maidens or faithful wives. To them, "straight" women were the victims, bound in the tyranny of heterosexual monogamy. To claim marriage was the same as prostitution was ridiculous. Marriage was a cruel form of sexual slavery that marked the wife as the exclusive property of one man. No wonder women were threatened by prostitution. As Donna observed, "You're jealous because your boyfriends come to us." For sex workers, that was the feminist double standard: "straight" feminists wanted to abolish prostitution in order to control men; it was male sexual freedom that women really feared, while complaining that women were merely sex objects.[59]

SEX AND PRAXIS

Praxis became the overriding question. The madonna/whore complex was the problem. Ending the premium on chastity would free all women from the stigma that attached to female promiscuity and that criminalized prostitutes. Moreover, the revolutionary availability of the Pill—and penicillin—permitted women to pursue sexual pleasure for recreation, not procreation, just as men had done for millennia. This definition of female equality challenged the core of the sexual double standard.

The question of commercial sex as a capitalist enterprise was an unanalyzed but salient issue in the debate. The sleaziness of new porn shops and live sex theaters, combined with an abundance of streetwalkers in Times Square, frightened several conference speakers, including some sex workers. There was discussion about the rise of massage parlors that "were relatively open houses of prostitution, most operating twenty-four hours a day." The porn industry had exploded in New York, and topless and fully nude bars were wildly popular. For many "straights" as well as some sex workers, the threat was not prostitutes per se, but capitalist patriarchy's exploitation of women's sexual labor and the crass commercialism of female bodies. As a result, there were feminists who could imagine that decriminalization might allow prostitutes to organize in women-run, non-exploitative cooperatives that maintained control over male clients and ensured workers' health and safety.[60]

This nebulous socialist-feminist vision came very close to capitalist-oriented legalization. Decriminalizing only the act of prostitution would permit governments to control commercial sex. States could levy taxes on sales or profits, whether from worker-owned or capitalistic enterprise. They would have the power to dictate women's lives by requiring work permits and tests for venereal diseases and employing other means of surveillance and control. Local governments could limit businesses to isolated zones, and restrict advertising and signage. Frightened by the recent legitimization of brothels in Nevada and troubled by the idea that governments could profit (through taxation) from the sale of sexual services, "straight" and sex-worker feminists alike questioned the trend toward legalization.[61]

But not everyone thought it would be so terrible, particularly entrepreneurially minded women who were in the business. Pauline Tabor, sixty-six, had owned a recently shuttered brothel in Bowling Green, Kentucky, since 1935. Her profile appeared in the *New York Times* two weeks after the conference:

> "I just wish they'd legalize prostitution," she said. "Honey, I'd donate money just to get things started. Be the best thing ever happened in this country. Save young fellas from forcing themselves on their girlfriends. Save old men from getting involved with their secretaries. Save everybody from getting V.D. It would be great."[62]

Even confronted with testimony from a woman with almost forty years of experience, it's doubtful that "straight" feminists or radical sex advocates would have agreed with Madame Tabor. Her support for legalization borders on the "sewer theory" of prostitution, as a necessary evil to "carry away the effluvia" of society. Tabor supported legalized prostitution to prevent the sexual exploitation of "good girls." That was not the sexual feminists Germaine Greer's fans imagined.[63]

Madame Tabor presumed that men needed sex more often than women, a proposition that smacked of male privilege and presumed women were passionless. But what did sex mean for feminists? There was no agreement. Ti-Grace Atkinson, founder of the Feminists, dismissed it: "Sex is overrated. If someday we have to choose between sex and freedom, there's no question I'd take freedom." Sex-worker activist Cheryl Overs dismissed separatist feminists who believed that without men, women's sexuality would be "loving, nurturing and not for sale. [The facts were] blatantly at odds with the word on the street, despite the ever-present highly edited testimonies from selected prostitutes."[64]

Sex worker Valerie Solanas offered a "far out" and iconoclastic analysis in her *SCUM Manifesto*, which appeared in 1968. Widely discussed and distributed, her essay forced readers to radically rethink the meanings of "equality" and feminist sexuality. Did "equality to men" mean that women would also foment war, capitalism, and rape? Many agreed with Solanas that centrist calls to socialize women as men's equals were problematic; by that logic, women would one day hold the same capitalistic, warmongering positions as men. That was not revolutionary at all.[65]

Importantly, Solanas challenged the popular psychoanalytic view that all prostitutes were masochists as a result of childhood sexual trauma. As a psychosis requiring psychiatric incarceration and rehabilitation, masochism justified stigmatization. The conference workshops reified this opinion. "J," the ex-prostitute turned psychology graduate student in Millett's *Prostitution Papers*, also clung to this analysis even as she struggled to refute it.[66]

The feminist sexuality of the future, as Solanas imagined it, explicitly rejected female sexual passivity. Indeed, Solanas advocated female dominance, with men of a SCUM auxiliary submissively pleasuring the women they served. Radical feminists in the 1970s categorically rejected the sexually assertive woman as a paradigm of female power—a Chaos or a Hecate—and instead embraced Gaia, the pacific earth goddess. (Perhaps it is not surprising that third-wave feminists, including sex workers, riot grrrls, burlesque performers, drag kings, roller derby girls, and Bettie Page wannabes would find the "sacred prostitute" and "dominatrix" images liberating and took pleasure not only in their own erotic performances but also paid to watch others to perform for them.)

Feminist celebrations of the goddess Gaia suggested the opposite approach could overturn the sexual double standard. Radical feminists such as Atkinson argued sex wasn't necessary at all. Others questioned the necessity of men. Anne Koedt's passionate claim that the clitoris was essential for female orgasm essentially destabilized heterosexuality. Clitoral stimulation and thus pleasure could be achieved alone, with a male or a female partner, or with technology, if one was so inclined. This solution avoided the sticky question of heterosexuality, or, alternatively, placing the responsibility of female pleasure onto the male partner. According to historian Jane Gerhard,

> Feminists claimed that women were entitled to both social and sexual independence. Women's desires, be it for emotional intimacy or for extended foreplay, for sex with men or with women, must dictate sexual practice. . . . Sexual self-determination, in turn, held the promise of full equality with men. Feminists in the late 1960s joined sexual liberation to women's liberation, claiming that one without the other would keep women second-class citizens.[67]

Soon, however, radicalized feminists would question sexual liberation, declaring it a chauvinist plot to sexually exploit women. Indeed, some had begun to theorize that the primary source of female oppression was the socialized and unnatural sexual desires of women to believe themselves "complete" only with a man. Thus praxis dictated sexual abstinence or separatist lesbian feminism.[68]

Koedt's seminal essay was required reading for feminists, but books about sex—philosophical, technical, and fictional—were everywhere. Herbert Marcuse's thick analysis of Eros and Freud (1966), Masters and Johnson's turgid "overnight sensation" *Human Sexual Response* (1966), Alex Comfort's *Joy of Sex* (1972), and adventurous novels such as Erica Jong's *Fear of Flying* (1972) shaped popular discourse about sexual shame and pleasure. Marcuse's observation about America's sex laws, "Repressiveness is perhaps the more vigorously maintained the more unnecessary it becomes," inspired a generation of critics and activists; several novelists explored these dilemmas in the 1970s.[69]

Sex workers understood shame and pleasure from their own authentic experience and from some clients who expressed shame about sexual desires that society viewed as abnormal. Many sex workers took pride in using their skills and openness to turn a session into a positive experience. "Straight" women's shame made sexual pleasure difficult; if a "straight" woman voiced her sexual desires, "she lost social respect." Making sex even more complicated for "straight" women was "socioeconomic subordination, threats of pregnancy, fear of male violence, and society's double standard [that] reduce[d] women's power in heterosexual relationships and militate[d] against women's sexual knowledge, sexual assertiveness and sexual candor," sexologist Leonore Tiefer later observed.[70]

Problems arose when "straight" women drew their own stilted, shame-filled sexual experiences to develop feminist praxis, as the epistemology of feminism required. The new sexology books by Masters and Johnson, though lauded as "scientific," were also blatantly sexist. A critical reading of these texts demonstrates an unsound research methodology and male-centered assumptions. Sex workers were the subject "others" in many of these studies. For example, Alfred Kinsey and his students hired prostitutes to study male sexual response, and wrote only about the men. They had no controls for female sexual expertise, nor did they collect data on the sexual response of the prostitutes they employed.

Masters and Johnson employed a similarly gender-biased methodology to construct their human sexual response cycle (HSRC), although they included female biological responses. As Leonore Tiefer more recently observed, HRSC emphasizes "the physical aspects of sexuality" and favors "a genital focus," thus privileging men's different sets of sexual values.[71] Anne Koedt would agree.

Again, however, Tiefer and Masters and Johnson did not collect data from sex workers, throwing the experiences of professional erotic service providers into the trash bin like so many used condoms. While female sex workers may share with "straights" the fear of poverty, sexual health, pregnancy, male violence, and social stigma, they cannot be sexually ignorant, passive, or shy, though they may act that way with clients. Expertise and openness is their stock in trade.[72]

The aggressive posture of sex workers at that 1971 conference challenged many of the assumptions held by "straight" feminists. Prostitutes weren't abject victims, nor were they ashamed of their work; they didn't make apologies. Organizers did not want to admit they were wrong, and clung to the trope of "the prostitute"—the representative Times Square hooker—rather than acknowledging the nonstereotypical feminists who participated. Even compassionate organizers like Millett failed to understand the issue, believing that the prostitute's "problem" (as she saw it) could be solved by "some fundamental reorientation in the self-image of the prostitute." For Millett and other "straights," prostitutes could be rehabilitated through feminist consciousness-raising. Then they would understand their own "sexual objectification as dehumanizing and degrading." Sex workers shouted back, "Get real!" Their problem was not self-image, but the real threat posed by the violent "pimp, police, and patron."[73]

Feminist sex workers agreed with their "straight" sisters that men conspired to keep women oppressed. Police and clients could be violent, although the police posed more danger. Police officers who extorted payments in the form of sex or cash were scumbags, and the contempt of doctors and nurses reduced them to walking vaginas. But rather than denouncing sex, these sex workers sought sexual freedom. They believed women should determine the value of sexual pleasure and free themselves of patriarchal control. "Hookers' Lib" was not "Women's Lib."

"Analysis paralysis" over the issue of prostitution threatened to blow out radical feminists' "sisterhood is powerful" umbrella. Fundamental disagreements over the primary source of women's oppression—men or sex—and the correct strategy for liberation—to control men or to liberate women's sexual expression—encouraged the idea that one particular (monogamous) position was more politically correct than another. Rage assemblies, rather than rap sessions, led to the feminist sex wars.[74]

CHAPTER 3

"MY ASS IS MINE!"

Call Off Your Old Tired Ethics

NEW YORK CITY FEMINISTS TALKED FOREVER, earning a reputation as the "roiling center of feminist theory" and strategy. San Francisco feminists organized. "It may be that the West Coast will get it together before we do in the East," Kate Millett wrote in February 1973 for the paperback edition of *The Prostitution Papers*.[1]

The organized sex workers' rights movement arrived in 1973, at the peak of the women's movement second wave. Sex workers seized on the opportunity to make their demands, organizing as feminists and demanding that "straight" feminists acknowledge that decriminalizing prostitution was a women's issue and a race issue. The near-demise of this movement came with the onset of rigid, "politically correct" identity politics and the anti-pornography movement of the 1980s.

Margo St. James founded COYOTE with her compatriot Jennifer James, a Seattle-based professor of anthropology, in May 1973. St. James was not a disempowered outsider, but an authentic member of the "victim class" of oppressed prostitutes who took it upon herself to speak out

---

"COYOTE": Button, c. 1973.

on behalf of her sisters. James was COYOTE's first research scholar and political adviser with a curriculum vita of academic publications and as experience organizing with the Seattle chapter of NOW and civil liberties groups, as well as lobbying for prostitution law reform in Washington State.[2]

St. James was the "Chairmadam" and spokeswoman for COYOTE. Even in a city full of hippies, beats, freaks, and folks who wouldn't have passed as ordinary citizens anywhere else, St. James's charisma made her stand out. Like Lenny Bruce and Dick Gregory, her stinging, witty observations of America's moral hypocrisies questioned authority. She combined the psychedelic play tactics of her friend Ken Kesey (the author of *One Flew Over the Cuckoo's Nest*) with the high camp of gay culture. Merry pranksterism scored the point: a "giant keyhole"—the better to snoop into citizens' private lives—was awarded to the "Vice Cop of the Year." Stunts like these charmed the public and the press while they disarmed politicians and policemen.[3]

Hookers' Balls and Hookers' Conventions were must-attend cultural "happenings" that drew politicians, drag queens, porn stars, the Hollywood elite, voyeurs, and the media. St. James and future supervisor Harvey Milk judged an Anita Bryant–look-alike drag show contest in 1977 to raise money for a Miami gay rights fund; a female-led rock band, Leila and the Snakes, performing between contest rounds. "Miss Leading" won; the runner-up was "Miss Ambisextrous."[4]

Cheeky public displays of sexuality tweaked the moral sensibilities of respectable citizens, but they were more than simple mischief-making. They were tactics in a larger movement seeking "respect for sexual freedom as a fundamental civil liberty." A pioneer group in that movement was the Sexual Freedom League, formed in the mid-1960s, made up of New York City activists who came together after working in the Communist Party, the Southern civil rights movement, or early homophile rights groups. Some joined the Gay Liberation Front after Stonewall, while other members migrated to the Bay Area, where they organized pansexual parties and nude wade-ins that added to the libertine reputation of "Baghdad by the Bay." Gays, whores, feminists, lesbians, and others who had yet to come out—including "straights" who hadn't yet discovered their own sexual secrets—would find comrades who were equally disgusted or frightened by the sexually repressive tendencies of

American society and law.[5] For this group of sex radicals, decriminalizing prostitution was an issue of freedom.

The public-policy changes COYOTE won in the 1970s chipped away at prostitution laws, making "the stroll" easier and sometimes safer. Particularly for women and transgender people arrested on prostitution charges, the abolition of mandatory venereal disease tests, mandatory penicillin therapy, and multiday jail quarantines ended some of the worst rights abuses. COYOTE also pressured public defenders to provide better representation for people accused of soliciting and prostitution, misdemeanor offenses that had been routinely plea bargained rather than contested.[6]

Though these were fragile victories and limited to a few cities, COYOTE's supporters viewed them as groundwork for a national movement to abolish all laws against prostitution. Realistically, however, this lone organization never had the members, money, or political power to carry out a major reform campaign in the states and through the courts, particularly as the country lurched toward the reactionary Republican leadership of Ronald Reagan.

Yet COYOTE was not a failure. It consistently pressured the feminist movement to pay attention to women's sexual freedom and condemned the censorious excesses of the anti-pornography movement. COYOTE was more than a dissident voice; its services and programs for "loose women" rejected the idea that sex was evil. It encouraged women to be angry about whore stigma and slut-shaming for pursuing sexual pleasure or trading sex for money. As St. James told Paul Krassner of *Rolling Stone* in 1974, "As a woman/whore, I feel equality will never be achieved until woman's sexuality ceases to be the source of our shame—until the men are forced to abandon their pussy patrols."[7]

COYOTE's broad assertion of a woman's right to sexual pleasure and to privacy was controversial from a legal point of view. Feminist and civil rights attorneys agreed in principle that, in time, the Supreme Court might decide favorably. The milestone birth-control case *Griswold v. Connecticut* (1965), the landmark interracial-marriage case *Loving v. Virginia* (1967), and the abolition of restrictions on the distribution of sexually explicit materials in *Miller v. California* (1967) provided a foundation, but not a building. Creating federal case law to support sexual liberty would take decades, and further political controversy erupted after the Court's privacy holding in *Roe v. Wade* (1973). Ratification of the Equal Rights Amendment had stalled by 1975, largely because activists for and against the ERA deliberately misrepresented the meaning of rights "on account of sex." Did "sex" refer to "women," gender, sexual orientation, or sexual behavior and who could use which restroom? Ultimately, COYOTE's efforts to work with mainstream and radical feminist organizations broke down over ideological and strategic differences about sex, privacy, commercialism, and criminalization.[8]

THE COYOTE TRICKSTER

San Francisco, the most populous "wide-open town" in the United States, had the history, culture, politics, people, and resources for sexual outlaws and social deviants to organize a movement for their liberation and rights, and Margo St. James was enmeshed in it. Part of the Beat generation, she had arrived in the city in 1959 from Washington State, where she'd married and had a son at the age of seventeen. Victimized in a police sting and wrongly convicted of prostitution, she had fought the system and won. She'd lived with the Beats in North Beach in the early 1960s, with the hippies in Haight-Ashbury in late 1960s, and with New Age gurus on a houseboat in Sausalito in the early 1970s. She identified as a feminist, a pot smoker, a jogger, and a supporter of many radical and offbeat political causes.[9]

St. James could almost laugh about it by the time COYOTE formed, but she was still angry about her arrest for prostitution in 1962, "the turning point of my life":

> I was a loose woman and always had people hanging out and smoking dope and partying. I was surrounded by dopesmokers and artists and poets who were just hanging out. My place was a crash pad, a crossroads for people of all classes and races.[10]

The North Beach beat cop watched the foot traffic going and coming from her apartment with suspicion, concluding that only a prostitute would have so many men visiting at all hours. The cop's "finky" brother, who worked on the vice squad, agreed. "They assumed that I must be charging and the vice squad came and solicited me in my own home. I didn't even say yes and they dragged me off!"[11]

Once in court, St. James proved that she knew too much about sex, but not enough about the law, to keep herself out of trouble. Perhaps she did not know that just the previous year, California had made prostitution and solicitation a criminal offense. The new disorderly conduct Penal Code 647(b) defined prostitution as "any lewd act between persons for money or other consideration." Asked by the judge to explain her generous hospitality, St. James proclaimed she was innocent of the charge of prostitution, adding, "Your Honor, I've never turned a trick in my life."

"Anybody that knows that language is obviously a professional," the judge declared, and found St. James guilty. As she remembered:

> In 1962 women weren't supposed to know what a trick was. That's all part and parcel of being intimidated by sex. We're not supposed to know, and if anybody mentions it, we're supposed to look down and blush.[12]

Just the accusation of prostitution was enough for St. James to be labeled "a whore." The judge pronounced St. James guilty not because she was making money but because her behavior fit the standard legal definition of a common prostitute—"female offering her body for indiscriminate intercourse with men, usually for hire."[13] This language criminalized women's sex lives regardless of whether she received "money or other consideration." To be a "free lover" was the same as a well-paid whore, and a threat to the family and civilization. In 1908, the Supreme Court had ruled on prostitutes:

> The lives and example of such persons are in hostility to the idea of the family as consisting in and springing from the union for life of one man and one woman in the holy estate of matrimony; the sure foundation of all that is stable and noble in our civilization.[14]

Even the liberal Supreme Court under Chief Justice Earl Warren hesitated to disturb that precedent. Laws in many states, including California, forbade "known prostitutes" and "known homosexuals" from working in or congregating in any place that held a liquor license. Like sex offenders today, they were prohibited from certain types of work, barred from public establishments, and required to register with the police. By 1962, there had been a series of confrontations between San Francisco citizens, police, and lawmakers over the notorious enforcement of liquor regulations. Inquiries into corruption stemming from police crackdowns on "known homosexual hangouts" led to gay men's formation of the Tavern Guild to fight against the harassment; the candidacy of the legendary Black Cat nightclub's star drag performer Jose Serria for mayor of San Francisco; and the transformation of North Beach particularly, into the "headquarters for homosexual America."

St. James's run-in with the police might be simply a minor historical coincidence, but there is a remarkable similarity between this early gay rights activism and the tactics used by COYOTE in the next decade. The stigmatizing arrest and conviction would turn St. James into a prostitutes' rights activist, with a starring role in maintaining the reputation of the city's Barbary Coast as a notorious neighborhood.[15]

St. James became a "known prostitute," situating her in the same offender category as convicted gay men, lesbians, and other "sex deviates." The bar where she had worked as a cocktail waitress fired her upon her conviction. Without regard to constitutional due process, the mere charge of prostitution (or homosexuality) made it difficult for someone to obtain legitimate employment or even rent an apartment.[16] St. James had a college degree, but no job skills. Her work options were severely limited. In 1977, she remarked,

> Fifteen years later I'm still unemployable. No one has ever offered me a job. People won't hire a hooker even if she's an ex-hooker. They think that you're going to start doing it on the table or something, so they won't trust you with their kids or anything like that.[17]

Only the bail bondsman and the attorney to whom she owed money were willing to give her odd jobs running errands and filing motions. Working in the Superior Court and central lockup on Bryant Street, St. James ran a gauntlet of sexual harassment and sexual propositions from men—the behavior that the radical feminists in New York had likened to prostitution: "The judges and the D.A.'s and what-have-you still kept hitting on me." Finally, after her car broke down, "I just started saying yes because I needed the money."[18]

Consider for a moment St. James's situation when she decided to turn herself out, and the rules she made for herself in deciding to accept a trick. Her work choices were restricted to menial low-wage jobs, her morality suspect, her wages practically garnished to pay off her bond and attorney fees. She was underpaid because of gendered wage discrimination and constantly offered money to have sex with her male supervisors and other men. Despite her consent, some feminists would conclude St. James was a victim of "patriarchy," since the hostile environment, combined with precarious economic conditions, narrowed her choices. But one could also blame capitalism or puritanical morality. And St. James set limits on how much money she earned and how many tricks she accepted, reserving her right to refuse an offer: "I would just do enough to pay the rent and stuff; I was never in it for the usual reason, which is to make lots of fast money."[19]

Working for the bail bondsman, St. James made friends with lawyers, detectives, sheriff's department employees, and jail personnel. The names and phone numbers of many of these men and women were later on the well-worn cards in her Rolodex. Vincent Hallinan was one name, a radical lawyer whose long career included a run for president on the Progressive Party ticket, founding the National Lawyers Guild, and defending Harry Bridges, the legendary president of the Longshoremen's Union. In his 1963 autobiography, *A Lion in Court*, Hallinan "argued for prison reform, against laws forbidding private consensual sex, contraception and abortion, he argued in favor of treating drug addiction as a medical condition and providing clean maintenance drugs to addicts, legalizing prostitution and against imperialism and American foreign policy." (St. James would tangle with his second son, Terence, thirty years later when he became district attorney.) Hallinan suggested St. James attend law school and, as she put it, "learn enough to file my own appeal."[20]

"I was driven. That arrest was like watching your relatives burn in the ovens. It's something you don't get over; you stay mad," she recalled. St. James enrolled in Lincoln Law School, then located in San Francisco. While she never earned a law degree, she successfully appealed her own conviction. Jerome Sack, dean of the law school, gave her assistance. He "agreed with me that the prostitution laws are discriminatory and unconstitutional" but advised her to   :r appeal focused on the problematic procedural aspects of her c. .e—the lack of evidence— rather than confront the constitutional issues. St. James won her case and wanted to defend other women accused of prostitution. Dean Sack advised her to "wait ten years" before trying to organize a movement.[21]

CALL OFF YOUR OLD, TIRED ETHICS

The early 1970s was a promising time to organize for prostitutes' rights. The United Nations declared the 1970s "the Decade of Women." US political trends, legal victories, state and local developments, and sexual attitudes had radically shifted since President Kennedy had spoken of the New Frontier. The political power of Democrats and progressive politicians in the Bay Area and Sacramento was at its peak. Under Chief Justice Warren, the Supreme Court's "equalitarian" revolution went a long way toward granting full citizenship to the disenfranchised and affirming the human rights of the disempowered.

The women's movement was in full swing, and despite stressful factional fights such as the 1971 prostitution conference in New York, it appeared that mainstream feminists had sufficient influence to convince lawmakers and judges to decriminalize prostitution. At the grassroots level, the multiplication of identity-based political movements, most centered on victimhood and oppression, made "hookers' lib" seem viable.

The "me generation" identity politics of the 1970s created a sense of solidarity for the women who called themselves "prostitutes, working girls, sporting girls, hustlers, hookers, and hos [whores]." Deviants were "coming out all over," as one influential sociologist described this uprising, defiantly rejecting the repressive attitudes of America's postwar era.[22] Questioning the authority of the medical, psychoanalytic, and juridical establishment, deviants and leftist scholars (including a young, queer Sorbonne philosopher named Michel Foucault) constructed alternative explanations for the problematization of social groups.[23]

Whores, queers, queens, dykes, wife-swappers, swingers, prisoners, bastards and love children, welfare mothers, ex-cons, hippies, sex fiends, pot smokers, and other longhairs surprised the "squares" and "straights" when they began to organize. The silent majority was probably discomfited by photos of these deviants splashed on the pages of the *San Francisco Examiner* and the *Chronicle*, but the source of their unease had less to do with the visible presence of "those people"—who'd been around a long, long time—than with those people demanding power and freedom.

Labeling a person "deviant" is an act of disempowerment; the social misfit doesn't deserve full citizenship and may be viewed as something less than human. Civil rights are reserved for normal members of society.[24] Historically, Foucault observed, immoral behaviors were often criminalized by the state and disciplined by the penal system. In the 1950s, US medical and psychiatric professionals began to call for decriminalization, claiming that deviants with psychopathologies needed care from medical professionals, not prison authorities. Stigmatization, however, remained a potent force in the process of socialization, encouraging citizens to shun or shame people who engaged in antisocial behaviors.

It took courage to come out and reject the label of "deviant" because public exposure often led to arrest or confinement in the psych ward. The economic and social penalties could also be severe, as St. James knew from experience. The mass uprisings of many different oppressed classes encouraged others to come out and to challenge the validity of the labels used to stigmatize them. Their forays into the public spotlight were essentially demands for equal rights as citizens, like most of the movements of the 1960s. As British historian Jeffrey Weeks observed,

> Transvestites, transsexuals, paedophiles, sado-masochists, fetishists, bisexuals, prostitutes and others—each group marked by specific sexual tastes, or aptitudes, subdivided and demarcated often into specific styles, morals and communities, each with specific histories of self-expression—have all appeared on the world's stage to claim their space and "rights."[25]

Rejecting the "deviant" label, activists asserted they were citizens whose rights were regularly violated when arrested for prostitution. "We're going for respectability," Lois Lee told the *Los Angeles Times* in 1978 during a Playboy Mansion fundraiser for her National Institute for Working Women (NIWW), formerly the California Association of Trollops (CAT).[26]

St. James hated slut-shaming, and fought it by flouting the rules and mainstream sensibilities. At the Condor, the topless club where Carol Doda famously performed, St. James packed the house on "Amateur

Topless Night" dressed up as a nun. (The nun costume had been a present from comedian Dick Gregory.) With the North Beach Catholic landmark, St. Peter and Paul Cathedral, a stone's throw away, she purposely thumbed her nose to those "Papal hypocrites" as she called them.[27]

A jogger, she ran the Bay to Breakers annual 12K race in 1965 before women were officially permitted to race. And she ran it nude. "No one, not even Jerry Garcia or Timothy Leary, was more hip than Margo," remembered North Beach Leathers founder Bill Morgan, who won the race that day.[28]

By the early 1970s, St. James's circle included Alan Watts, the philosopher of the counterculture on whose Sausalito houseboat WHO (Whores, Housewives and Others) held its first meeting, and the novelist Tom Robbins, who nicknamed her the "Coyote trickster." "Indian legends describe the trickster as always giving people exactly what they want," wrote Jennifer James. "Margo describes the coyote as nature's most promiscuous animal."[29]

Another friend was Richard Hongisto, the newly elected liberal sheriff of San Francisco. Hongisto's campaign had been built largely on the distrust liberal San Franciscans had for their metropolitan police, and although he would try public confidence later, in 1972 he was the Bay Area's newest political darling.[30] Still furious about the way she'd been treated by the police, and knowing Hongisto had brought together "the liberal groups in town," St. James cornered the sheriff to ask "what it would take to get NOW, and gay rights groups to support prostitutes' rights":

> He said that we needed someone from the victim class to speak out,
> and that was the only way the issue would be heard.
>   I decided to be that someone . . . [31]

St. James's conviction for prostitution a decade earlier made her a member of "the victim class." Hongisto recognized that identity politics required authenticity: only the voice of someone who "had been there" was authoritative; no phony could validate the experience of a discredited, "stigmatizing condition." For St. James and others in COYOTE, speaking out was "an act of self-affirmation."[32]

COYOTE formed in May 1973. "We were terrified and electrified and empowered when we announced the formation of the first prostitutes'

rights group in the United States in history," St. James told a new generation of activists thirty-five years later. The actual May date is usually
given as Mother's Day, though St. James has also cited May 1, International Workers' Day. More recently, she joked that COYOTE was founded
one year after FBI director J. Edgar Hoover's death (May 3, 1972) "because
everyone wanted to make sure he was actually dead."[33]

The group's purpose was "to provide a loose union of women—both
prostitutes and feminists—to fight for legal change." In 1973, COYOTE
was one of several liberal groups that wanted to expand the right to privacy in the wake of *Roe v. Wade*; the National Gay Task Force and American Civil Liberties Union's Sexual Privacy Project also began initiatives.
COYOTE asserted that women who worked as prostitutes should have
the same citizenship rights as "straight" citizens. As sociologist Valerie
Jenness observed in her 1993 book:

> The prostitutes' rights movement is in line with this historical mo-
> ment, as well as compatible with numerous other constituencies
> emerging to be publicly counted, treated as legitimate, and granted
> rights of citizenship.[34]

To get COYOTE running, St. James used her remarkable persuasive
skills and twirled her formidable Rolodex. She'd learned that "if you're
interesting and you have a good rap, people are willing to take you to
dinner." Or they will donate money or volunteer. She gathered together
"reputable" citizens who gave COYOTE credibility and money, and recruited professionals to provide services, information, and expertise.[35]

St. James persuaded the public relations firm that had handled Hongisto's election to volunteer their services, then

> decided to reconnect with the lawyers and bail bondsmen I had
> known and I hoped the hookers would join me. . . . A professor
> at UC gave me some good leads and resources. Another old friend
> got a job as a jail doctor, so I had inside information from him and
> from the girls.[36]

Jennifer James, a recently minted PhD in urban anthropology, became COYOTE's academic expert, developing factsheets and statistics to

counter the common myths about prostitution. James had conducted extensive ethnographic research on streetwalkers for her dissertation and had joined with several attorneys, including Marilyn Haft, director of the ACLU's Sexual Privacy Project, to map a legal challenge to the constitutionality of prostitution laws beginning in Washington State.[37]

St. James's gift was her charisma, manifested in her thoroughly outrageous speaking style and her networking skills. When she made the rather far-out proposal to decriminalize prostitution, she made it sound both rational and amusing. She convinced influential, knowledgeable women and men to donate their skills and support. In an era when the civil rights of almost every oppressed minority group seriously mattered, liberating prostitutes sounded like fun.

Hustling for funding, COYOTE's mission received validation with an initial $5,000 grant from San Francisco's Glide Foundation, known for its social justice work and community action organizing. The grant allayed the discomfort some people might have had about St. James's frequent criticism of religious "hypo-critters." With the money, COYOTE organized the first prostitutes' conference in 1974 at the Glide United (Methodist) Church in the Tenderloin, just two blocks from Compton's Cafeteria. Another $5,000, awarded to COYOTE in 1975, came from Stewart Brand's Point Foundation, devoted to using the profits from the *Whole Earth Catalogue* to help build a better world. In contrast, the $1,000 donated to NIWW/CAT from the Playboy Foundation was simply a token.[38]

St. James didn't want to "organize" or build an activist membership core; she had little experience with grassroots organizing. Adapting the "back of the yards" strategy expounded by legendary organizer Saul Alinksy would have meant working the streets talking to women, posting flyers, and passing out literature. That wasn't St. James's style, though later, Gloria Lockett, who would become COYOTE's codirector, used street organizing to talk to hard-to-reach people in the Tenderloin and the Fillmore about AIDS, condoms, and safer sex. Both women persuaded a lot of sex workers to join COYOTE. St. James told the *Harvard Crimson* in 1976, "It takes about two minutes to politicize a hooker."[39]

In the early years, COYOTE took a laissez-faire approach to organizing by providing a safe space for sex workers to meet and talk and find support. Local and national underground papers ran notices of meetings and events. COYOTE's contact information was passed out by the

Haight-Ashbury and the San Francisco Sex Information switchboards, at the Tenderloin's free medical clinic, the Glide Information Center, and other social services and referral centers. *Off our backs* and other women's newspapers across the country listed COYOTE's twenty-four-hour emergency telephone number in their community directories.

It wouldn't be surprising if the emergency number for COYOTE's Survival Line for Independent Prostitutes (SLIP) had been scratched deeply in the wall by the inmates' telephone at central booking on Bryant Street, next to numbers for bail bondsmen. SLIP offered immediate legal assistance when any woman was arrested, provided court-appropriate clothing, and taught survival skill classes in jail.[40] COYOTE also had a bail fund, created with money raised from its Hookers' Ball; the project was intended to free women from exploitative pimps. St. James often answered the SLIP line herself because she was always in the office.[41]

The grassroots reality for many was that the crime of prostitution created a huge victim class of women with overlapping legal, social, economic, health, family, and education issues. In the Bay Area, COYOTE created social welfare programs and assistance services that were urgently needed and successful, even if some were provided haphazardly.

From phone calls, letters, and rap sessions, St. James and volunteer Priscilla Alexander, who joined COYOTE as a volunteer in 1976, heard from sex workers in the city and soon from around the world, as word of COYOTE spread. There were complaints about police harassment. In San Francisco, everyone complained about the mandatory three-day quarantine of female prostitutes for venereal disease. Many needed help raising bail; others wanted a better lawyer than the overworked one assigned by the public defenders' office. Others hoped COYOTE could do something about violence, sexual coercion, and threats they experienced from the police, clients, and other men. Access to competent health care, abortion services, reproductive health services, and even basic sexual information were also requested.

COYOTE's programs were radically different in their approach to sex workers' problems. The few services available for female offenders, like those for unmarried pregnant women, tended toward the Victorian; the missions of the Florence Crittenden Homes and the Magdalene Homes were to instill sexual shame in wayward women and girls. COYOTE shifted the paradigm. It didn't seek to rescue and rehabilitate "fallen women" by training them for minimum wage jobs and a life of piety. They wanted women to be "conscious": to be angry and willing to do something about the way society and the law treated "loose women." COYOTE offered a radical critique that affirmed women's anger and let them know they weren't alone in their experiences of whorephobia and slut-shaming discrimination.[42]

COYOTE held rap sessions for women to share their experiences of working on the streets and behind closed doors, adapting feminist consciousness-raising methods. It organized "whore conventions"—first in San Francisco (1974), then in Washington, DC (1976), and finally internationally in Brussels and Amsterdam (1985 and 1986). Locally, it put together educational programs and cultural events to raise money for other projects. As St. James described her efforts,

> Usually I rush out and hustle up money after my project is already under way. I ask somebody for money, teach a sexuality class or a dance class, put on some bizarre flea market—any kind of hustle like that works to get a little cash flow.[43]

When the phone rang, St. James answered it, whatever time the call came in. "I'm getting phone calls in the middle of the night from some hysterical hooker who is in trouble." She dealt "with stuff and emergencies as they come in. That way I don't have to say, 'I'm sorry I can't help you right now; I've got something else to do.'" Working "eighty hours a week," St. James practically lived in COYOTE's Tenderloin office because whatever money she raised or earned from speaking went back into the organization. She couldn't afford an apartment or a car; she belonged to the YWCA so she could shower at midnight and rode a three-speed bicycle.[44]

Over the years, COYOTE acquired other staff, mostly unpaid as well. Priscilla Alexander, the daughter of New York City organizers, a Bennington College graduate, and a former English teacher, spent her "spare time" as a word processor in order to work for COYOTE and NOW. She provided St. James with much-needed assistance, taking up the research work that Jennifer James, by then a tenured professor at the University of Washington Medical School had done previously.[45] Georgia Wilkins was a volunteer speaker-organizer; she, along with "a double handful of other hard workers" formed the core of COYOTE's San Francisco membership and staff.

The issues and grievances sex workers identified would have overwhelmed an organization with the staff and resources of the national ACLU. But in those hopeful times, St. James and the volunteer staff did what they could. COYOTE couldn't organize a campaign on every issue, but St. James could talk about them, and the *COYOTE Howls* newspaper could report them. The growing list of crimes committed against prostitutes strengthened the case for decriminalization.

PUSSY PATROLS

The prostitutes' rights movement made decriminalization its goal. Though COYOTE did not engineer the abolition of all laws against prostitution, it was not a "failure," as sociologist Ronald Weitzer claimed in 1991.[46] Movement goals are always idealistic; like utopian fiction, goals provide people with a vision of a world not yet achieved, but one that is within the realm of possibility.

St. James argued that "hookers' lib" was fundamentally tied to women's control over their bodies, a privacy issue, and a fight against the racial profiling of black and Hispanic women as prostitutes. Decriminalization served as a political frame that people instantly recognized in a decade when lawmakers sought to reduce or abolish penalties for "victimless crimes" including abortion, alcohol and drug use, vagrancy, and consensual sex between unmarried adults.

Statistical data and social science evidence gathered and analyzed by James and later by Alexander provided St. James with facts about the injustices that sex workers faced. They gathered stories from victims and identified women and men who were penalized by society's "old, tired ethics." St. James used the media well. Print reporters loved her sound bites, and her frequent appearances on national television, a medium particularly suited to her charisma, were especially popular on the new daytime talk shows of the 1970s. She was always prepared to "show the facts":

> Margo meets her interviewers with Xeroxed copies of papers by psychiatrists, sociologists and lawyers, all tending to demonstrate the laws on the subject are indefensibly biased in favor of the

hooker's customer who never gets arrested and against the hooker who often does.[47]

St. James made a strong case for decriminalization. Ten years after appealing her case, she could focus on the constitutional issues.

In late 1973, COYOTE launched its first major campaign, a public education drive denouncing the racist and sexist biases of prostitution arrests. Selective enforcement of prostitution laws meant that the police unconstitutionally targeted women, instead of enforcing the law equally. California law was gender neutral: both women and men were prohibited from soliciting for prostitution. Yet women were 90 percent of those arrested; when police arrested men, the charges against them were routinely dismissed in exchange for their testimony against the alleged female prostitutes. (Men who solicited men were charged with sodomy, not prostitution.) The tricks were not getting caught.

St. James's media interviews hit particularly hard against the profiling of black and Hispanic women as prostitutes, detailing not only racial discrimination by the police but also the racial discrimination by the commercial sex industry. She told a reporter in 1973:

> Half of the women in the county jail are there on sex charges— political prisoners, arbitrarily chosen by society to pay its dues for sexual guilt. Most of them are black, another aspect of discrimination—minority women being forced to work on the street due to the fact that the hotels and massage parlors are owned by white folks who won't hire them or let them hang out.[48]

Sweeps of street-based women netted only those most visible to the public, but represented just one-tenth of all workers in the sex industry, according to COYOTE estimates. An ACLU attorney used FBI Uniform Crime Reports to show that it was "seven times more likely that prostitution arrests will involve black women than women of other races."[49]

Those reports did not reveal how many were transwomen, poor, older (or underage), or casual laborers. COYOTE activists recognized the ripple effects that these disparities had on racial attitudes. Prostitution arrests reinforced the racist stereotype that women of color were more sexually promiscuous and immoral than white women, and supported public policies of discipline and control, including forced sterilization, public welfare cuts, and increased "law and order" patrols in poor neighborhoods.

To feminists and the general public, St. James presented COYOTE as a reform group, educating people about the sexual double standard embedded in the enforcement of prostitution laws. It took two people to commit an act of prostitution, yet police unjustly persecuted women for male carnality, while men were rarely arrested. Most state laws were gender neutral, but Alaska, Indiana, Louisiana, North Dakota, and Wisconsin made prostitution a crime only for women who "sold" sex; another ten states made it a crime for men to "buy" it. Despite these variations, it was "totally discriminatory" that prostitution laws punished mostly women.[50]

Gloria Steinem, Susan Brownmiller, Florynce Kennedy, and Ti-Grace Atkinson were among the well-known feminists who supported decriminalization, agreeing that all forms of legal discrimination against women needed to end. The equal protection clause of the Fourteenth Amendment prohibited singling out one class of citizens for a crime. Alaska's discriminatory law was overturned in June 1973, and challenges had been filed in other states. Gender-neutral laws also had to be enforced equally: punishing only women for soliciting violated their constitutional rights. Demands for equal protection—and equal punishment—justified a resolution calling on states to decriminalize prostitution at the 1973 National Organization for Women convention. "What the women's liberation movement had in mind . . . was ending the double standard," recalled Karen DeCrow, NOW president from 1974 to 1977. "If women craved and adored sex also, it could hardly be used for barter."[51]

Consent required that women were empowered to negotiate sex for pay or for other consideration, including adoration. St. James raised this point and other objections that divided feminists and legal reformers. When solicitation is criminalized, women are endangered because they cannot barter sex for pay in explicit terms. For that reason, all consensual sex, whether for pleasure or for profit, should be viewed as a private matter between adults. Like sodomy, prostitution should be regarded as a victimless crime, since both parties consented; it was a matter of sexual freedom. Legal reformers, including the ACLU and the American Bar Association agreed, but some "straight" feminists balked. Though they supported privacy to advance abortion rights, gay rights, and perhaps sexual freedom for women, to say that prostitution was a private matter might condone sadomasochism, polygamy, pederasty, and other repulsive sexual behaviors.[52]

COYOTE and "straight" feminists shared concerns about violence against prostitutes but fundamentally disagreed about its causes and prevention. St. James and Alexander held that the whorephobia and slut-shaming promoted by criminalization aggravated violence because it made prostitutes vulnerable and fearful about fighting back or reporting crimes against them. Brownmiller and other prohibitionists viewed prostitutes as exploited women whose very existence perpetuated violence against *all* women because they were "females [who] may be bought for a price."[53]

Decriminalization was a difficult issue for feminists. The split over issues of privacy, sexual freedom, and violence led to further disagreements about pornography, public sex, and third-party management. Straight liberal feminists who saw patriarchy (but not the state) as the culprit turned into prohibitionists who advocated stronger laws and revised police tactics to stop sexual exploitation. That meant greater risk for sex workers. Future COYOTE codirector Gloria Lockett was arrested for "pimping" when a vice cop caught her holding cash that another woman had earned. Racism, Lockett said, meant that she was accused of felony pimping while police charged the white women with simple misdemeanor prostitution.[54] Even when confronted with injustices like this one, prohibitionists continued to believe stronger enforcement of pimping laws would help exploited women.

THE TRICK IS NOT GETTING CAUGHT

The COYOTE campaign against prostitution laws initially focused on selective enforcement. St. James hit hard on the gender and racial disparities of arrests in her public appearances, and pushed the matter further with pickets at the city's prestigious hotels to protest against police entrapment. When the US Supreme Court ruled that indigent citizens accused of misdemeanors were entitled to legal representation, public defenders were instructed to investigate and represent people accused of soliciting and prostitution, jamming court dockets. In court, COYOTE helped to abolish mandatory VD quarantines by proving that only women, not male clients, were kept in jail. COYOTE almost convinced the San Francisco Board of Supervisors to direct the police to issue citations for 647(b) violations. The resulting turmoil pushed newly elected mayor George Moscone to announce a moratorium on prostitution prosecutions in January 1976.

Eleven months later, the district attorney and police chief decided to start arresting sex workers again, and began raiding sex shops and sweeping the streets. But in December 1976, a San Francisco judge dismissed soliciting charges against thirty-seven women because the police had failed to arrest any men, in blatant disregard of constitutional law. COYOTE pushed harder on sex discrimination issues. St. James publicized the lack of pretrial diversion programs for women, and demanded development of alternative sentencing programs as well as training programs designed specifically for female ex-offenders. There was talk that COYOTE would offer its own programs, but the money never materialized. Proposition 13, cutting government budgets across the state of California, as well as growing public hostility over coddling criminals and generous entitlement programs, cut off the possibility of public funding for COYOTE.

Arrest statistics proved only that the police focused on street-based workers, St. James continued, and didn't reveal the race discrimination in the commercial sex industry or the "straight" businesses—the hotels and bars—that facilitated private sex work. The vast majority of sex workers worked "indoors" as call girls, escorts, massage parlor workers, and performers in peep shows and strip clubs, and almost all of them were white. Law enforcement tended to ignore indoor sex businesses, legal and illegal, which employed mostly young white "co-eds" and "girls" to attract higher-spending white clients. By the mid-1970s, places that offered a half dozen or more girls on one shift might include one or two "exotics"—Asian, African American, or Hispanic women. Employers mixed racial prejudice with class prejudice, arguing that the more women of color working in an establishment, the more downscale it appeared.[55]

Bars and hotels where women met dates on their own often refused service to black women, despite federal and state civil rights laws. "You couldn't hang around with other Black girls," Gloria Lockett recalled. "You had to hang by yourself or with other white girls, because if you were hanging in the Fairmont or the Hyatt, the people working there were more apt to bother you if you were with another Black girl."[56]

COYOTE also held public demonstrations to protest against entrapment. "It's well past time for whores to organize. The homosexuals organized and now the cops are afraid to harass them anymore," St. James told the underground newspaper the *Phoenix* in September 1973. "The homosexual community in San Francisco has gotten politically organized—just as the hookers are trying to do with their pickets and they put enough pressure on City Hall to stop entrapments."[57]

Most startling about the protests was not the picketers, by now a rather normal sight, nor COYOTE's witty picket signs. It was the public demonstration itself. Like the protests organized by Gay Activists Alliance (GAA) at the White House in 1965, a *political* protest by public women and their allies was bold—even in San Francisco, where it was hard to avoid streetwalkers outside of hotels.

In San Francisco and Seattle, security guards frequently harassed and even expelled escorts and other sex workers from hotels and other public places. The practice raised questions about the gender and racial profiling tactics used by police and raised larger questions about discrimination in public places. The Association of Seattle Prostitutes (ASP) had picketed the Roosevelt Hotel because it gave free rooms to the vice squad so they could entrap women working as escorts, both as call girls and on the street.

For a week, St. James, along with perhaps two dozen women and men, picketed San Francisco's major convention hotels, calling attention to their cooperation with the police for prostitution sting operations:

> The hookers looked like liberated housewives and the vice cops looked like the Mod Squad. The hookers and their friends were members of COYOTE. They had come . . . to picket the place for being finky and providing vice-coppers with free rooms to entrap their sisters . . .
>
> It was noon and the first day of a week-long picketing campaign to bring public attention (and hopefully indignation) to bear on the increasingly frequent use of free rooms in fancy downtown hotels as "lurid set-ups" to which the vice-coppers bring suspected hookers . . . So Coyote's campaign got underway in the light drizzle with at least 20 pickets, half a dozen vice cops and six or eight newspaper and television reporters at hand.[58]

Their targets were the Hilton Hotel on the edge of the Tenderloin, the Hyatt Regency on Embarcadero, and the Bellevue Hotel and the Stanford Court on Nob Hill, all of which gave the vice squad free "entrapment" rooms. Detectives would bring up women from the street, telephone escort agencies and ask for someone to be sent to the hotel, or arrange outcalls with massage parlors and encounter studios. Once in the room, detectives negotiated sex for money with the women. Few sex workers knew what rights they possessed or how to prevent entrapment. Some believed, naively, that they were not breaking the law in the "privacy" of a hotel room. Others had been told that vice cops couldn't take off their clothes, so they made new clients strip before negotiating. Even worse was the plight of women whom police officers had tricked into sex before arresting them. Caught in these stings, many complained bitterly, but had no means to fight back.[59] As an added insult, men would joke, "If you have sex with a prostitute and don't pay her, is it rape or shoplifting?"

COYOTE pushed the Board of Supervisors to change the way police handled solicitation and prostitution offenses. Current law required arrest and detention, amounting to a revolving door that flooded the courts, enriched bail bondsmen, overwhelmed public defenders, and cost taxpayers $5 million each year. As an alternative, St. James suggested citations, a policy that had been adopted in Eugene, Oregon, a couple years earlier. According to Jennifer James's research, there were no major compliance problems during the first year it was in effect. San Francisco should do the same, as it already did for small quantities of marijuana possession, making prostitution a misdemeanor offense. With the money the city saved, as well as the fines collected, COYOTE or another social service organization could create a "scholarship fund for women in the life who are interested in achieving alternative means of survival."[60] Building on the concessions won in the legal arena, St. James turned her attention to prison health policies.

COYOTE's most significant victory in the 1970s was to end mandatory VD quarantining of women charged with prostitution. The practice, a holdover from World War II–era public health campaigns to keep military men "clean," was based on a dubious medical proposition. According to the American Social Hygiene Association, the main advocate for the policy, the spread of VD to the general public could be prevented by testing women picked up on prostitution charges for gonorrhea and syphilis, quarantining them in jail, and forcing them to take penicillin injections for three to five days until the test results came back. The policy presumed nonmonogamous sexual relations were the cause for sexually transmitted infections (STIs) and viewed prostitutes the vectors of disease. Quarantines, advocates believed, would force the patient to be sexually abstinent during treatment with the new "wonder drug."

Women complained constantly about the quarantine. "You had to be examined for VD before you could get out of jail," St. James testified. The city's required, medically unjustifiable penicillin prophylaxis injections violated women's civil rights because it subjected them to punishment before conviction. It reinforced whorephobia because it presumed women were the carriers of diseases, not their male clients. Exams for VD could be brutal; though they were the responsibility of the prison physician, the actual exam could be performed by someone without medical training. (Indeed, some women said they knew more about gynecological care than the staff.) Adverse drug reactions went untreated, as did the predictable yeast infections most women develop after antibiotics. (This was when the Boston Women's Health Collective recommended nystatin or topical gentian violet to treat vulvovaginal candidiasis, and years before the FDC approved 2 percent miconazole nitrate for over-the-counter sales.) As an added insult, according to St. James, "9 out of 10 prostitutes do not have VD."[61]

COYOTE's press release on the quarantine was a snappy response to a stupid policy. Coercing prostitutes into "unnecessary treatment for VD" for the protection of "innocent wives" addressed only half the problem. St. James suggested "the husband should also be considered promiscuous and be examined and quarantined as the women are." Once more, St. James used the press to publicize the problems of sex workers and framed her point to emphasize sexist hypocrisy. And COYOTE filed suit with the assistance of cooperating attorneys.[62]

In 1975, the California Supreme Court held that the quarantine requirement applied equally to customers. Enforcing the decision, an Oakland court judge ordered "several men to spend five days in jail awaiting the results of their venereal disease tests." When law enforcement officials considered the consequences of incarcerating men as well as women "the practice was immediately discontinued." The strategic beauty of demanding selective enforcement of prostitution laws was that many men did not want to face the shame women routinely endured, nor would they calmly tolerate the prospect of losing three to five days of work.[63]

Women arrested on 647(b) prostitution charges almost never exercised their right to a trial before a jury of their peers. Most agreed to pay a fine or plea-bargained to a lesser charge; some were simply held overnight and released the next (Monday) morning to get them off the streets for a weekend. These were misdemeanors, for which people served time in the local jail, not in state prison. As a result, though there were thousands of arrests for prostitution every year, neither the courts nor the public defenders' office took the charges seriously. Further, the court had no duty to provide an attorney to those who could not afford one; *Gideon v. Wainwright* (1963) guaranteed legal representation only for felonies.

In 1972, the US Supreme Court ruled that indigent clients were entitled to counsel for any misdemeanor crime for which the punishment exceeded six months. Even with the ruling, women were having difficulty obtaining representation. Court-appointed attorneys rarely questioned the evidence presented by vice officers or pursued selective enforcement claims. COYOTE pressured public defenders to exercise due diligence in defending women, rather than routinely pleading guilty. The courts and the district attorneys, faced with the prospect of going to full trial, began dropping charges.[64]

The threat to overload the system by forcing the courts to meet the full extent of their constitutional obligations gave COYOTE another victory. Other groups of second-class citizens were forcing both federal and state governments to meet their needs during this period. Welfare rights activists engaged in mass defiance and disruption campaigns to force human services agencies to treat the poor with respect and dignity, and to make the system provide all the benefits to which they were entitled. Prisoners went on strike and defied their wardens while their advocates filed thousands of legal complaints about inhumane treatment. As Frances Fox Piven and Richard Cloward argue, for a short time, such movements forced elites to concede to poor people's demands.[65]

San Francisco's policies on female prostitution, commercial sex businesses, and gay and lesbian rights changed after the close mayoral election in December 1975. The new mayor, George Moscone, with his new police chief, Charles Gain, and Attorney General Joseph Freitas, announced in

January 1976 that they would cease to prosecute prostitution cases. De facto decriminalization changed the city's landscape at a historic moment when feminist and conservative "anti-smut" forces were starting to coalesce. Hotel owners and developers, fronting through a concerned citizens group, also mounted a campaign to abolish the sex businesses and street prostitution that, they claimed, degraded and cheapened the city.

Sex workers, opponents said, started to migrate in massive numbers to the "wide-open town" in 1976. The origins of this new "roving band of gypsy whores"—and whether it actually existed—are uncertain. Some claimed they were recently displaced Times Square streetwalkers; Gloria Lockett suggested that women who'd been working in Oakland and San Jose started strolling Union Square instead because they no longer risked arrest. "It was quite a time," St. James told a reporter in 1994. "The girls were lined up four abreast in front of the St. Francis hotel on Union Square." "It was wild and wonderful," agreed Robyn Few. "We were everywhere and making crazy kinds of money."[66]

But the party ended when Freitas and Gain abruptly rolled back the de facto decriminalization policy in December 1976, and restarted street sweeps and entrapping workers in adult sex shops and topless dance clubs.[67]

In response, and with the support of attorneys from the ACLU of Northern California and the San Francisco Citizens' Council for Criminal Justice (a group fighting against the construction of new jails), COYOTE identified at least two dozen plaintiffs and filed twenty-six lawsuits against the state prostitution laws. They also educated the Queen's Bench, the California women's bar association, and women judges. St. James and her lawyer allies asked the group to review carefully the evidence in prostitution cases. Three judges, including a past president, volunteered to "participate in the women's political caucus and [provide] peer counseling to prostitutes."[68]

Judge Ollie M. Marie-Victoire, who usually assigned cases to other municipal judges, decided to hear prostitution cases herself. After listening to charges against thirty-seven women, she asked the prosecutor— Where were the men they were accused of soliciting? There were none, because the police hadn't arrested any customers. Angered at the blatant legal discrimination against prostitutes who, she pointed out, were largely non-white and "economically disadvantaged," Marie-Victoire began dismissing the cases. She contended that "an intentional, purposeful, selective enforcement policy of the San Francisco police department" led to numerous arrests of prostitutes, while permitting their white, middle-class customers to go free.[69]

COYOTE was overjoyed by the ruling; St. James, as well as the National Organization for Women, publicized it widely. Judge Marie-Victoire "suddenly became a heroine to the women's movement" wrote the *New York Times*.[70]

Off our backs, the radical feminist newspaper in Washington, DC, thought the judge didn't go far enough, however, scolding Marie-Victoire for ruling only on procedural issues rather than striking down the law on constitutional grounds. The reporter dismissed the judge's suggestion of "equal entrapment" because arresting male clients did not address the real issue. The "criminals are neither the prostitutes nor the customers who pay for their services," *oob* opined. "The economic and social system" was the root cause, because it "creates the conditions that drive women into prostitution."[71]

Male members of the bar did not accept Marie-Victoire's liberal stance for gender equality. The assistant district attorney for vice crimes, Joe Rusoniello, told a reporter there was no reason to arrest men because, "The customer is not involved with the commercial exploitation of sex, at least not on an ongoing basis." Newly elected District Attorney Freitas and other senior judges wanted to disqualify Marie-Victoire, the immediate past president of the Queen's Bench Bar Association, for "prejudice." A Superior Court judge ordered her to recuse herself from four pending cases. In the interim, the women whose cases had been dismissed also filed suit, believing that the next judges to hear their cases would be hostile to their claims.[72]

Nevertheless, the campaign against selective enforcement questioned the fairness of prostitution laws in court and in the press. St. James's leadership generated public awareness and popular support to "do something" for oppressed sex workers. In a time of expanding legal equality for once-disenfranchised citizens, as well as widespread suspicion about police practices and corruption, St. James's media appearances began to shift the public narrative about prostitutes, pimps, and pornography.

"The Establishment" began to take note. The American Bar Association in 1976 voted on a recommendation that state legislatures "repeal all laws which prohibit commercial sexual conduct between consenting adults in private." Though the American Law Institute had called on states to decriminalize private consensual sex in 1959, the new language recognized that commercial sex should also be a private manner. State lawmakers such as Massachusetts representative Barney Frank had already introduced legislation, saying "Who goes to bed with whom is none of the government's business."[73]

Despite concerted efforts to discipline Judge Marie-Victoire, her criticism of selective enforcement persuaded other judges in the city and elsewhere to order changes in police practices. The result was a new campaign that targeted male clients. Prostitution prohibitionists called on police to enforce gender-neutral laws and arrest men who perpetuated sexual slavery. Their demands coincided with those of liberal activists who wanted law enforcement agencies to hire more women and minorities. Police departments across the country now needed female decoys to arrest men for soliciting. "Pinking" the police meant hiring women as officers, and for Norma Jean Almodovar an opportunity to join the Los Angeles Police Department as a traffic cop (though after experiencing years of sexual harassment in the Hollywood Division, Almodovar found more "honest" work as a call girl).[74]

Everyone, from the Black Panthers to the American Nazi Party to the Gay & Lesbian Advocates & Defenders (GLAD) complained about selective enforcement and police entrapment in the '60s and '70s; the civil rights of gays, women, and people of color were mainstream issues, legitimized by a widely shared perception of police corruption and incompetence. Lawyers representing women accused of prostitution routinely made a selective enforcement claim, primarily based on their client's female gender and sometimes on race. A 1979 lawsuit claimed bias on the basis of gendered heterosexuality, offering a new twist that was deeply entwined in the city's sexual politics.

Attorney Gil Eisenberg, whose firm often represented COYOTE members and other people in the sex industry, successfully demonstrated a prima facie claim of discriminatory prosecution based on heterosexual orientation in *People v. Municipal Court of San Francisco* (1979). The case claimed that the city failed to arrest gay men who worked as escorts or in bathhouses for prostitution, and subjected only women with male clients to prosecution. Private investigator Jack Webb, a retired SFPD detective and another old friend of St. James's, alleged the protection given by city officials to gay sex business owners was the result of large cash contributions to their election campaigns. Though the case failed on appeal, primarily because the district attorney's office refused to release requested records, *People* suggests how the political power of the local gay rights activists solidified in the transition from George Moscone's administration to that of Mayor Dianne Feinstein.

HOOKERS HELPING HOOKERS

Women who were victims of violence received assistance from COYOTE. St. James had earned a private investigator's license after law school, which she used to assist women in pressing charges against their assailants. As she explained, police detectives were reluctant to press charges when the plaintiff worked in the sex industry. By gathering evidence first, St. James could pressure the District Attorney's Office to file charges.

"Peggy," a "working girl" who advertised in the *Berkeley Barb* newspaper in 1977, called St. James when she was assaulted by client Floyd McCoy. When she arrived at his apartment, McCoy "grabbed her, pushed a gun in her face, and promised to 'teach her a lesson.' Peggy fled, with McCoy in unsuccessful pursuit." The police, however, refused to arrest McCoy. Eleven weeks later, the body of Jenny Chang, an honors student, was discovered "dead—nude and beaten—at the San Francisco State University Library, where McCoy was employed."[75]

Along with Asian American women's groups in the Bay Area, COYOTE rallied to demand the prosecution of McCoy. During his trial for assault with intent to commit rape, assault with a deadly weapon, and false imprisonment, "an effective support group developed substantial evidence contradicting McCoy's defense testimony," *off our backs* reported. The support group's efforts led McCoy's attorney to claim his client "the victim of a conspiracy." The conspiracy appears to be from the bench: the judge permitted the defense to question "Peggy" about her occupation and rejected evidence supporting the rape and gun possession charges. The jury convicted McCoy only of simple assault.

Many people rightly believed McCoy had gotten off very lightly, but his conviction signaled that prostitutes could also be victims of sexual assault and that they could have their day in court. Police skepticism remained high, however, and female victims were forced to run a gauntlet of examinations. "Peggy" had to pass a lie detector test before the police would take her statement, and hospitals did not routinely stock or administer rape test kits until the early 1980s. "Good girls" and "bad girls" were judged the same. If a case went to trial, the victim's entire sexual history could be discussed: the law presumed the rape victim was a slut who asked for it. Feminists, angered by the evidence presented by Susan Brownmiller in *Against Our Will* and elsewhere, lobbied hard for the adoption of rape shield laws that prohibited defense attorneys from introducing evidence about the victim's prior sexual behavior.[76] In fact, though, Brownmiller suggested that prior relations between the victim and the accused might be taken into consideration.

In San Francisco, COYOTE sought another definitive shift in the way the criminal justice system treated female sex workers. Alternatives to incarceration and pretrial diversion programs had been created primarily for male and juvenile offenders; programs for women were almost nonexistent. Criminologists noted that female offenders' crimes were either too severe to warrant leniency (killing an abusive husband or partner was a capital offense, not self-defense), or petty misdemeanor offenses—primarily shoplifting, check kiting, and prostitution—that though repeated, did not necessitate interventions by the system.

By the early 1970s, with federal money from Nixon's war on crime, social services in a few cities began to experiment with pretrial diversion programs specifically targeting women. In Boston, the federal Law Enforcement Assistance Administration funded a program in the Division of Female Offenders that regularly interviewed "arrested women, looking for those who are interested in changing their lifestyle." Eligible women from ages seventeen through twenty-six received access to counseling, housing, and day-care and health services during the ninety-day program. Prisoners' advocates noted with skepticism "the staff's tendency toward condescension," which was also reflected in the program's criteria for participation. The program "would reject, for example, a satisfied and successful prostitute." Counseling "tries to provide women with knowledge about their bodies and urges them to 'broaden their horizons,' so they don't see themselves as mere sex objects." To successfully complete the program, women had to persuade program counselors they had seen the error of their sinful occupations, before charges against them were dropped.

The way the justice system treated women offenders was criminal, COYOTE charged. The lack of community services or alternative sentencing programs designed for women made the problem worse. The state offered male ex-offenders with several prerelease and anti-recidivist programs. St. James wanted programs designed specifically for female offenders, whether they had been convicted for prostitution or other crimes. Women engaged in prostitution because they needed money; poverty—not childhood sexual trauma or psychoses—was why they broke the law.[77]

COYOTE's approach to assisting sex workers challenged the century-old reform paradigm in which middle-class, Christian, feminist, or public health charity workers attempted to rescue prostitutes from moral degradation. When St. James spoke at Harvard University in 1976, the *Crimson* reported:

> Evidently, the complaints and needs of those in the trade have been submerged for too long without channels for expression or counter-action, and COYOTE is the first attempt to respond from within. This is no bunch of holier-than-thou reformist outsiders trying to barge in and clean up—COYOTE is hookers helping hookers.[78]

COYOTE volunteer Georgia Wilkins was a hooker helping other hookers. She was twenty-four and the mother of two children. Wilkins moved to San Francisco "because of COYOTE," though she hadn't done sex work for five years. "I wanted to work politically so women would stop getting the brunt of it," she told an *LA Times* reporter in 1976. Her harsh experiences working on the streets of Seattle had been alienating because they brought home "that whore-madonna myth" emphasizing the line between good girls and bad girls. After attending a COYOTE meeting, Wilkins said, "Now I feel like I'm sort of both. If there is such a thing. Because I'm a mother, a worker for women's rights and a hooker."[79]

Like St. James, Wilkins saw clients only when she needed the money, not as a full-time career. Her current work as a call girl was a very different experience from her earlier years working in the streets. "The support from the other women makes it easier," she said, because of the camaraderie. They were strong women, who knew "when you have to pretend having intimacies with so many people, it's going to be trip on you."

As a speaker for COYOTE, Wilkins wanted people to adopt "a more realistic viewpoint, instead of blankly saying [prostitution] isn't good."

> People, because they are morally afraid of it, don't have a clear view and aren't educated enough to know what it is. We aren't saying it's good. But there is a real need for it. Those guys [clients] wouldn't be there it there wasn't. And women have their need of it too, for a lot of reasons. And we're saying that women should have the rights to their bodies.

Another reason she volunteered for COYOTE was because she was concerned her children would be affected by society's disrespect for sex workers. As a mother, she wanted them to be "really strong, independent kids" who wouldn't be embarrassed about their mother. "And if society will let them, I think they will understand. That I have to do certain things to survive."[80]

Wilkins's nuanced and complicated understanding of sex work underscores COYOTE's intersectional approach to services. Decriminalization, or, more accurately, changing the way law enforcement handled prostitution cases, helped improve conditions for women who wanted to continue working. By participating in COYOTE, sex workers realized they could constructively challenge the violence and social ostracism they had experienced. Indeed, by the mid-1970s, "coyote" became slang for an independent working woman who did not rely on a pimp.

Better transition programs, including job training, pretrial diversion, and alternatives to incarceration, could stop the permanent stigmatizing of women arrested for prostitution. As convicted sex offenders or "known prostitutes," they became second-class citizens or less, who could be legally barred from many types of jobs, housing, and other programs and services. Providing a real alternative would help women get out of "the life" if they wanted to and give them the opportunity to earn decent wages and the respect and independence that came with a good job.

In the late 1970s, some COYOTE members started to discuss another unmet need—what might they do for women who wanted business advice about how to set up their own businesses or wanted COYOTE to recommend a good place to work? Some thought COYOTE should provide training to beginning sex workers, give advice about unlicensed sex work businesses, or offer information about avoiding arrest and working more safely on the streets. It might even teach clients how to be nice to sex workers: a much more pleasant way to deter the men who constantly called the office in the mistaken belief COYOTE would give out members' names and phone numbers. If experienced sex workers shared their knowledge, everyone might benefit.

Assisting women who wanted better working conditions was a greatly needed service, but COYOTE could not risk "pandering" charges. As long as prostitution remained illegal, COYOTE could not tell others how to commit a crime. The dirty tricks of police and the FBI were known by then, and no one wanted a COYOTE member or the entire organization entrapped for criminal conspiracy or running a house of prostitution. The realization that someone could be arrested for these felonies—which seemed possible with revelations about the FBI's Counter-Intelligence Program (COINTELPRO)—forced COYOTE to review its programs. The chilling effect nixed some organizing projects and services for hookers to help hookers.[81]

COYOTE never developed the institutional structure or financial resources to decriminalize prostitution through the political or legal process. It did not have the large activist membership, pots of money, powerful political allies, and other resources to launch a campaign to change the law on a state-by-state basis. Not even advocates of the Equal Rights Amendment, with all their resources and support, managed to persuade thirty-eight state legislatures to ratify the constitutional amendment. St. James had a message and a vision that appealed to many in this liberal era, but COYOTE did not possess the power.[82]

"IF I CAN'T DANCE . . ."

"If I can't dance, I don't want to be in your revolution," anarchist and sex-worker advocate Emma Goldman said. Though she said it in 1911, most "serious" organizers paid little attention to creating a joyous movement culture for people to express themselves with dance, music, poetry, mural-painting, and other forms of people-friendly art. Even in the 1970s, white leftist and feminist activists mistrusted the effectiveness of "the art of protest." And as everyone knew, feminist activists were hatchet-faced gorgons who lacked a sense of humor.

But no one ever called "Chairmadam" St. James grim. Even when voicing anger about the wrongs done to prostitutes, she managed to make people smile or laugh. To prove sex workers weren't "mindless, lazy and diseased," she climbed Pike's Peak in Colorado. She became one of the few feminist spokespeople that journalists actually wanted to talk to, along with her frequent ally, Florynce Kennedy, New York City black lesbian feminist attorney and founder of the Feminist Party. Media inundated the Chairmadam with requests for interviews and comments on almost every issue, knowing that her charismatic personality and wit made good copy. Paul Krassner reported in *Rolling Stone*, jabbing mainstream and underground press alike, "Margo St. James turned the finest trick of her life when she turned this prurient interest of the media upon itself to spread the message of the hookers convention."[83]

The first National Hookers' Convention, held in June 1974 at Glide Memorial Church in San Francisco's Tenderloin, was nothing like the New York feminist conference on prostitution three years earlier. Tweaking propriety, St. James pulled her "finest trick" with a simple, mimeographed poster that read, "Our Convention Is Different: We Want Everyone to Come"; and to make sure people understood the double entendre, a line drawing showed female fingers stimulating an aroused clitoris and labia. The poster hit the sweet spot between popular culture and controversy while paying tribute to COYOTE's newest supporter, Betty Dodson, who was liberating masturbation like St. James was liberating hookers. As historian Leslie Fishbein noted, the poster

> simultaneously mocked the traditional anti-sexual preachings of organized Christianity [and] asserted the right of even prostitutes to satisfaction independent of their services to males, and echoed the growing concern of feminists with the clitoral orgasm and its implications for nonpatriarchal female pleasure.[84]

As the local host, COYOTE organized entertainment and serious discussion. Also attending were representatives of the Association of Seattle Prostitutes (ASP), of which Jennifer James was a member; and the Prostitutes of New York (PONY) that had formed to fight for sex workers hurt with the "clean up" of Times Square.

Over one thousand people attended, reported *off our backs*, and about a quarter of the attendees were journalists. The feminist media—like the rest of the media—were frustrated in their attempts to talk to real live prostitutes. They hounded anyone who stood out: A "sister of mercy," who may or may not have been an actual nun. A young woman with "her hair in a huge platinum Afro and a tiny silver bow in her nose" (who complained of all the photographs taken of her). St. James finally took the podium to explain there were "several professional women" around, perhaps as many as one hundred, but none of them fit the "1950 slut image" or the stereotype of a whore. Most of the women in the audience were "dressed casually in jeans and with little makeup," reported the *LA Times*. "We look just like everyone else," said St. James. Then she outed "two rows of plain-clothes police" to identify the faces of men who might try to entrap prostitutes attending the conference.[85]

Reverend Cecil Williams took the pulpit to welcome the delegates, the press, and everyone else to his church. As a community organizer since the early 1960s, Williams had led efforts to challenge police harassment and violence. In 1967 or so, "three Black prostitutes were brutally beaten by police," Williams recalled. "We formed a citizens' action group, got medical reports, began filing [law] suits and the door began to open." To Williams, the church's social justice mission meant helping everyone to fight for their rights.

Williams understood from this experience that decriminalizing prostitution was both a women's issue and a race issue. Police got away with brutalizing street-based sex workers because so many were women of color. Race discrimination by "plush hotels" that refused entry to black prostitutes led to a racially skewed pattern of arrests and sentencing: though they represented only two out of five women arrested on prostitution charges, 62 percent of those sentenced were nonwhite. The biggest danger to women of color was the police, not the pimps, not the customers, not even street criminals.[86]

After the invocation to "get it on" from Reverend Williams, "uhuru guru" Flo Kennedy gave the keynote address, wearing a "green pith helmet and floor-length lavender cape." "What is this shit that's going on between the whores and the police?" she asked. Kennedy broke down the situation in New York City. Commissioner Murphy had decided to harass street people, the "prostitutes, homosexuals, minorities, and women." That way no one paid attention to the real criminals like Mayor Lindsay and midtown business owners. "In this society you have to suck your way to power and the politicians are the real whores and pimps."[87]

"My Ass Is Mine!" sang a chorus of women, including several law professors, who joined St. James and Kennedy:

> When I'm out to take a walk, some guy says he wants to talk
> And my way proceeds to block, I get real sore
> 'Tho I know I speak real fine, that ain't what is on his mind.
> I'm another piece and he's just trying to score.[88]

With the singing, the band, the drag queen nightclub singer, the feminist comedienne duo, five belly dancers, St. James, Kennedy, and the meeting and greeting among the delegates, "the convention, it became clear, was not much of a convention at all but an event, a happening." The schedule ran well behind, and the planned two-hour panel discussion on decriminalization became a quick, twenty-five-minute summation.

But at that point, the first National Hookers' Convention faced unanticipated heckling from a sex worker angry that the women had not included him. "What about the rights of *male* prostitutes?" a "thin, red-haired young man" demanded. Operating within the framework of sex discrimination, the prostitutes' rights movement understood "sex" oppression as a women's issue. The movement welcomed all women and, importantly, recognized that racism made the experiences of women of color in the sex industry worse. But it was for sisters. "It's a gentleman's trip," as Lucia, another delegate, said. "A man propositions you, a man jails you, and a man bails you out." And she wanted to keep COYOTE for women. "COYOTE finally gave us something of our own."[89]

Men were welcome guests at the Hookers' Masquerade Ball, however. COYOTE's first public cultural event, held in October 1974, was advertised as "the social event of the year for heterosexuals, bisexuals, trisexuals, transsexuals, nonsexuals and other minorities who feel they are discriminated against." It was a relatively small affair, with only three hundred people in attendance, but everyone commented on the costumes. "Hot-pink pasties, g-strings, sequins and nudity adorned the raucous proceedings—but the drag queens reportedly outdid the rest."

In this, said one ball-goer, "Once again it's proven that men end up on top." The proceeds went to COYOTE's bail fund.[90]

In anticipation of the 1975 ball, COYOTE called a strike in solidarity with two hundred prostitutes in Lyons, France, who had occupied a church to protest police abuse. In accordance with the 1949 United Nations declaration, prostitution was decriminalized in France, but *les flics* refused to investigate complaints of violence, used debauchery laws to arrest women, and threatened to take away their children. The French strike had forced the national government, including President Valéry Giscard D'Estaing, to seriously address their issues.

COYOTE's ball attracted Bay Area politicians and Hollywood elites, including director Francis Ford Coppola and *Klute* star Jane Fonda. With this event, St. James established her reputation as cultural-political broker. In 1978, COYOTE's Hooker's Masquerade Ball attracted twelve thousand people to the San Francisco Cow Palace.[91]

The cultural force of the Hookers' Balls and Hookers' Conventions tended to overshadow COYOTE's organizing work, legal cases, service programs for sex workers—even its protests, such as the "loiter-ins" held at both the Republican and Democratic National Conventions of 1976. Even today, reproduction posters advertising the COYOTE balls of the mid-1970s remain in demand. COYOTE volunteers tended to dismiss the events, seeing them as public relations rather than the site of real political work. COYOTE volunteer organizer Georgia Wilkins said that "the bizarre image" of the event didn't help the public view of prostitution.[92]

The tension between realpolitik and cultural politics diluted COYOTE's impact and the movement's progress at the time. Feminists, mainstream and radical, as well as other activists on the new left were able to dismiss St. James's efforts to include women's sexual freedom in the feminist agenda. No matter how often she and other COYOTE members appeared at national and international women's conferences, they weren't accepted as legitimate members of the women's movement.

Yet COYOTE's positive long-term cultural influence was vast. Like the Cockettes, the Radical Faeries, and other transgressive tribes of the era, it inspired third-wave feminist sex workers and gender-bending queer sex radicals in later decades. Ironically, they too would fight against the mainstream gay rights lobby for visibility, challenging its focus on the rights of respectable citizenship.

For a time, women in San Francisco's sex industry enjoyed better treatment and haltingly created a framework for human rights. Yet it is doubtful that the prostitutes' rights movement would have won decriminalization in the 1980s, even if AIDS had not shifted COYOTE's priorities. The feminist anti-pornography movement's power was perversely amplified by Reverend Jerry Falwell's Moral Majority and other Christian conservatives, who posed formidable barriers to the rights of prostitutes. Activists of the 1970s created a movement based on human rights and cultural politics that would help sustain the cause as the first mysterious flush of Kaposi's sarcoma cases began to appear in San Francisco and New York City.

CHAPTER 4

"RESISTING THE VIRUS OF REPRESSION"

Disease Vectors and Sexual Experts

"THE PROSTITUTE STUDY" DIDN'T require participants to be sex workers, and most of the 180 women who volunteered for it had never done sex work. But the 1986 study was the first federally funded effort to focus specifically on AIDS among women. The women scientists who conducted it didn't focus on whether female sex workers could be vectors for the disease. Their goal was to determine the prevalence of AIDS-related retrovirus (ARV) in a large cohort of women; they also wanted to identify how seropositive women became infected.[1] Indicative of the sexism in medicine, when male AIDS researchers heard about a study to track the virus in women, they assumed the subjects were prostitutes. The story of the prostitute study tells us a lot about American public reaction to sex, women, and a previously unknown retrovirus.

Tagging the research as a prostitute study at least recognized female sexual agency. In the 1980s and 1990s, stories about women and AIDS focused on women as caretakers and nurses of dying (gay) men,

---

"This Condom Is Legal": Condom package, designed by No Condoms as Evidence Campaign, distributed at the International AIDS Conference, Washington, DC, 2012.

or on AIDS babies, as though mothers were merely human incubators. Women didn't get AIDS, the doctors said: white gay men presented with Pneumocystis carinii pneumonia (PCP) and Kaposi's sarcoma (KS), the two primary indicators of advanced infection; women didn't. Women's health advocates were skeptical. For years, they had demanded that the scientific establishment pay attention to women as medical subjects, and objected to the presumption that white male bodies were the norm.[2]

With the emergence of AIDS, some women redirected their fight, challenging assertions by the Centers for Disease Control and Prevention (CDC) that women could not contract Gay-Related Immune Deficiency (GRID), as it was first called. The "prostitute" tag suggested that some women, or at least some bad girls, could become infected because they shared similar sexual (read: promiscuous) lifestyles. Whether women could infect men or other women, and how transmission occurred, was unknown. No one mentioned condoms, because condoms were for prostitutes. Hospitals routinely reused needles. Most sexually transmitted infections could be cured with penicillin. So, it seemed an unplanned pregnancy was a woman's biggest worry, but there were plenty of birth-control methods available.

AIDS was a mystery. In the 1980s, scientists tried to unravel it by applying existing theories of disease, but those theories explained AIDS only after eliminating far too many outliers. Risk groups, lifestyle, sexual promiscuity, and identity—socially constructed classifications for human beings—left out a lot of people, including women whose bodies reacted to AIDS differently than male bodies; doctors did not associate recurring yeast infections, pelvic inflammations, cervical dysplasia, and other conditions with AIDS.

Too late, more than a decade after the first mortality report in June 1981, medical researchers began to accept that the human immunodeficiency virus (HIV) demanded a revolution in scientific thinking to understand its transmission and prevention. In 1996, there were more than half a million people living with AIDS in the United States; another ten years later, almost 600,000 Americans had died from AIDS-related causes.[3]

Epidemiologists had the clues to solve the mystery of AIDS by 1987. An investigation into the sexual histories of ten soldiers diagnosed with AIDS or AIDS Related Complex (ARC) at Walter Reed Hospital in Washington, DC, in 1984 suggested how transmission occurred, but doctors did not ask the right questions of the infected soldiers. Eight of the men, "reported sexual contact with prostitutes in various parts of the world, one had had multiple female sex partners in New York City, and one had had sex with a woman from Haiti."[4]

This was "proof" that women could infect men through heterosexual transmission. To Walter Reed doctors, it was obvious that prostitutes and Haitian women were disease vectors. They were wrong. A slew of angry letters poured in to the editors of the *Journal of the American Medical Association* criticizing the epidemiological claims of the study, but the idea that women infect men stuck.[5]

The Prostitute Study was the second clue to solving the mystery of AIDS. Presented in 1986 by Dr. Constance Wofsy, Dr. Judith Cohen, and their associates at San Francisco General Hospital, the study discussed the extreme difficulty of isolating ARV in vaginal or cervical secretions, throwing into question female-to-male transmission through unprotected, heterosexual intercourse.[6] "Promiscuous" sexual behavior did not explain how women became infected. The only behavior shared among the study's 180 participants with confirmed ARV was injection drug use; the criminalization of drug paraphernalia meant that users were more likely to share hypodermic needles.

With the availability of a blood-testing method (ELISA), the Prostitute Study, truthful responses from the Walter Reed soldiers, and other federally funded research, by fall 1986 scientists had the data to identify how the virus moved from one body to the next. Reviewing the construction of HIV by epidemiologists, medical historian Gerald Oppenheimer argues these studies should have ruled out lifestyle and identity as explanations for transmission: "The concept of high-risk membership should have actually withered away, replaced by the notion of *high-risk activities.*"[7](Emphasis in original.)

Had a public-health education initiative begun then, openly talking about condoms, sterile needles, safer sex, and taking steps to overcome resistance to their use—as sex workers started telling each other and their clients in 1983—an untold number of deaths and HIV infections could have been prevented. Instead, CDC researchers and political leaders continued to focus on risk groups. They warned citizens about AIDS among homosexuals, heroin users, Haitians, hemophiliacs, and hookers, the "4-H Club."

There was initial disagreement over whether the fourth "h" identity group should be hookers or hemophiliacs. The CDC chose the bleeding disorder that affects males almost exclusively. But the press chose to hunt for infected sex workers. In 1983, the *San Francisco Chronicle* managed to link AIDS with race, prostitution, drug use, criminality, and bad mothering in a story about Elizabeth Prophet, brought from county lockup to the AIDS ward. The deaths of her two children from "pneumonia" were only later connected to her HIV positive status.[8] Women didn't get AIDS; they just died from it.

Activists in COYOTE recognized they had to respond to AIDS. Margo St. James and Priscilla Alexander knew their members' lifestyles were more similar to those of promiscuous gay men than those of low-risk female heterosexuals. Warnings about "homosexual" men were vague too, since the sex trades included male hustlers—who might or might not be gay—and transwomen, as well as many injection drug users. The queer lives of sex workers, their clients, and their lovers, rarely fit neatly into Kinsey's static scales.[9] If lifestyle was indeed a factor for AIDS, then sex workers and others with sexual differences were at risk.

COYOTE was committed to protecting the health and welfare of sex workers. It was one of the earliest feminist organizations to teach safer sex to women and to recommend condoms for protection against disease. In 1983, even before the story about Prophet appeared, St. James and Alexander had begun to warn women "about a mysterious disease that was affecting gay men," COYOTE member Carol Leigh recalled. "And they insisted that I use condoms to protect my health."[10]

Alexander had read accounts of prostitution and disease; Judith Walkowitz's 1980 history of the impact of the Contagious Diseases Act on prostitutes in Victorian England showed how incurable sexually transmitted infections threatened the rights of sex workers and all women.[11] Alexander remembered thinking, "By the spring of 1983, AIDS began to pose serious problems for lesbians, gays, bisexuals and other sexually stigmatized groups, by setting the stage for major civil rights violations . . . I figured prostitutes would in some way become involved."[12]

Alexander, Leigh, and other sex workers were AIDS activists from the start, joining with other women to address the medical and political challenges of the disease and pushing the feminist sex wars into the background. After a decade of work for decriminalization, they did not want the human rights of sex workers sacrificed in the name of public health. From the early 1980s through the mid-1990s, COYOTE faced four major battles. First, to prevent the spread of AIDS, it needed to know the role of women in seroconversion, and to do that, to actively participate in medical research. Second, it needed to find ways to protect people in the sex industry; it taught them how to best protect themselves and the health of their clients and their intimate partners, and developed community programs to carry out that education. Third, COYOTE had to turn around attempts by the commercial media and medical researchers to blame female sex workers for spreading AIDS to heterosexual men. Fourth, it tried to stop laws criminalizing HIV-positive people, especially measures singling out sex workers—women, transwomen, and gay men—as disease vectors despite contrary scientific evidence.

In this 1980s version of *The Real World* reality show, sex workers did all this after Ronald Reagan and a reinvigorated Republican Party swept into Washington on an election "mandate." The new morality agenda celebrated family values with "the entire right-wing social agenda": abstinence-only sex education, "no promo homo," parental notification for reproductive services or venereal disease treatment, prayer in schools, and more. Prohibitionist feminists aligned with moral conservatives to make war on pornography and radical sex.[13]

The timeline of AIDS and AIDS activism changes when viewed from the perspective of sex workers, who were marginalized by white gay male movement leaders. ACT UP activist Sarah Schulman criticized the "gentrification" of AIDS advocacy that occurred as organizations professionalized their services and fund-raising, but sex-worker activists must still fight for the right to speak freely and receive money. Grants and government funding to educate and prevent AIDS have allowed sex worker–focused groups to institutionalize, to eventually meet at biennial International AIDS Conferences and harm reduction meetings, and to form the International Network of Sex Work Projects (NSWP) in 1990. But the result often looks more like a poor woman's fixed-up ranch facing foreclosure than the professionally rehabbed and decorated city brownstone of a married gay professional couple.

The current generation of community workers, safe-sex educators, peer counselors, health paraprofessionals, and student interns working with sex workers may have become petty bureaucrats whose salaries are paid with government funds. But they can also be civilly disobedient activists who break laws to prevent harm. They may distribute clean needles and syringes or hand out crack kits in violation of drug paraphernalia laws. They talk to youth in the sex trades to help them obtain shelter and necessities, and break trafficking laws. Some might provide medications, such as emergency birth control or post-exposure prophylaxis (PEP), without a prescription. Outreach workers may occasionally obstruct justice simply by letting folks on the stroll know the police are a few blocks away, or ignore mandatory government "pledges" that prohibit bureaucrats from supporting sex work. Their activism may not change official policy, but it does save lives.

"DANGEROUSLY CRAZY ABOUT SEXUALITY"

"The time has come to talk about sex," scholar-activist Gayle Rubin announced in 1982:

> To some, sexuality may seem to be an unimportant topic, a frivolous diversion from the more critical problems of poverty, war, disease, racism, famine, or nuclear annihilation. But it is precisely at times such as these, when we live with the possibility of unthinkable destruction, that people are likely to become dangerously crazy about sexuality.[14]

Rubin's paper, "Thinking Sex," written for the Barnard College sex conference, offered a framework for analyzing the social structure of erotic desire and sexuality that was separate from gender oppression and feminism. Stigmatizing people with sexual differences, and others who engaged in stigmatized sexual practices such as sex work, as "dangerous and inferior undesirables" led to medical policing and criminalization by the state.

Mapping a radical theory of the politics of sexuality, Rubin critiqued the position taken by sexual moderates who tried to avoid the excesses of anti-pornography feminists. In this middle ground, citizens condescendingly "defend the rights of erotic nonconformists to political participation." However, if a means to "normalize" the nonconformists' behavior should appear, moderates would expect the fixing to commence forthwith. In the interim, sexual moderates favored "consent," as St. James used the term, to argue the case for decriminalization and rights. But as a legal construct, Rubin notes, consent conveys a privilege "enjoyed only by those who engage in the highest-status sexual behavior."[15] People engaged in low-status sexual behaviors, such as street-based work, trading sex for drugs, or working without an escort license, remain criminals. A radical theory of sex, Rubin suggested, would favor sexual pluralism and erotic justice.

Other sex radicals, intellectual, indigenous, and otherwise, were also devising political theories of their own sexual cultures. In the ferment of analyzing the construction of sexuality and gender, race, and sometimes social class, theorists didn't free themselves from the trap of identity politics, preserving a kind of biodetermined nationalism that at first somewhat eased progressives' fears of expanding state power. In the face of the AIDS epidemic, the belief that certain semiprivileged groups were most at risk would demonstrate the deadly dangers of identity politics.

The effort to understand HIV demanded paradigm shifts in science, medicine, public policy, and the social organization of sexuality. Sexual behaviors had to be understood as separate from culturally constructed identities, "not [as] something we are, but something we do." Conflating "homosexual" identity with high-risk practices, CDC leaders asserted in October 1986 that "frequency of exposure"—a polite way of saying promiscuity—increased the "likelihood of transmission."[16]

"Frequent exposure" and "promiscuity" confused a scientific problem (What factors are causally responsible?) with a moral and political one (Who is accountable?). It was also sexist, based on a double standard that judged women's sexual behavior on far stricter terms than men's. A San Francisco study of "sexually active women" looked for "women [with] five or more partners in the past three years." That would have qualified one in five women students at UC Berkeley. In a letter to the *Lancet*, Dr. Joyce Wallace of St. Vincent's Hospital in Greenwich Village defined gay male promiscuity as "more than 50 partners a year"; in a popular women's magazine, one author claimed some gay men "had as many as 50 sexual partners a week."[17]

"Sex" seemed even more complicated. Government officials didn't use explicit language until 1987 when US Surgeon General C. Everett Koop's AIDS report recommended universal sex education and condom use. But Republican senator Jesse Helms slapped down that moderate

effort with his 1988 "no promo homo" amendment prohibiting HIV/
AIDS education programs that could "promote or encourage . . . sexual
activity, homosexual or heterosexual."[18]

Federal funding for the first national scientific survey of sexuality,
urgently needed to understand how people organized their sexual-social
networks, got hung up in a congressional sex war. Conservatives demanded changes in survey methodology, targeted populations, and even
what terms the researchers could use, as the Family Research Council
and the National Gay and Lesbian Task Force disputed what percent of
the US population was "gay."[19]

In the time of AIDS, "politically correct" identity politics among
progressive activists could be as "dangerously crazy" as the sexual policing advocated by moral conservatives. The confrontational tactics of
AIDS activists, demanding that researchers recognize the people whose
diseases they were trying to dissect, led to accusations that they were
introducing politics into scientific discourse.[20] But disruption was essential. AIDS was both a cultural signifier and a medical condition; acknowledging that symbiotic relationship was the only way to identify
potential research biases, scholar Paula Treichler argued:

> Nature and culture, reality and language, are interactive; they con-
> stitute each other. What this does not mean, however, is that nature
> and reality are fixed, certain, and unyielding while culture and lan-
> guage . . . are . . . purely arbitrary, or accidental.[21]

Science can only be as rational as social discourse permits.

Long ago, scientific thinking organized people into hierarchical
classes based on perceptions of their "natural" characteristics and intellectual abilities; such mismeasures of man (and woman) became identities that conferred political privileges and social class according to group
membership. Racialized, gendered, sexualized, and classed identities also
worked as devices with which scientists and the public assessed a person's
potential for diseases such as syphilis, sickle-cell anemia, breast cancer,
hysteria, and Tay-Sachs. Individual behaviors and talents, the intersectional availability of opportunities and structural disabilities, counted
only as curious anomalies, the exceptions that proved the rule. To suggest otherwise would destabilize scientific authority.

Now we know that HIV does not discriminate, but to solve its mystery, scientists and civilians had to discard much of what they thought they knew about bodies. They had to learn that a scientific "fact" can be a social construction; words describe only what people observe or instruments measure. The fact of the body does not predict its social behavior. Until quite recently, the view of "fixed bodies" dominated. Men were men, women were women, transgendered people were suspect, and the intersexed were from outer space.

From the body came identity, which was used as a proxy for behavior: women were gentle and communal, black people were musical and muscular, gay men were artistic and promiscuous, and lesbians were butch and asexual. The scientific certainty that gay people were born that way gave power to political claims—one of the most persuasive arguments in the gay rights movement said that it was unjust to discriminate on the basis of biology or genetics. Sexual identity was not a culturally constructed "preference" from which gay people might someday be cured—made "normal" through medical invention, marriage, or some 12-step program. AIDS showed us how to have theory in an epidemic if we were daring and radical enough to scrape off the labels so stubbornly glued to the jars of our bodies.

We now know that AIDS is not HIV, but the end stage of a viral infection that attacks the body's immune system, damaging white blood cells and making them unable to fight off other diseases. Living in semen and blood, the retrovirus moves between bodies through mucous membranes and open wounds. In North America, the primary modes of transmission are penetrative vaginal or anal sex without an impermeable barrier and shared hypodermic needles and syringes. It is "insanely difficult" to become infected through oral sex; HIV in body fluids cannot pass through healthy unbroken skin. For HIV-positive mothers, azidothymidine (AZT) can reduce the chances that they will pass the virus to their babies in the womb or through breastfeeding. Antiretroviral drugs can prevent further damage to the immune system and reduce viral loads to undetectable levels.[22] There is still no cure, but if a condom breaks (or there is no condom), a course of post-exposure prophylaxis (PEP) drugs can prevent an HIV infection if taken within seventy-two hours.

While scientists struggled to understand HIV, fear raged, propelled by ignorance and stereotypes. We now know that many of the CDC's early warnings were wrong, yet a 2011 survey by the Kaiser Family Foundation concluded that "myths about modes of transmission remain stubbornly persistent" among the general public. People still believe that drinking glasses, toilet seats, and swimming pools can be the source of an HIV infection.[23]

Some myths have been exposed: there is no "rugged vagina" endowed to resist the virus, and intravenous drug users don't bond over a "ritual" sharing of hypodermic needles. Honest, open discussions about sex are good, but people also need power to negotiate safe and fair terms, and some are less nimble on sexual terrains. Condoms, water-based lube, and clean needles work; Nonoxynol-9 and spermicides do not. Bathhouses and brothels are excellent sites to hold adult conversations about sex, pleasure, and health. And sexual pleasure comes in many forms. But these social science lessons took years to accept.

From the first mention of AIDS in the *Morbidity and Mortality Weekly Report (MMWR)* in June 1981, the CDC constructed it as a sexual disease that affected white gay men. Identity, not virology, would determine the course of scientific research and public policy for the first two decades. "Homosexual" served as trope for frequent, loveless, and unnatural sex practices, one that easily flexed to include all gay men, regardless of their actual sexual behavior or "lifestyle." In this modern time, the medical profession effectively swapped the recently invented "homosexual" for the historic "prostitute": a person who engages in promiscuous sexual intercourse.

Sex and high-risk lifestyles caused AIDS, the medical experts said. "The fact that these patients were all homosexuals suggests an association between some aspect of a homosexual lifestyle or disease acquired through sexual contact and *Pneumocystis* pneumonia in this population."[24] In the opinion of the CDC, "promiscuity"—a term conveying morality, not scientific exactitude—was dangerous. It did not consider the unexplained clusters of pneumonia deaths among young and poor inner-city African Americans and intravenous drug users as AIDS related.[25]

Scientists and straights seemed predisposed to believe in a gay cancer. CDC epidemiologists had just completed a Los Angeles–based study documenting a high incidence of sexually transmitted infections among gay men who sought clinical care. This research presumed that viral transmission was "a biological process within a determinate social

matrix." At the time, medical literature spoke of the "pathetic promiscuity" and "supposed hedonism" of homosexuals, implying a connection
between diseased bodies and psychosexual behavior. This is how many
straights understood "identity."[26]

People with AIDS were constructed as "homosexuals." They might
be called "faggots," "punks," or "sissies" by "straights," but doctors saw
them as mostly well-off urbanites, and almost all were white, making
them (fairly) respectable citizens who had been medically "compliant"
patients who followed doctors' orders in earlier studies. Because clusters
of gay men presented with PCP or KS infections, CDC epidemiologists
assumed there was a connection between these rare diseases and identity,
and consciously manipulated some early AIDS cases to make them fit
into the category of gay men.[27]

Women didn't present with these same diseases, and doctors failed
to fully investigate the causes of their illnesses. At New York City's Riker's
Island jail in 1981, young women, many of them African American and
Latina, were dying of pneumonia and other respiratory infections that
their immune systems couldn't fight.[28] Chaplain Eileen Hogan saw the
pattern early; Dr. Wendy Chavkin in the New York Public Health Department alerted the CDC about an unusual outbreak of candida (thrush)
at the jail. The inmates' shared histories of intravenous drug use, alco-
holism, prostitution, inadequate housing, incarceration, poor nutrition,
and medical neglect failed to interest the CDC, and no thorough investigation was done. "Jailhouse diseases" aren't copiously documented by
prison medical staff. On the outside, when women sought emergency
room treatment, doctors failed to report their conditions because they
were women, presumed to be medically noncompliant, uninsured, or
simply hysterical.[29]

Hookers and junkies may have been noncompliant, but women knew
something was wrong. Ignoring the doctors' ignorance, inmates at Bedford Hills Correctional facility in upstate New York initiated a program
to educate, support, and advocate for each other, with permission of
prison officials. AIDS Counseling and Education (ACE) "emerged from
nothingness with a need to build consciousness and save lives," former
prisoner and AIDS activist Katrina Haslip wrote.[30] ACE's work to create
a peer-education program for women in prison and after their release
(ACE-Out) transcended every identity label.

The women in Riker's Island and Bedford Hills didn't have many allies. For black women, the connection of HIV/AIDS with "promiscuous,
irresponsible and involved in illicit sexual activity such as prostitution"
undermined the civil rights quest for respectability, political scientist
Cathy Cohen argued.[31] Among conservatives—black and white—the
AIDS-related deaths of women could be blamed on their bad choices, not
systemic social injustice or the failure of medicine to see past poverty and
race, past identity.

They might have received better treatment if they had falsified their
sexual histories, like the soldiers in the Walter Reed study falsified theirs.
The doctors assumed soldiers' integrity and self-discipline, but the men
were covering their asses from the military brass. Their sexual and
health histories were self-reported, with no guarantee of confidentiality.
If they admitted to high-risk lifestyles—having sex with men or injecting
drugs—they faced dishonorable discharge, losing careers and GI benefits.[32] So the soldiers recycled the warnings they'd heard about sexually
transmitted diseases and blamed women for their infections.

Though AIDS remained identified as a disease of gay men, the Walter Reed Study led to news stories about heterosexual AIDS in 1985. Public confidence in science and government spokesmen began to crack. In
New York City, a health department epidemiologist ominously warned,
"50,000 to 100,000 women around the country, perhaps 40,000 in New
York alone, may now harbor the AIDS virus."[33]

The Reagan administration was forced to respond. Concerned about
the fitness of military personnel (but not civilians), the Pentagon announced that all new recruits would be tested. In February 1986, the
White House quietly instructed Surgeon General Koop to prepare a report on AIDS.[34] And while President Reagan had yet to mention AIDS in
public, the CDC and National Institutes of Health (NIH) began to fund
scientific research on women and AIDS, viewing promiscuous women as
a potential new risk group.[35]

"PROSTITUTES ARE BEING SCAPEGOATED FOR AIDS"

If a man could contract AIDS because he had "frequent homosexual con-
tacts with various partners" as the *MMWR* claimed, was there a heterosexual analogy? Could women who had frequent sex with various male
partners also be at risk? The medical literature didn't discuss male sex

workers. All "homosexuals" were male; no distinctions were made as to transwomen, bisexual men, "gay for pay" hustlers, or those with other sexual differences.[36]

Sex-worker activists understood that public leaders historically blamed "undesirables" for disease and social problems. Dolores French, founder of Atlanta's Hooking Is Real Employment (HIRE), an affiliate of COYOTE, recognized the potential for backlash:

> [W]e realized that, as working prostitutes, we faced an almost in-surmountable challenge . . . In 1984, heterosexuals were still go-ing on their merry way, not caring or even knowing about safe sex, thinking of AIDS as something that happened to *those people.* But we prostitutes knew that, sooner or later, AIDS would spread into the heterosexual community and that when it did not only would we be blamed, but if history were any guide, we would also be ar-rested, quarantined, and worse.[37]

The 1984 COYOTE convention in San Francisco, held a week before the Democratic National Convention that nominated Walter Mondale and Geraldine Ferraro, was billed as a "Women's Forum on Prostitutes' Rights." But politics and political theories weren't on the agenda; attend-ees were more concerned about how to prevent AIDS for themselves and their clients. French wrote,

> We considered ways to get the word about safe sex out to as many working women as possible because, if a man frequents prostitutes, he usually frequents a lot of prostitutes.[38]

French had a better grasp of male clients' sexual behavior than CDC officials. But French, like almost everybody else at the time, thought that HIV behaved like other viral infections, moving from one body to the next through body fluids, perhaps even by touch or through the air.

Sex workers had integrated safer sex into their practices decades ago. How to prevent unwanted pregnancies and diseases is among the first lessons, if not the first lesson, learned in the profession. Taking care of one's own health and determining a client's health is a skill set that has been passed down for generations. But ideas about "responsibility" for preventing conception and disease had shifted with the availability of the Pill and other birth-control methods. In the sex industry, many prostitutes and clients continued to use condoms, a holdover from World War II, when the Armed Forces insisted on using them to prevent syphilis and gonorrhea among servicemen.

The continued stigmatization of venereal diseases, however, led to occupational and class biases against routine condom use. Street and brothel workers were more likely to use condoms, or charge more money for sex without, but high-class services expected women to use the Pill. Sydney Biddle Barrows, the "Mayflower Madam," did not allow escorts to use condoms because they were "good" girls, and their clients from the "best classes" of men—class, presumably, being a 100 percent effective prophylaxis.

Barrows did, however, teach her workers how to do a precoital visual inspection, a "dick check," for open sores, rashes, warts, or crabs. She also compensated them when they chose not to have sex with a client for health or safety reasons. This introduction to worker safety in the sex trades was common long before AIDS. But AIDS required new methods. Lesions from Kaposi sarcoma served as a telltale sign, but KS is an end-stage disease. No one could visually identify HIV in a prospective partner. Sex workers demanded more information.[39]

AIDS posed a threat to sex workers because the government might adopt the repressive policies of the past. In the 1980s, there were calls for quarantines, mandatory testing, contact tracing for everyone identified with HIV, and public registration of all prostitutes and licensed brothels. But attitudes toward prostitution had hardened, making the political landscape different from earlier times. Rather than regarding sex trade as a "necessary evil," the moral conservatism so deeply embedded in the Reagan era turned toward abolitionism: the goal was to wipe out pornography, prostitution, and all promiscuous behavior.

The public sex panic was not confined to the Republican Party; in San Francisco, Mayor Dianne Feinstein, feminists, and gay activists also participated. "Acquired Surveillance-System Efficiency Syndrome (A.S.S.E.S.) is sweeping our community with guilt and repression," read an ironic 1983 protest flyer against the public sex panic in San Francisco. The city's "red light abatement" campaign began before AIDS and was aimed at (heterosexual) massage parlors, encounter studios, after-hours clubs, and other places suspected of prostitution or of making fraudulent offers of sex for pay.[40]

"The uptight 'good girl' who took over as mayor has turned her cops loose on prostitutes and made their lives worse than it's been in years," said Margo St. James.[41] In 1984, good girl Feinstein, *Chronicle* reporter Randy Shilts, and others successfully shut down gay bathhouses, leather-sex bars, and sex clubs, claiming a public health emergency.

Public health policies for preventing HIV in Nevada's licensed brothels weren't concerned about public morality, but on protecting the interests of brothel owners and the state's tourism industry. They were hardly silver examples of enlightened progressive health policies. Legislators wanted to ensure that workers, in French's words, would "be controlled and tested and 'made safe' for clients." She was correct to worry "that the government would end up treating prostitutes like a commodity."[42]

In Nevada, medical inspections and work licenses were supposed to prevent sexually transmitted infections before AIDS. For that reason, brothel owners did not permit workers to demand condoms.[43] Nevada was one of the first states to criminalize sex workers with AIDS, and in March 1986, it was also the first state to adopt mandatory AIDS tests for brothel workers. Of course, the workers, not the owners or the state, had to pay for the tests. A year later, after realizing that a clear test was only good until the next time a person had an unprotected encounter, the Nevada board of health established a mandatory condom policy.[44]

If hooking was to be regarded as real employment, Dolores French and other COYOTE members wanted to know whether sex workers would have rights as employees. Despite licensing, states did not recognize prostitutes as workers entitled to employee and health benefits as blackjack dealers, bartenders, and Vegas showgirls were:

> [I]f a woman [working in a Nevada brothel] is found to be AIDS antibody positive, she isn't given any kind of unemployment or offered worker's compensation. She is simply kicked out of the state of Nevada. And the men, meanwhile can go to brothels assured that the remaining women are "clean."[45]

As a civil rights issue, the early years of fighting against AIDS discrimination focused mostly on issues faced by gay men, the "people" with AIDS" (PWAs). Their first successful lawsuits recognized HIV as a legitimate disability and entitled PWAs to protection under federal civil rights laws. A California man won workers' compensation benefits in 1987 after proving that his employer condoned "recreational sex" with "native women" in Zaire, where he claimed he contracted HIV.[46] Health-care workers, police officers, and fire department personnel have won compensation for HIV contracted in the line of duty; one can only hypothesize the conditions and proof needed for a sex worker to win workers' compensation benefits based on seroconversion.

In California, sex workers led action on AIDS and AIDS-related issues, primarily because COYOTE and the United States PROStitutes Collective had laid the organizational groundwork. People arrested on prostitution charges were singled out in the nation's first mandatory AIDS testing law. Priscilla Alexander and Gloria Lockett participated in developing the first general population survey of AIDS among women. In San Fernando, the Adult Industry Medical clinic opened in 1998, providing industry-standard STI and HIV testing and general health care for performers.

There were pockets of activity elsewhere too. In Seattle, sex workers won a grant from Kings County to conduct peer-run street outreach and health education campaigns.[47] In Atlanta, Dolores French was one of the first sex workers to openly serve on an official government commission considering the public response to prostitution and AIDS.[48] The chair and other members valued her knowledgeable and articulate contributions, supporting her even after her arrest for "operating an escort service without a license" in March 1985 (a charge almost never made). The press called the commission's recommendations—methods curbing street prostitution, for city-funded, voluntary testing for HIV and STIs in exchange for reduced sentences, as well as safe-sex education for sex workers—"pragmatic" and "thoughtful," but ultimately, the commission was another lost cause.[49]

French could wow the World Whores' Congress with a hilarious condom demonstration, but folks back home in Georgia were not impressed. The chairman of the state AIDS task force wanted mandatory testing of all convicted prostitutes, and dismissed concerns about constitutional rights; another member, a pediatrician, called safe sex "a figment of the imagination" and claimed one prostitute could infect "5,000 unborn babies" in five years. Attorney General Mike Bowers, who had just successfully defended the state's sodomy law in the US Supreme Court, said he would soon issue an opinion on the matter.[50]

New York City led the nation in AIDS cases, and from the mid-1980s through the 1990s, the Gay Men's Health Crisis and the AIDS Coalition to Unleash Power (ACT UP/NY) dominated local politics. ACT UP's "base was that of the well-educated, white, gay male of Manhattan who had sophisticated knowledge of New York's culture, politics, and art"; many, it should be noted, traded sex as workers and as clients.[51] Though they did not identify as "sex workers," they used their expertise to teach people "how to have sex in an epidemic," refusing to abide the restrictive counsel for sexual abstinence or long-term monogamy.[52]

New York health advocates issued conflicting statements regarding AIDS and prostitution. In 1982, Dr. Joyce Wallace found two sex workers (in a group of twenty-five) with "compromised immune systems, including one who quickly developed full-blown AIDS." But, she later conceded, "there is almost a complete overlap between drug use and prostitution."[53]

Public health officials in New York City and State warned against violating the civil rights of prostitutes after Randy Shilts wrote alarmingly about salesmen taking the disease home to Cincinnati. Don Des Jarlais, an epidemiologist in the New York State Health Department, endorsed needle exchanges as a risk-reduction practice, and at the 1986 international prostitutes' rights convention in Brussels, announced with professional authority, "The bottom line is that AIDS is spread by behavior, not labels."[54]

Labels still mattered, though. The Women's Committee of ACT UP/NY might have become a token; the CDC claimed that only 9 percent of AIDS cases were women, and many believed they were all "perverse" women at that. An article in *Cosmopolitan* magazine in January 1988 seemed to confirm this view of perversity by claiming that (white) heterosexual women were in "no danger of contracting AIDS through *ordinary* sexual intercourse." The committee struck back with a protest at the Hearst Building, where the women refused to negotiate with the police, changing the way all future ACT UP demonstrations organized.[55]

Iris de la Cruz—"Iris with the Virus"—was diagnosed a few months before the *Cosmo* article appeared. In twenty years, she had lived through motherhood, drug use, street work, reviving Prostitutes of New York

(PONY), rehabilitation, then methadone and a job as an emergency medical technician; doubtless she'd seroconverted years before she looked "like the national AIDS poster child."[56]

Through her mother, Beverly Rotter, de la Cruz got involved in AIDS activism, and for three and a half far-too-short years, she was everywhere: writing a column for the People With AIDS Coalition newsletter, speaking at the ACT UP women's demonstration at the Department of Health and Human Services in Washington, DC, in October 1990, demanding that HIV-positive women be made eligible for disability compensation.

But AIDS still wasn't a "women's" issue. Even as the number of US women with AIDS climbed, people believed that promiscuous lifestyles tied the risk groups together, focusing attention on prostitutes—historically associated with disease and danger—rather than sexual practices. The mass media perpetuated this idea with headlines such as "Hookers Carrying AIDS."[57] The rights and health of sex workers were never the issue; public opinion said the disease was just punishment for their promiscuity, just as it was for gay men.

Nor was the public concerned about the health of African American women when President Reagan talked about a "Cadillac-driving welfare queen" more often than the six thousand men and women who had already died from AIDS-related illnesses. Yet in 1986, the majority of women affected with AIDS were African American (51 percent) and Hispanic (20 percent), and most of them were between thirteen and thirty-nine years old.[58] As for the rights and lives of seropositive injectors, male or female, Reagan's "war on drugs" turned them all into criminals. Good (white) girls just said no to sex and drugs.

The wives of the Cincinnati salesmen described by Randy Shilts weren't worried until "heterosexual AIDS" endangered their health and their children. As mainstream women's magazines focused on heterosexual white women, the public turned away from dangerous women of color and drug users toward sympathetic "traditional" families. White women, as potential victims rather than as perpetrators of an epidemic, aroused political action playing on gendered racial differences. The dark, drug-addicted sexual bodies of the underclass needed tough-love discipline and welfare cuts. But the have-it-all career women and suburban mothers also required discipline. Integral to the conservative Christian social agenda, premarital chastity, marital fidelity, and family values were promoted as its version of safe sex, offering more protection against AIDS (and abortion) than condoms.[59]

The US Public Health Service (USPHS) counseled citizens in 1986 that sexual abstinence and long-term mutually monogamous relationships were the best ways to prevent infection, and it still does. This advice, based on moral values, further criminalized sexual differences. In 1987, the USPHS recommended HIV testing and counseling for all "homosexual men, IV-drug abusers, persons with hemophilia, sexual and/or needle-sharing partners of these persons, and patients of sexually transmitted disease clinics [and] male and female prostitutes."[60]

Coupled with fear and stigma, today HIV is a status offense in thirty-four states.[61] HIV-positive status now turns people into sexual offenders; prosecutors don't have to prove someone with HIV intended to or actually transmitted the virus to obtain a conviction. In many jurisdictions, spitting or biting is a crime, even though saliva does not carry HIV.[62] Prostitution is a misdemeanor but becomes a felony if sex workers are HIV positive.[63] Though positive clients are also violating HIV exposure laws, there is no known conviction. Indicative of transphobia, the first felony convictions of HIV-positive sex workers in the Bay Area were transwomen. But the press and the government continued to warn people about "prostitutes."

COYOTE reframed the debate to stop the scapegoating of sex workers. Priscilla Alexander discarded the term "prostitute" and started using Carol Leigh's term "sex worker." This linguistic tactic shifted attention to a sex-positive image, removed from the ancient image of prostitutes as reservoirs of infection and as vectors of disease. Sex workers became potential "sex experts" who could serve as frontline educators to a hard-to-reach adult population that knew little about safer sex. By the early 1990s, HIV researchers adopted the term, acknowledging a need for cultural neutrality, as they also adopted "MSM" for men who have sex with men and later employed "survival sex" and "exchange sex" to refer to people who traded sex for drugs or other necessities.[64]

Understanding sex work and AIDS required factual information, not tropes. In January 1984, Alexander attended the first National Organization for Women Lesbian Conference, where civil rights attorney Katy Taylor warned delegates that the crisis would affect them, that it was already affecting them.[65]

Five hundred people showed up at the San Francisco Women's Building in October 1984 for a meeting organized by the Women's AIDS Network at which Priscilla Alexander and Gloria Lockett were recruited as representatives for sex workers. In June, Lockett recalled, COYOTE had organized a national "Feminist Alliance on Prostitutes' Rights," which brought together "about 50 people, prostitute supporters, advocates, working prostitutes, and ex-prostitutes" who met at Margo St. James's place in Mill Valley.[66]

Lockett was working as an interviewer for Project AWARE (Association for Women's AIDS Research and Education) and recognized that its research model didn't provide informants with more than a condom. It needed more focus; "something more definite had to be done with prevention and education."[67] After many monthly "rap groups," exploring what sex workers could do about AIDS, they founded the California Prostitute Education Project (CAL-PEP) in 1985. Created and run primarily by women in the sex trades, CAL-PEP's prevention programs were street-based. It was "an easy transition from street walker to street worker for the ex-prostitutes."[68]

CAL-PEP's street outreach taught sex workers about safer sex, and its staff taught researchers how to create studies with a truly representative sample of women with "promiscuous" sexual histories, paid and unpaid. Drs. Constance Wofsy and Judith Cohen were studying the purported link between sex work and AIDS to "define whether it's a big issue, a little issue, or a non-issue."[69]

Only one-third of the participants were sex workers, but Wofsy and Cohen collaborated with CAL-PEP volunteers to design a pioneering, feminist research project that would become a model for future studies. Sex workers developed recruitment strategies and outreach materials for a cross-section of women, rather than focusing on women in prison, jails, and AIDS wards, as other studies did. To create a safe space for participants, respect their dignity, and ensure anonymity, counselors were women like themselves who could also provide medical and social service referrals, and met people near their homes rather than in AIDS clinics. Most importantly, fearing they might be duped into a new Tuskegee Syphilis Study, sex workers demanded that researchers share the results with them.[70]

Alexander and CAL-PEP did their own interpretation of the results before presenting them to the public. The data confirmed a difference between women who used intravenous drugs and those who did not: sharing needles accounted for almost all of the women's positive ELISA tests, the rest had (male) lovers who injected drugs. The research also revealed that HIV transmission was more likely unilateral from male to female; there were no confirmed cases in which women infected men during sexual contact.

In 1988, Cohen, Wofsy, and Alexander published an article summarizing all of the existing research, recommending that public health agencies endorse safer-sex education and promote the use of latex condoms for sex workers, even with their intimate partners. Of key concern should be IV-drug users who, because of their addictions, were less likely to insist on condoms.[71] Despite the high number of HIV-positive street-based workers in New York City, Alexander noted elsewhere, infection rates among heterosexual men remained low. "A street prostitute is likely to see eight guys a day—that's 1,500 a year," she said. "Given these numbers, if it was going to happen, we would have seen it by now."[72]

Though the CAL-PEP study showed unsterile needles were the more likely vector for AIDS transmission, politicians and the press continued to claim, like the Walter Reed doctors, that prostitutes were spreading AIDS to heterosexual men. As director of the National Task Force on Prostitution, Alexander disputed the "infected hooker spreads AIDS" myth in newspaper columns, press releases, and elsewhere. In New York City, advocates like Katy Taylor worked with outreach workers from the Judson Memorial Church to draw press attention to increased harassment and violence against sex workers by police and civilian men. Instead, the media launched a hysterical search for new heterosexual culprits.

The rush to test all arrested sex workers with a view toward criminalizing seropositive women and men in the sex industry was an ineffective means for preventing the spread of AIDS, warned Wofsy, Cohen, and Alexander. When brothels were closed during World War II, syphilis and gonorrhea skyrocketed because "non-professionals" did not use condoms and did not understand alternative prophylaxis methods. Testing might sound good, but did not ensure clients' health and ignored the civil rights of sex workers. Yet mandatory and routine testing as well as criminalizing HIV-positive sex workers was exactly what lawmakers chose to do.

CRIMINALIZING SEX

In the fearful climate of the 1980s, COYOTE did not have the resources to win a legislative or court battle against the criminalization of seropositive sex; indeed, very few lawyers in the civil liberties or gay rights establishment were willing to take up that fight on behalf of sex workers.[73] During the sex panics of the 1970s over gay teachers in public schools and modest civil rights laws protecting gays and lesbians, conservatives set the terms of the debate. To quell the panic over "homosexuals," conservative gays and lesbians led the campaign to distance themselves from their identities as sexual beings. They believed that aiding others with sexual differences, as Gayle Rubin suggested in 1982, could undermine efforts to win gay civil rights.

Jerry Falwell of the Moral Majority and Donald Wildmon of the American Family Association were just two of the religious right leaders to condemn the "disease-carrying deviants [who] wander the streets unconcerned possibly making you their next victim."[74] In 1984, Dr. James Fletcher, editor of the *Southern Medical Journal*, quoted St. Paul on "the due penalty of their error" and opined, "a logical conclusion is that AIDS is a self-inflicted disorder for the majority of those who suffer from it."[75]

Georgia Attorney General Gary Bowers shared the belief that deviant sexual practices were dangerous to public safety. He defended his decision to appeal the court's ruling in Michael Hardwick's criminal sodomy case to the Supreme Court, arguing that "the law would help reduce the spread" of AIDS. In *Bowers v. Hardwick* (1986), the Court announced that homosexuals had no constitutional right to sexual privacy. In a 1987 public opinion survey, 43 percent of respondents believed AIDS was just punishment for a person's behavior.[76]

The political rise of the Christian Right did not rely solely on homophobia. It also attacked pornography, recreational sex, public sex, and abortion, the central issues of sexual freedom. Among Pat Robertson's acolytes and Jerry Falwell's disciples, disgust over sex outside of marriage was based on the religious ethics of Southern Protestantism. Sexually arousing and sexually explicit images and literature were obscene; religious ideals should prevail over freedom of expression. Sex for purposes other than procreation (including homosexual and hetero-sexual sodomy) undermined holy matrimony. Abortion and contraception were wrong not only because life began at conception but because they permitted women to escape just punishment (bearing and raising a child) for their sexual sins.

And of course, prostitution encouraged men to violate their marriage vows—although that hardly stopped a string of fundamentalist ministers from hiring sex workers, female or male, depending on their predilections. Pentecostal evangelist Jimmy Swaggart, whose television ministry reached an estimated eight million viewers in the mid-1980s, was found with sex worker Debra Murphree in Lake Charles, Louisiana, in 1988, one of several women he hired regularly in and around Baton Rouge.[77] In his confession to church elders, Swaggart also admitted he was "addicted" to pornography. Three years later, the California Highway Patrol stopped Swaggart with Rosemary Garcia, another sex worker. Answering the typically inane media question about why she worked for Swaggart, Garcia echoed bank robber Willie Sutton, "He asked me for sex. I mean, that's why he stopped me. That's what I do. I'm a prostitute."[78]

Murphree and Garcia protected themselves, insisting Swaggart use condoms, a safer-sex precaution that neither he nor his fundamentalist brethren were willing to allow members of their congregations—or the public, if they could help it. However, "straight" feminists at the time did not exhibit the same sense of self-preservation as these sex workers. Ignoring their basic disagreements with the Christian Right, feminists from the anti-pornography movement welcomed the final report of Attorney General Edwin Meese on pornography in 1986, which called for stronger enforcement of federal legislation that restricted the sale of, and access to, sexually explicit images.[79] They made stranger bedfellows than Sheriff Hongisto and St. James had a decade before.

The rise of the anti-pornography movement led to a particularly stressful period for sex-worker activists, who felt battered from the Right and the Left. For radical feminists, fighting pornography was the next logical step in their critique of patriarchal violence. Classless in its analysis of the employment issues and the actual labor conditions of sex workers, their movement focused almost exclusively on men who, they believed, were engaged in a global conspiracy to dominate women.[80] Their targets were not merely the producers of pornography but also its distributors, consumers, and even male (and sometimes female) performers. The infamous slideshow created by Feminists Against Pornography used emotional appeal to incite activists, a tactic copied by contemporary anti-sex-trafficking activists. Noticeably absent in these years was any female-authored feminist critique of gay porn; and criticism by men tended toward self-flagellating essays about the wrongs of heterosexual porn.[81]

The first San Francisco demonstration organized by Women Against Violence in Pornography and Media (WAVPM) targeted Broadway, the heart of the city's commercial sex district. Angry marchers elbowed their way into the encounter parlors, topless clubs, and peep shows, harassing and threatening the working women and men. Demonstrations at the Mitchell Brothers O'Farrell Theatre in the Tenderloin kept customers from entering. WAVPM members were pleased with their success, but the exotic dancers who worked there were not. US PROS Collective sent WAVPM a cease-and-desist demand in 1983, insisting that it stop interfering with their livelihoods.[82]

Arrests for soliciting and prostitution increased in the 1980s, and police rounded up street-based workers—female, male, and transgender—on harsher charges as part of the war on drugs. Prosecutors dug up old laws designed to regulate prostitutes and prevent the spread of communicable and venereal disease, along with midcentury anti-terrorism statutes that criminalized the possession of "infectious" agents. Prosecutors charged HIV-positive sex workers with attempted manslaughter, even when the accused "used condoms with every client and no client tested positive."[83]

On the far end of the political spectrum, Lyndon LaRouche put an initiative on the California ballot in 1986 classifying AIDS as a communicable disease, triggering "Typhoid Mary"–type quarantines by local officials. Over two million people cast ballots in favor of the initiative, 29 percent of the total vote.[84] With clear support for stronger political action, legislators filed dozens of bills; most blatantly discriminated against HIV-positive people. Despite activists' efforts, two bills passed. The first, passed in 1988, endorsed by the state's powerful prison officers' unions, mandated AIDS testing of all prisoners and allowed officials to quarantine anyone who tested positive, though it did not provide for specialized medical care. The second, sponsored by conservative Republican

Senator John Doolittle, amended the sexual offenses statute and was copied by legislatures in Georgia, Florida, Utah, and Nevada.[85] It made soliciting and prostitution a felony on the second offense if the accused tested positive, and carried a sentence of up to three years in prison. By 1994, "20 people, including 12 women and eight men" were imprisoned on felony prostitution charges, according to San Francisco NOW activist Teri Goodson.[86]

COYOTE, with ACT UP/SF and support from public health workers, fought against these laws, but the landscape had shifted since June 1988, when President Reagan's Commission on the HIV Epidemic called for criminal sanctions against anyone who "engaged in behavior which is likely to transmit" the virus. Carol Leigh, Priscilla Alexander, and others did what they had done earlier, testifying before Doolittle's judiciary committee in Sacramento, lobbying Assembly members, and meeting them in their home districts.[87] Sharon Kaiser, COYOTE education director and CAL-PEP's social worker, handled the press and public relations. Even Speaker Willie Brown, whom St. James had known since the early 1960s, was unable to pull one of his famous legislative maneuvers to prevent passage of the Doolittle bill.[88]

Frustrated and angry, Leigh, dressed as Scarlot Harlot, led three hundred sex workers in June 1990 in a street march on the Sixth International AIDS Conference meeting at the Moscone Convention Center. Inside, the marchers protested the exclusion of women from AIDS research while lawmakers targeted sex workers as disease vectors. Leigh, filmmaker Dee Dee Russell, Vic St. Blaise (founder of *Whorezine*), and Rebecca Hensler of ACT UP/SF were some of the sex-worker and AIDS activists who also blocked the steps of San Francisco City Hall in a last attempt to stop implementation of mandatory testing.[89]

Civil liberties advocates had already filed an injunction to stop mandatory testing before the bill went into effect in January 1989. Grace Lidia Suarez, an attorney with San Francisco's public defender's office, filed suit on behalf of COYOTE member Heather Love and ten other convicted sex workers (eight women and two men) and won a stay of execution while the court considered the bill's constitutionality. In Love's case, the court upheld the law as a "special need" to protect public health and safety. California's Supreme Court refused to hear the case in 1991, and testing began.[90]

But the scientific grounds cited by the court were unsound, even specious. The USPHS based its recommendations on moral values, discarding CDC-funded research that threw into serious question assumptions about heterosexual transmission:

> Male and female prostitutes should be counseled and tested and made aware of the risks of HIV infection to themselves and others. Particularly prostitutes who are HIV-antibody positive should be instructed to discontinue the practice of prostitution. Local or state jurisdictions should adopt procedures to assure that these instructions are followed.[91]

The gender-neutral language made HIV transmission appear bidirectional, similar to syphilis and gonorrhea. Yet there was no conclusive evidence, and no confirmed cases in 1987 or when the case was decided in 1990, that women infected men through vaginal intercourse. There was only *suspicion* of possibility, based on the myth that the promiscuous lifestyle of certain risk groups spread HIV to "innocent victims."

Further, the *MMWR* guidelines and California law did not take into account the wide variety of services offered by sex workers, female and male, instead presuming that vaginal or anal intercourse without a latex condom were standard. Sexual behavior and client interests had changed significantly since 1981, as the legislative record showed. Carol Leigh and Gloria Lockett testified that clients and workers now asked for safer-sex practices, fantasy scenes, mutual masturbation, and hand jobs. The inclusion of "male prostitutes" collapsed many kinds of male sex workers but in intent, targeted homosexuals. The suggestion that sex workers discontinue the practice implied that money, not blood or semen, was the transmission route. The law remains in force.[92]

In May 1991, a felony case against an "L.A. Hustler With AIDS" began. Three months later in August, a thirty-five-year-old woman was convicted of felony prostitution in Contra Costa County. In October, San Jose police profiled a "transvestite" with twenty-one previous prostitution convictions who they knew was HIV positive. After they saw "him" "waving at and making eye contact with lone male motorists," police followed him to a hotel and busted down his door (which *Bowers* permitted). There they saw "Diana" providing oral sex with a condom. The judge denied bail, saying, "[H]e poses an 'extreme danger' to the community."[93]

HUMAN RIGHTS AND HARM REDUCTION

Sex workers had reason to view the medical establishment and scientific research with suspicion. Historically, public health officials had targeted prostitutes as the source of sexual diseases in the general population and had enacted vicious and violent regulations to police women working in the sex industry, and other women suspected of loose morals. Health-care workers and women's rights activists rarely treated sex workers humanely, although there were exceptions.

Researchers at prestigious institutions tended to view sex workers as dumb broads, perhaps more valuable than lab rats, but not much more. Alfred Kinsey and his colleagues hired female prostitutes to study male sexual arousal and response. At first, female sexuality didn't interest them; when they decided it might be an interesting topic, they chose to study normal wives not tramps.

Logically sex workers could have provided professional expertise to the sexologists, but they were rarely consulted nor was their knowledge regarded as authoritative, except perhaps on issues of deviant sexuality. As Gail Pheterson remarked, "Rarely are stigmatized behavior patterns studied in dominant social groups or even in legitimized subordinate groups such as 'wives.'"[94] Scientists were no more enlightened than their fellow men, believing that any woman who degraded herself through prostitution must be unintelligent, but then many assumed that *all* women were brainless.

In the 1960s and 1970s, the feminist health movement and the efforts by African American groups ranging from the Black Panther Party to the Congressional Black Caucus adopted a critical stance toward health and science, questioning professionals' preferential treatment of WASP males and their old boys' clubs. Challenging everything from the absence of women and minority students in graduate and medical schools to the use of black and female bodies as guinea pigs for medical research, activists used identity politics as a hammer to break down doors and change the system.

They also created alternative health-care clinics and developed models of care based on information sharing and collaboration between patients and medical workers. The Boston Women's Health Collective, the Emma Goldman Clinic in Iowa City, the Black Panthers' Peoples' Free Medical Clinics, the Tenderloin Free Clinic, and free and sliding-scale clinics across the nation targeted the particular needs of their populations, needs that had long been ignored by the Establishment. Feminists challenged the presumption that women's health should focus primarily or exclusively on reproductive health, since it presumed that women existed merely to reproduce "mankind" and that the quality of their own lives were immaterial. These developments profoundly shaped the way progressive activists responded to the AIDS epidemic.

The political crises of the early 1980s threw sex-worker activists and everyone else on the Left into disarray. A mere dozen years after its founding, COYOTE members felt like everything was rolling backward. Old allies abandoned the sex workers' rights movement, turning almost completely against decriminalization, withdrawing to fight other battles. Feminists of all types split over issues of sexuality, gender, and bodily self-determination. The low level of women's involvement in HIV/AIDs issues is sometimes attributed to the image of the disease as gay, white, and male.[95]

The identity framing of a virus that had, even then, infected thousands of women and men, heterosexual and different, black and white, obscures the tireless work of women; before forming ACT UP/NY's women's caucus, its leaders had all worked in the radical, queer, and lesbian wings of the abortion rights movement. Through their AIDS activism, women also confronted anti-pornography feminists who successfully suppressed safer-sex literature for lesbians and straight women.

The political disenfranchisement of sex workers forced activists to rethink their strategy. For COYOTE, the polite tools of civic activism—petitions, letter-writing, telephone calls, visits to elected officials' offices, testimony in legislative hearings, written comments on proposed regulations—no longer seemed to work. Public education and outreach to women's groups continued through the National Task Force on Prostitution, directed by Priscilla Alexander. She turned to HIV awareness and prevention, producing scholarly articles, public-policy reports, and the path-breaking anthology *Sex Work* in 1986.[96] Alexander and Gloria Lockett took turns attending meetings of the Women's AIDS Network.

The shift in COYOTE's work in the 1990s gave rise to a new generation of activists more willing to claim "deviancy" and sexual differences as rights, central to challenging racial injustice. Scholars might claim COYOTE "failed," but these new activists cared little for the politics of respectability, its underlying normalizing cultural tactics, or the citizenship framework that had determined the earlier organization's strategy. They weren't interested in winning rights for some, recognizing that decriminalizing only prostitution would likely penalize other forms of sex trades. They wanted more.

Sex-worker activists and sex radicals repositioned their demands in the philosophy of universal human rights, employing the language of harm reduction. They organized community-based services to address basic needs as well as online communities and DIY media to discuss sex work issues. For some in the movement, there was no reason to engage in the confrontational political style that had characterized earlier clashes with lawmakers. As community-building and cultural work took precedence, there were fewer reasons to engage elected officials at all. Politicians were not their allies, though they continued to be their clients.

Controversy accompanied the shift from the feminist identity of COYOTE to CAL-PEP's human rights and harm reduction focus. After nineteen years of working as a prostitute and several more years interviewing sex workers and other women for Project AWARE, Gloria Lockett recognized the shortcomings of prevention education. Talking only to sex workers was not enough, and supplies shouldn't be limited either. In African American communities, working women shared their limited resources, including syringes and needles, among closely knit "family" networks and lovers.[97] Effective HIV prevention had to include people in those networks.

Lockett also saw that HIV, police crackdowns, and violence against sex workers had changed the way people worked; many wanted different careers but didn't have the necessary educational credentials, social networks, or job skills. Robin Laylon, another former prostitute, created Women Emerging in 1988 to help sex workers transition out of the industry through counseling, job training, and placement.[98]

With a new, fully equipped mobile van, CAL-PEP focused on the Tenderloin and Polk Street neighborhoods. There, volunteer outreach workers, former and current sex workers, opened shop for anyone who wanted hot food, a place to sit, or someone to talk to, as well as HIV testing, safer-sex tips, or supplies. Counselors from Women Emerging offered advice too.

Lockett encouraged family and friends to participate in CAL-PEP programs, perhaps the earliest example of HIV education to recognize that street-based hustling among African Americans is organized differently than in low-income white and other ethnic communities. Opening up services to the community, regardless of gender or sexuality, earned the trust of the street-level community and brought in people who had never considered accessing CAL-PEP.

Providing nonjudgmental services required careful attention to language and services. Under Lockett's direction, CAL-PEP stopped talking about "prostitutes' education" and said "street outreach"; "PEP" became Prevention and Education Project. Under its current mission statement, CAL-PEP serves "hard-to-reach, high-risk populations . . . who have limited access to healthcare [with] pioneering effective prevention strategies in street outreach and mobile HIV/AIDS, STD, and hepatitis testing— using cultural relevance, humility and grace as our guiding principles."[99]

White feminists on CAL-PEP's board objected to Lockett's decision to open up programs to men and others in the Bay Area. They also thought Lockett had abandoned the sex workers' movement by joining with Women Emerging. In fact, CAL-PEP never stopped educating prostitutes. It still provides services to women and men doing street-level work, though they often don't identify as "sex workers." Given their experience with police and the views of family members or church leaders, "hard-to-reach, high-risk" populations aren't likely to seek assistance from an organization valorizing sex work, just as many men refuse to access services for gay men. In rewording its mission statement and retooling its programs, CAL-PEP rejected the limitations of identity politics and embraced human rights–based harm reduction principles.

In some cities, public health officials began to invite sex workers to participate in policymaking, though inclusion remains more of a novelty than routine. These dialogues acknowledged that nonprofit groups as CAL-PEP, Washington, DC's HIPS (Helping Individual Prostitutes Survive), New York City's FROST'D (From Our Streets with Dignity; later the Foundation for Research on Sexually Transmitted Diseases), and others had extensive street knowledge and access unobtainable through other channels. In exchange, sex workers' groups benefited from public health officials' scientific authority, political power, public funding, and access to medical supplies and services. In several key struggles, the recommendations of public health authorities on quarantines, mandatory testing, and patient privacy persuaded legislators. And when laws couldn't be stopped, public health workers could moderate their impact. Many turned a blind eye when community health activists began handing out clean needles and syringes; some are rumored to have even provided the supplies.

Proactive advocacy brought other results. In 1992, Priscilla Alexander went to the International Labor Organization in Geneva, where she developed health and safety standards for people in the sex industry. After Alexander returned to the United States, she and Margo St. James joined with the Exotic Dancers Alliance (EDA) and San Francisco's STD Prevention and Control Department, headed by Dr. Jeffrey Klausner, to open the St. James Infirmary. The model for a peer-led occupational health and safety clinic for sex workers was first conceived in 1985; St. James wanted to "disprove all this bullshit about how we were the spreaders of disease and stuff."[100]

Ironically, the state's mandatory HIV testing law gave St. James the leverage to obtain start-up funding from the city for the clinic. In 1998, she heard from a woman in jail whose blood had been drawn without her consent. Recognizing the incident could turn into a political fiasco for the city, she got a meeting with Klausner, who had experience with sex-worker health issues in Seattle. Efforts were already under way to transfer regulation of massage establishments from the police department to the public health department, at the suggestion of Johanna Breyer and Dawn Passar from the EDA. St. James, Breyer, Passar, Carol Leigh, and other sex-worker activists had previously worked together on Mayor Willie Brown's Prostitution Task Force and in the Harvey Milk Democratic Club. With their political experience and constituencies, and the support of the public health department, even conservative members of the Board of Supervisors couldn't vote against funding.[101]

In June 1999, the St. James Infirmary opened, offering a holistic model for health-care services: "compassionate and non-judgmental healthcare and social services for all sex workers while preventing occupational illnesses and injuries through a comprehensive continuum of services."[102] Today, former, transitioning, and current sex workers staff the clinic and board, while director Naomi Akers helps to shape new research, an SJI priority.

Human rights–focused advocacy for health care has given activists new tools to better the lives and health of sex workers. In 2010, Penney Saunders and Darby Hickey from the Best Practices Policy Project and attorneys from the Sex Workers' Project of the Urban Justice Center evaluated health-care and HIV services in the United States, invoking Article 25 of the Universal Declaration of Human Rights, which recognizes that all people have the right to adequate health care.[103]

With support from other sex-worker groups, they submitted their compliance report to the UN High Commissioner on Human Rights in Geneva, giving evidence that for people in the sex trades, the United States failed to ensure even minimum standards of care: "Sex worker friendly services . . . are few and far between . . . and significantly underfunded. The criminalization of sex work and drugs directly undermines the ability of sex workers to protect themselves from HIV infection and, in a broader sense, alienates these communities from the support needed to defend their health and rights."[104]

The prostitutes' rights movement that St. James had led through the mid-1980s drew on the traditions of the civil rights movement, relying on civic engagement and pushing for recognition and legal reforms through legislatures and courts. Early legal victories had seemed to promise more significant gains in the future. But HIV/AIDS changed the political and legal landscape. Sex workers had to resist the virus of repression. They did so with admirable skill. COYOTE and CAL-PEP facilitated much-needed research on HIV transmission, even as sex workers confronted sex panics on both the Right and the Left that sought to criminalize consensual sex, commercial sex districts, and seropositive status.

Peer educators and outreach workers in CAL-PEP and other non-judgmental community-health groups strolled the streets and loitered in residence hotels to hand out sterile syringes and supplies. Public-health authorities adopted a "don't ask, don't tell, don't pursue" policy toward these underground actions. Harm reduction began because people were willing to engage in acts of civil disobedience to save lives, defying laws that made possession of drug paraphernalia a crime.

Feminist groups were curiously absent from AIDS advocacy. Though HIV affected women and feminist health issues central to HIV policies and research, the mainstream women's movement generally ignored a crisis framed as a gay men's issue. Instead, after the death of Nancy Reagan's friend Susan G. Komen, they took up breast cancer as "their" disease cause, intertwining a pink ribbon with the red AIDS ribbon in symbolic solidarity.

AIDS was the leading cause of death for men ages twenty-five to forty-four when Bill Clinton was elected president in November 1992; when conservative Republican Newt Gingrich became Speaker of the House three years later, AIDS was the leading cause of death for men and women in the United States between ages twenty-five and forty-four. In 1992, the number of deaths in the United States from AIDS-related illnesses peaked at 75,457.[105] There were no more "risk groups": everyone who had sex or shared blood was at risk. Lessons about "safe" sex—using condoms and finding pleasure in alternative sexual expression—gave way to sermons about "safer" sex that emphasized abstinence, monogamy, and long-term commitment. No wonder so many gay moderates joyously celebrated Hawaii's brief recognition of same-sex marriage in 1995. Government had rewarded gay and lesbian couples in exchange for sexually respectable behavior.

Sex-positive activists and costumed whores zapped hypocritical politicians, promo-ed homos, defended abortion, and performed "obscene" art. Such cultural interventions were tools to counter the trend toward "punitive fidelity." They insisted that "women be active subjects of desire, constructing sex in order to be safe."[106] They recognized Monica Lewinsky as one of their own. The president himself might claim, "I did not have sex with that woman," but an unpanicked radical analysis held that Bill and Hillary had a right to (heterosexual) marital privacy, including the choice of an open relationship.[107] It also recognized that "sex" includes oral sex, one of the least risky forms of sexual pleasure, though the cigar raised a question.

Sex workers may not have decriminalized prostitution, but they destigmatized sex and the commercial sex industry. Why shouldn't people talk about sex? In those pre-"cocktail" days, when AIDS made sex literally a life-and-death matter, plain talk about sex saved lives. That's what Dr. Joycelyn Elders, the US Surgeon General, thought when she suggested during a talk for World AIDS Day in 1994 that sex education in school might discuss masturbation as a form of safe sex.[108] But Congress (and Health and Human Services Secretary Donna Shalala) wanted abstinence-until-marriage sex education, and the press misrepresented Elders' remarks, raising the image of children jacking off in class. Ten days later, Clinton, mired in sexual politics of his own, accepted the Surgeon General's resignation.[109] In defense of self-pleasure, activists Carol Leigh, Dorrie Lane, and Dee Dee Russell rallied to nominate "Elders for President," attracting support from hundreds of Christmas shoppers in the tourist heart of San Francisco. In 2010, women of color, who represent one-quarter of all American women, accounted for 82 percent of all female HIV cases in the United States, more than the number of incarcerated African American, Hispanic, and Native American men (a not-unrelated fact).[110]

President Obama's national HIV/AIDS strategy, issued in 2010, still prioritizes gay men and MSM as risk groups. The plan does not address how the criminalization endangers sex workers and drug injection users, making them more vulnerable to abuse, less able to negotiate condom use.[111] Now we know about HIV but have yet to make policy based on its lessons.

CHAPTER 5

"ASSEMBLY-LINE ORGASMS"

Organizing the Sex Market

FOR THE NEW BOHEMIANS, the kids, and the homeless who squatted in Alphabet City in lower Manhattan in the 1980s, the sexual revolution and gender-bending broke down the stigmas about sex work and sex workers. Annie Sprinkle, Penny Arcade, Shelly Mars, and Karen Finley performed for the downtown in-crowd. Leathermen and transwomen strolled the Meatpacking District; runaways and throwaways plied their tricks on the Chelsea Piers. Gay white men ruled the West Village, though many did so from their hospital beds at St. Vincent's. In Times Square, "you could get anything there. You wanted to meet someone, get laid, make money, get high? No problem."[1] Queers, punks, and rappers maxed out their amplifiers to protest gentrifying landlords in Washington Square, thousands acted up at City Hall against Mayor Ed Koch's AIDS policies, and more shouted down the Christian conservatives and Cardinal O'Connor's strident family values tirades.

In the postindustrial city, tongues were untied, Paris burned, Nola Darling "got it," and Salt-n-Pepa smacked back "Who is the tramp?"[2] No

---

"Outlaw Poverty Not Prostitutes": Button, from St. James Infirmary, San Francisco.

matter how high-tech the lynching, black youth knew the significance of race had not declined. The arrival of crack cocaine had led to a free-for-all underground war among distributors and sellers for market dominance and control of the drug. Newspapers focused their stories on stray bullets killing children, "crack babies," and Reagan's "Cadillac-driving welfare queens." Yuppies, buppies, and guppies complained about crack-heads, "wilding" black teenagers, and gay bashers, a crime-ridden city bonfire of rap, crack, and hos.

Public sexual culture was under attack as officials used the AIDS crisis to close down gay bathhouses and other sex businesses.[3] Public health advocates did not bother all that much with clubs patronized by heterosexuals. The peeps and the porn stores were being battered by urban redevelopment schemes, new technology, and anti-porn feminists and religious zealots. Deindustrialization accelerated the decline of public sexual spaces. Middle-class and working-class men stopped dropping by the local strip club after work to watch the girls and have a drink or two. Instead, they drove home—sober—to the safety of cable TV, VHS or Betamax, and to porn BBSes (bulletin board systems) shared on dial-up modems.

Telecommunications, video, cable television, and the Internet had radically transformed the sex industry by the end of the 1990s. Digitization offered users porn in the privacy of their homes and hotel rooms. VCRs, then cable, provided an easy, private—if at first expensive—voyeuristic experience. "Porn made the VCR a household word," observed sex columnist Jayme Waxman.[4] Chat lines and bulletin boards were another entry into sex markets, paid and free. Cybersex appealed to a new consumer demographic of wired women, though entrepreneurs didn't acknowledge the demand. As public sexual expression came under renewed attacks from the Meese Commission on pornography, Congress, and Christians, technology shifted from a novelty to a necessity, a workaround to avoid public shaming for heterosexual, gay, female, and alternative sexualities.

The privacy of cable and the false anonymity of the web were stiff competition for the titty bars. In Times Square, some were the last hold-outs from the earlier decades of burlesque that had been shuttered by Mayor Fiorello LaGuardia during World War II. The peep shows, triple-X theaters, and strip clubs on Eighth Avenue and Forty-Second Street had just weathered another round of repression that almost halved their numbers to sixty-five by 1983; by 1998, only nineteen "seXXX" shows remained.[5] Like Norma Desmond said about the movies, the stages got smaller. The "raincoat crowd" came for lunch, but Times Square at night was perceived, wrongly, as dangerous (the crowds prevented muggings, although they provided plenty of people to distract the pickpocketing victim). One might get anything there because organized crime and the cops controlled the neighborhood.

In midsize and big cities across the country, downtown sex districts were rundown and dangerous. The carpets were old, the drinks watered down, and the "girls" older. In 1985, Mothers Against Drunk Driving won its battle to raise the legal drinking age to twenty-one, which in turn kicked out the kids, co-eds, and the frat boys.[6]

Hugh Hefner, an early investor in cable television, had shuttered all his Playboy Clubs and hotels by 1988.[7] The 1950s and '60s style of the tits and titillation had become passé as strip clubs and sex businesses scrambled to innovate in the 1970s and diversify in the 1980s. To compete against porn and "performance art," commercial sex businesses got a gimmick or got rawer. Joani Blank found the gimmick, opening Good Vibrations, the "first sex-positive, woman-friendly adult store in the country," in 1977 as a clean, well-lighted place in San Francisco. Instead of video booths, she provided a try-out closet for sex toys.

In Times Square, the stores turned into XXX-rated Walmarts, selling adult novelties and pornographic videos and magazines, in addition to their private video booths and live, nude sex shows. Show World, the legendary peep palace of Times Square, created a "trannie" stage in its rabbit warren of adult wares and illusory celebration of heterosexuality.[8] Customers could "lunch" on the dancers who opened their legs in those pre-AIDS days. African American and Latino transgender performers and hustlers ruled bars like Sally's Hideaway until they fell during Mayor Rudy Giuliani's war on sex.[9]

In rust-belt towns like Erie, Pennsylvania, Pap's Bar did business as "Kandyland" and hired nude exotic dancers to entertain its unemployed, white working-class patrons. The city council passed a new zoning ordinance to shut it down, claiming that sexually oriented businesses were responsible for rising crime and other negative secondary effects in the abandoned neighborhood. No one mentioned, at least in public, the negative secondary effects of local factory closings when NAFTA went into effect.

But on Wall Street, greed was good. Corporations merged while raiders engaged in hostile takeovers of profitable firms, sold off assets, shut down factories, and sent manufacturing first to the new maquiladoras on the Mexican border, then to China. Bankers, lawyers, and stock traders made millions, partying all night on coke—and sometimes crack—with Manhattan call girls. Tracy Quan's fictional heroine "Nancy Chan" married a banker, but that didn't stop her from jet-setting to Europe with her clients or worrying about her friends who were busy organizing "trollops."

In Erie County, the recession of the early 1980s devastated the local economy; by 1983, unemployment was 14.3 percent. Even after the recovery, the closing of mills and plants meant lower wages as workers shifted to service jobs.[10] Pap's Kandyland provided jobs to some of the unemployed; women, young and older, danced to support their families as benefits and welfare dried up.

Working-class and poor people weathered joblessness and cheese lines, while Reagan held up the want ads to show how many jobs were available. People like to say that hard times drive women and men into the sex industry, claiming that economic desperation explains their "ruin." The growth of the commercial sex industry in the 1980s and 1990s, however, cannot be explained simply by an expanded labor pool or by the collapse of public morality. Commercial investment, market expansion, and increased consumer demand for bread and circuses are reasons for its growth. Buyouts meant Hooters, Scores, and Spearmint Rhino were hiring, while the local department stores—Wanamaker's, Woodward & Lothrop, Jordan Marsh, Kaufmann's, Burdines, Rich's, Marshall Field's—gobbled up by Federated Department Stores, laid off thousands.

The people who found jobs in the new sexual economy entered workplaces that increasingly resembled work in other sectors of the new service economy. They were often corporate owned, MBA managed, quarterly-profit driven, hostile to unions and government regulation, and dependent on a compliant, low-skill, high-turnover labor force composed of temporary and marginalized workers. Under these conditions, exploitative worker-management relations led to greater resistance and labor activism.

Resistance, individual and collective, is powered by desires for autonomy and better working conditions. The legal jobs available in the commercial sex industry literally shelter sex workers from the dangers of working on the streets and can offer a sense of security, privacy, and camaraderie. But the shelter is sometimes just a house of straw, offering less protection than a bus shelter on a rainy night. Exploitation of workers—forget the sex part—is made worse because *everyone* who could do something—managers, owners, labor boards, regulators, and elected officials—can't forget the sex part. They're whores, they aren't workers. But sluts have united, and unions have focused on pay and working conditions.

The few examples of labor organizing in the sex industry suggest that unionizing sex workers is at least as difficult as decriminalizing prostitution. Yet the stumbling blocks are not so dissimilar from those in other industries dependent on contingent labor, independent contractors, low wages or piece rates, and high employee turnover.

Nor are many of the problems faced by workers in the sexual economy unique. Complaints about sexual harassment, race discrimination, disregard for OSHA rules, and violations of wage and hour regulations are supposed to be under the jurisdiction of various government agencies, though bureaucrats have been reluctant to expend their limited resources. Police sometimes seem to be the only officials to care about the way dancers or spa workers perform their jobs.

Tricking dancers to solicit for prostitution, or raiding spas in search of suspected trafficking victims is not the kind of "government assistance" that sex workers want. Workplace fairness has been an issue for largely nonunionized workers in nail salons, home health care, day-care centers, nannies, and domestics. Notably, these jobs often draw from the same female labor pool: immigrants (documented and not), poor women of color, women who are undereducated or without English language proficiency, those with criminal records, and women who provide primary support for their families—the globalized workforce that can be defrauded into coercive labor contracts.

Workers in today's commercial sex industry are deeply affected by five major trends that began in the 1980s: technology, anti–public sex crusades, globalization, urban redevelopment, and neoliberalism have changed business practices and sexual cultures. Corporate investment in sex businesses led to diversification and vertical integration as management embraced digital technology and cost controls to increase profits. Videos and the Internet inspired people to explore sexual alternatives, while the reinvention of strip bars as "gentlemen's clubs" made live sexual entertainment legal and available to customers without raincoats.

Employment in the sex industry has grown rapidly as a result. Legitimate "paycheck" jobs in the porn industry and exotic entertainment clubs have reduced only some of the stigma associated with prostitution in earlier times. Technology has enabled virtual strangers to negotiate intimate experiences before they actually meet, in exchange for cash or a simple NSA (no strings attached) hookup.

Demand for quick, paid sexual encounters remains, but clients *and* workers increasingly seek the "girlfriend" experience or some variation of it. The "boyfriend" client has also been around forever (that was why those British great houses retained so many footmen) yet these days he appears to be regarded more with appreciation than suspicion. Client demands for quality time with another person have subtly reshaped working conditions and workers' views of their jobs in some sectors.

"BIG AND WEIRD AND VARIED"

The sex industry is big and weird and varied, and there are a lot of different issues that face people who are in the industry by circumstance, choice, or coercion. The industry is not a monolith and there are lots of things that need to be done to improve the lives of the people who work within it.

— Audacia Ray[11]

It can seem sometimes that there are more occupations in the commercial sex industry than there are sexual proclivities. As of 2010, perhaps half of all sex workers in the United States were employed, in one way or another, in the commercial sex industry. There are escorts, brothel workers, professional dominants, telephone sex operators, strippers, exotic dancers, sensual massage workers, webcam entertainers, porn models, adult film performers, and specialists of all types, genders, colors, shapes, sexualities, and fetishes.

It's a job; it pays the bills. Some people like the work, some don't, and many have mixed feelings. There are good and bad bosses. It's a service industry with decent, indifferent, and horrid customers. It's an entertainment industry for tourists and locals. There are fights and there are birthday parties. The sex market, with its legitimate, quasi-legal, and illegal businesses, is a huge, diverse sector of the US economy that even conscientious prohibitionists might have difficulty avoiding.

The industry includes "all of those legal and illegal adult businesses that sell sexual products, sexual services, sexual fantasies, and actual sexual contact for profit in the commercial marketplace."[12] In the 1970s, the sexual revolution forced businesses to innovate. Customers could buy "time alone with a girl in private" in a waterbed demonstration store, a nude encounter studio, massage parlor, or with a private dancer in a club or its back booth or back room. By the 1990s, the licensed venues for sex and entertainment in San Francisco included "strip clubs and erotic performance theaters, erotic film and video production, porn magazine publishing and phone sex switchboards, commercial parties and sex clubs."[13]

Sex businesses were traditionally located in designated urban sex zones; many of the "strips," "blocks," and "zones" were hard by turn-of-the-twentieth-century red-light districts. On the corner of Broadway and Columbus Avenues in San Francisco, just up from the old Barbary Coast, was a topless shoeshine booth across from City Lights bookstore and fully nude dancers (and Carol Doda) at the Condor on the other corner. Bourbon Street in New Orleans was only two blocks from Storyville. In Washington, DC, "the Strip" was just up the street from "Hooker's Division," where US General Joseph Hooker's Civil War camp followers set up houses of prostitution that flourished until World War I.

In the twenty-first century, sex businesses are located everywhere and online. There are strip clubs, peep shows, gentlemen's clubs (with cabaret-style theaters and food and beverage services), pornographic film studios, pornographic photography studios, live-sex websites, escort agencies, spas, saunas, massage parlors, brothels, phone-sex services, Internet chat rooms, bathhouses, and BDSM dungeons. A new generation of desperate housewives have even become "Goddesses," hosting sex-toy parties and "passion parties" to model and sell lingerie to other women. Toys in Babeland, the Seattle-based "sleaze-free, sex-positive" store, offers *Fifty Shades of Grey* how-to classes, based on the best-selling romance series.[14]

Sex businesses haven't always been this diversified or open. The expanded marketing strategies are responses to new sex markets. New zoning laws forced the dispersal of sex-oriented businesses in the 1980s. New technology to disseminate pornographic images and texts has historically forced "real sex" establishments to compete, and not because geeks and nerds are big players in the sex industry. Consumer demand for pictures of naked people and of naked people having sex, and for-real people who will get naked and have sex for money, spurred more innovation. Polaroid cameras gave people instant images. The drugstore clerk never saw the pictures, giving the photographer and subject privacy from the prying eyes of film developers and the police.[15]

In the early 1970s, escort and outcall services became much easier to set up and operate with the advent of call forwarding, paging services, and direct-dial telephones.[16] By the early 1980s, pagers, faxes, message services, and digital answering machines, as well as the first generation of cell phones, gave some sex workers even greater independence, allowing them to screen and set up dates directly with customers. Escort agencies, spas, and massage parlors still depended mostly on local magazines, newsweeklies, and the yellow pages to advertise, but in the late 1980s, many advertised on cable television, some using 1-900 numbers to charge and screen prospective clients, though the interface was less than perfect. When the web went public in 1992, independent escorts built their client books by building their own websites, allowing them to work without depending on outcall services and agencies.[17]

Consumer demand for technology exploded when HIV became a "heterosexual" disease. The phone-sex industry offered "real live girls," a selling point when the only safe sex was aural, even when the "real live girl" read a script and in reality looked nothing like the caller's fantasy. Credit card customers could also dial-a-porn or call adult chat lines directly.[18] Phone sex was facilitated by low-cost multiline call centers and the creation of premium rate 1-900 or 1-976 exchange numbers, which split the charges between the phone company and the call recipient.[19]

Cheap videotapes and video players flooded the market in the early 1980s, offering customers erotic entertainment in the privacy and security of their homes. They also represented a safe-sex alternative for the AIDS-phobic purveyor. Porn could be rented or purchased at neighborhood stores; there was no need to venture into the "few segregated public spaces, the seedy book shops and triple-X theaters" still around.[20] The ubiquity of VHS tapes, players, and cameras helped to democratize media access and production, and created a big fad for amateur porn featuring real people.

Tellingly, by 1987, women accounted for 40 percent of the estimated hundred million X-rated videotapes rented each year.[21] Blurring the traditional lines between "good" and "bad" girls, video gave female consumers direct access to porn, but whether they were renting it for themselves or to watch with someone else was a matter of debate. Mainstream producers routinely dismissed business proposals and film scripts presented by women in the industry, repeating the mantra "Women don't buy porn." The San Fernando Valley whizzes also overlooked the market of men looking for new narratives.[22]

Feminist porn stars recognized there was a market for sex-positive films. In the "Golden Age of Porn," Candida Royalle, Veronica Hart, Gloria Leonard, Annie Sprinkle, and Veronica Vera were "the original 'Sex and the City' girls" who remained in New York rather than migrating to Southern California.[23] Candida Royalle founded Femme Productions in 1984 to "create erotica from a woman's perspective."[24] "Porn images and movies have changed remarkably little from the formulas of the early stag films to the films of the golden age," Royalle recently observed. Good porn, women producers say, focuses on women's authentic sexual experiences, "HER experience of sex, HER pleasure, and HER orgasm."[25]

Lesbian porn for dykes and femmes was an untapped market until Debi Sundahl, Nan Kinney, and "Lesbian sexpert" Susie Bright started publishing *On Our Backs* in 1984. "Produced with stripper money," it was "dedicated to tweaking the prudery of puritanical feminist publications like *off our backs*."[26] It inspired Jackie Strano and Shar Rednour to create SIR Video (Sex, Indulgence and Rock 'n' Roll), whose films *How to Fuck in High Heels* and *Hard Love* (2000), among others, featured "tattooed, variously sized, butch and/or femme women [to] show that sexiness is about what you do, not how much you can conform to the generic Playboy-model mold."[27] Winning awards from the Adult Video Association (AVN) showed the Valley whizzes that alt porn was a market too.

Cybersex, Usenet, camgirls, online porn, and escorts' websites were yet more competition for the brick-and-mortar commercial sex industry. At first (1979–1992) everything was "free," after the layout for computer, modem, and perhaps a separate phone line for dedicated Internet access. The chance to "meet" sex workers through Internet chat rooms was a powerful draw even in the pre-HTML days, when it was mostly "talk and type" BBSes; photographs could be downloaded, sometimes name-linked to individual sex workers, many of them not. Perhaps it goes without saying that the models didn't receive royalties or payment for their images. America Online, Prodigy, and other graphical user interfaces created another boom in 1992, making access easy for less technically inclined subscribers.

"Though the golden years of camgirls were brief, they coincided with the rise of the web itself," reminds Melissa Gira Grant, a pioneer in this genre of sex work. Camgirls changed the picture, graphically. JenniCam started in 1996; by 2000, there were thousands of women and men "camming," some for free, some for pay. Some were "company girls" paid by the minute on sites like Danni's Hard Drive. Danni Ashe, the webmistress, had been working as a stripper and nude model (her pictures were on Usenet). She taught herself HTML and launched Danni.com in July 1995; within a month, her site had more than a million hits per day. By 1997, the website grossed $2.5 million annually.[28]

"Hanna" described working for sites like Danni.com. The free portion of the site was "seduction, flashing, and toys" to encourage viewers to buy one-on-one time with a performer. Hanna earned $1 of the $5–6 per minute paid by the customer, but nothing for the free portion. The customer "directed" her performance as though he were producing porn, a situation that ignored the cam girl's "comfort level or personal desire," Hanna recalled.[29] Some sex workers, however, became skilled at directing, even creating, their customers' desires.

In one island of the web, sexy women geeks were creating explicit and erotic material, sometimes free of charge, or for a voluntary "donation" or paid subscriptions. Sex-worker communications activist Audacia Ray argues:

> Small-scale, women-run businesses are the majority of the online porn industry in the cultural sense. The idea of a woman running her own site seems more personable and sexier than a corporate entity. Though the good old boys still have the industry mostly in their pockets, independent women's sites get a lot of attention, both prurient and financial . . . The somewhat ludicrous freedom of choice on the Internet has led to the development of niches that are sometimes difficult to imagine even in jest, but has created a window of opportunity for many women with the entrepreneurial nudie spirit.[30]

Gira Grant, Ducky DooLittle, and other girls—and except for a scattering of gay camboys, it was all girls—worked independently. They showed it was possible for any girl with a digital camera, a computer, and an Internet connection to perform online.[31] Their self-reliance also gave them the freedom to do their own thing. Many riffed on the performance art of Annie Sprinkle; Gira Grant, known online as "Shakti," tapped into the Sacred Prostitute or Holy Whore trend of the 1990s.[32]

Critics in academia, politics, and the media derided camgirls as narcissists, rather than techies, workers, or performers. Gira Grant points out that camgirls used LiveJournal, chat rooms, and Internet mailing lists to discuss these issues, build community, and teach each other programming skills. "It was more a boot camp in 'How to Make the Web' where you could show up sometimes in your pajamas."

Some indies figured out how to make a "nekkid" buck online. iFriends created an online network and a system for taking credit card payments, letting operators set their own prices. "Furry Girl" and other niche operators built on demands for alt-porn and fetish specializations.[33] Furry Girl describes her site as "amateur porn created by a real gal with a hairy pussy, hairy pits, and hairy legs"; she has also established very strict limits on what she will, and mostly what she won't, do. People who want to "know her better" would have more luck supporting SWAAY (Sex Work Activists, Allies and You), a project she founded to educate the public about sex work.

SuicideGirls.com was launched by "Spooky" and "Missy Suicide" in 2001 as a social networking site (before Friendster and long before Facebook). Their DIY-approach website featured tattooed and pierced punk, goth, and emo girls and the boys who wanted to connect with them. Early on, a reviewer in *Bitch* magazine wrote that SG models looked like "cheerleaders with makeovers from Hot Topic," but hundreds of portfolios were sent in weekly from young women vying for the daily "New Modern Pin-up Girl" picture or the weekly feature model that, in 2002, paid the rather paltry sum of $100 to $200.[34]

The "world wild web" had a good run, but it did not last. Just a few years after the web became accessible to anyone with a modem and dial-up access, Congress enacted the first federal "decency" statute, though it was struck down just one year later. Waves of fear-mongering about Internet pornography were often based on allegations of child exploitation and, more recently, sex trafficking, led Congress to consider dozens of laws. Most have been struck down or modified by the courts, but under current law it is extremely complicated for independent website operators to post pictures of naked people.

Section 2257 of the Child Protection and Safety Act of 2006 imposed so many recordkeeping requirements that most US-based websites cannot meet the new burdens, which include making accessible to the public records of every photograph and film posted online, along with two forms of legal identification from the performer proving that he or she was eighteen at the time the image was made. For some, it seemed the only recourse was to move out of the United States, as transman pornographer Buck Angel did for a time. It turns out that porn, streamed as live erotic entertainment, can be offshored with a high-speed connection as easily as a Mumbai-based customer help center.

Profits in the commercial sex industry have been attributed to the cultural taboo it still represents. Demand for sexual entertainment seems almost recession-proof. People will find the money for escapist fantasies whether it's a Hollywood blockbuster, a new computer game, or a night at a strip club. Prohibitions against prostitution may contribute to the industry's profitability, but the data—when sex workers' experiences are included—are not conclusive. But profitability is the reason why blue-chip Wall Street firms, including General Motors and AT&T, invest in it.[35]

Job growth in the commercial sex industry in the 1990s contrasts sharply with the massive layoffs and wage cuts experienced by unionized workers and office workers in other sectors of the economy. Personal services and intimate labor are face-to-face, body-to-body work. Some contact is fleeting and some demands more durable relations. Besides sharing the same general labor pool, personal service workers are generally hired and paid in a similar way: as temporary or independent workers, with flexible or indeterminate hours, and no benefits or wage guarantees.

MSNBC dubbed Hugh Hefner the "Walt Disney of adult entertainment," but "Hef" created a successful business model copied by other publishers and club operators. By 2001, Rick's Cabaret, the Penthouse Club, Scores, Déjà Vu, Million Dollar Saloon, and others had operations in major US convention cities; Larry Flynt's Hustler Clubs, including

Barely Legal, are part of his privately held corporation, with fourteen clubs in the United States and elsewhere.

MBA-managed sexual entertainment emporiums are just one sector of a publicly traded industry. Vertically integrated and with a global reach, some are media corporations that market their stars on club stages, print media, websites, and adult films produced in their house studios. Others focus on hospitality, offering food, drinks, entertainment, party rooms, limo services, and more. But a strip club cannot be operated like a Holiday Inn franchise, though there are customers who expect the carpet to match the drapes. Even loyal VIPs at Rick's Cabaret think chorus lines of a dozen double-D blondes in plastic platforms are monotonous.

Corporate investment and the competition it inspires for independent operators have fundamentally changed commercial sex. When a club changes workers' pay scales or creates an enticing new product, everyone else in the business copies it. To ensure distinctiveness, strip club chains and adult product stores use strategic marketing schemes to promote their brands. Frequent-buyer discounts and various membership schemes encourage customer loyalty. Logo merchandising by Hustler, Playboy, and other companies have created another revenue stream. It should be noted that these do more than promote the brand: they also "domesticate" commercial sex, encouraging women to entertain at home and further blurring the line between public and private sex.[36]

Government attempts to shut down public sex venues have forced business owners to fight back, drawing on deep pockets to wage costly court fights against restrictive zoning and merchandising regulations. The Free Speech Coalition (FSC) and the Association of Club Executives (ACE) are trade associations with offices in Washington, DC, and various state capitals that track industry issues. ACE advises clubs on strategies to fight zoning restrictions; FSC, partnering with the Electronic Frontier Foundation and the ACLU, has often successfully challenged federal Internet censorship laws.[37] Notably, however, the Supreme Court ruled against them in *Erie v. Pap's TDBA Kandyland* (1997). Justice Sandra Day O'Connor wrote that communities may ban nude or partially nude dancing because it had "deleterious effects" on "public health, safety and welfare . . . [which creates] an atmosphere conducive to violence, sexual harassment, public intoxication, prostitution, [and] the spread of sexually transmitted diseases."[38]

Increased government regulation is one reason for the McDon-aldization or Disneyfication of the commercial sex industry. For independent businesses, the costs of these lengthy regulatory fights were too great; like independent porn websites after 2257 went into effect, they too shut down or drastically altered their operations. Sex panics—over AIDS, street-based prostitution, child pornography, sex trafficking, or whatever else—were another contributing factor. San Francisco activists blame AIDS hysteria for the closing of public sex venues, but by focusing only on the bathhouse controversy, they overlook a larger pattern.

Crackdowns against street-based sex workers, and then arrests for prostitution and related crimes at indoor venues in the late 1970s, preceded the bathhouse closures.[39] Real estate developers were itching to rebuild, from Union Square to the Tenderloin, but Mayor George Moscone held them in check. Then Moscone and Supervisor Harvey Milk were assassinated in November 1978. As a supervisor, Dianne Feinstein had made deals to redevelop the city, while publicly aligning herself with WAVPM. When she became mayor, San Francisco's sex districts north of Market vanished as other real estate moguls turned their attention south of Market, to the gay male/queer leather community's sex zone known as the "Valley of the Kings."[40]

People who relied on San Francisco's public sex districts for work and for pleasure were the first witnesses to the destruction that would follow in the 1980s in Times Square, Boston's Combat Zone, Chicago's Old Town and Near North Side, Vancouver's Downtown Eastside, Hollywood, and elsewhere: a real estate land grab disguised as the end of public tolerance for undesirable street people and public sex.[41]

In New York, Mayor Rudolph Giuliani manipulated uptown's disgust over Times Square's sex theaters and porn stores, pushing the "XXX Zoning Law" through a protracted court battle that forced the remaining places out of business. The best place to see "The Life," wrote Tracy Quan on Salon.com, was at the Ethel Barrymore Theatre, where the hit musical of that name was "unashamedly sentimental about Times Square prostitution circa 1979." By 1998, as a result of the "quality of life" crusade, a visitor to Times Square "would be hard pressed to find a drag queen, a cruiser, or even a massage parlor." Nothing stood in the way for real estate moguls who had contributed heavily to Giuliani's election to redevelop.[42]

BUMPING AND GRINDING ON THE LINE

Technology empowered some sex workers to seize the means of production, but their goals were making profits through new markets, not improving labor conditions in the sex industry. Former porn stars such as Nina Hartley, jenna jameson, and Stormy Daniels have gone into business for themselves, taking control over their images and their profits. Hartley, who won more adult video awards than any other performer, has turned her filmmaking skills and her nursing degree into a career educating adults about sex. Jameson opened her own strip club, while Daniels became a film producer, director, and political activist in her home state of Louisiana.

Performers who worked for Candida Royalle, jameson, Tristan Taoromino, or SIR Productions describe a daily grind that isn't much different from working in the mainstream pornography industry. After Dylan Ryan filmed her first porn video, *Champion* (Blowfish Video, 2005), she described the work as tedious, "far less sexy than I had imagined. We started and stopped a lot. . . . But, thankfully, no one expected me to give extreme fake moans."[43]

Undoubtedly, the blonde, blue, and boobed standard models were fewer in number than the diversity of tattooed, pierced, hefty, hued, transgendered, and unusual. Some may say that women directors are better to work for because they tend to be more involved than the makers of the assembly-line productions of the Valley. But new technology or not, it is a business, and labor—talent—is a cost.

Labor conditions in the commercial sex industry are as variable as they are in other industries with large numbers of "unskilled," transient, predominantly female workers. Management views "girls" as temporary laborers, not skilled entertainers. This view is reinforced by the sexism of the "straight" working world in which women earn 73 cents to every dollar earned by men, and by the social, political, and cultural stigmatization of sex workers that views them as expendable and disreputable.[44]

Writing about their work in strip clubs, peep shows, and other commercial settings, dancers gauge job satisfaction using measures that couldn't be answered in the stereotypical academic women's studies question, "What's a nice girl like you . . . ?" Indeed, scholars might elicit better answers if they asked, "How's the money?" Or, "If you were in charge, how would you run this club?" In twenty years of dancing and activism, Jo Weldon has given a lot of interviews:

> While every interviewer asks me whether I was sexually abused as a child, none of them ever asked me a single question about the financial mindset, or even the financial motivation, involved in my decisions to work in the sex industry. No one—including the interviewer, who is not doing research but is curious about my job—has ever asked me if my parents argued about money in front of me, if I got an allowance, if I had a job in high school, if I was raised to value money as a form of status or simply as a means to an end and so on. This makes me question the socially acceptable assumption that leads researchers to believe that the questions they are asking are worth asking.[45]

Some authors are business-minded, even purely mercenary, and these reasons are overlooked. At the same time, when a sex worker gives altruistic reasons, justifying her job choice because she wants to save her parents from paying for college, or because she has children to support, the sexism goes unremarked. Men can just make money. Women can only make good money to support someone else.

Some sex workers boast of the power they feel in taking control over their own sexual pleasure. Their transgressive, bad girl views get labeled as sex-positive feminism. But sex workers who enjoy the power they have in controlling men's sexual pleasure might get thrown back into the deviant pool.

Dancers like to brag about that one "$1,000 night" or wish for their own $1,000 night, but the take-home is usually much less; a good weekend night might be $400 for most women. Once they pay the stage fee and the DJ fee, tips out to the bartenders, the barbacks, the barker, the bouncers, and the taxi fare home, they've still earned more than working an eight-hour shift at McDonald's. But "stripper money," for some unresearched reason, spends faster.

It's not a labor of love to manufacture sexual pleasure, it's work. Whatever the joys of personal liberation, they are tempered by the physical and psychic labor necessary to produce "assembly-line orgasms." That alienation—the same alienation experienced by other industrial workers—can make the work feel mechanical and routine. "Miss Mary Ann," a peep-show dancer at the Lusty Lady in San Francisco, wrote of the routine involved in working for a peep-show audience in 2002:

> The job has always been defined in MY mind by the repetitive manual labor it demands. Punch a time clock, spot an open window, make eye contact, pout, wink, swivel your hips a little, put a stiletto-clad foot up on the window sill to reveal an eye-full of your two most marketable orifices, fondle your tits, smack your ass, stroke whatever pubic hair you haven't shaven off, repeat these ten steps until the customer comes, then move on to the next window, repeat the process until your shift's over, punch out. Some call it the fast food of the sex industry: we produce assembly-line orgasms.[46]

Repetitive motions, dangerous conditions, special footwear, and sticky polyester and polyurethane uniforms and costumes are routine in the sex worker's working environment. It's one thing to explore intimacy with a chosen partner in the private security of a home, it's quite another to pleasure a virtual stranger in public.[47] And it's even more difficult to repeat that routine three, five, eighteen, thirty times a shift for two, five, or seven nights a week in a club or a hotel room or a brothel—or their own house, for the lucky ones. Those who aren't so fortunate work outdoors, such as Jill Brenneman, who recalled working in cars where "I got to give blow jobs from under a steering wheel or over a gear shift. I got to suck a gear shift during doggie style sex for twenty bucks"; or on the street, giving "a blow job in the rain while [I was] half naked, on my knees in some alley in Cincinnati."[48]

Theoretical discussions that posit sex work as gendered performances of eroticism or pleasure-giving tend to forget the sweat, muscle fatigue, and blisters, much as Edgar Degas's paintings of gas-lit ballerinas do not reveal their disfigured feet in harsh photographic detail. Whether it is appreciatively called "art" or critiqued as a "performance," sex work is physical work that, like other work, can take a tremendous toll on the body. The top-earning dancers are fit and strong gymnasts with the endurance levels of marathon runners.[49]

Athletic shoes aren't the footwear expected of exotic dancers and female sex workers. Perhaps the most (un)surprising result of the dancer survey conducted by Naomi Akers, director of the St. James Infirmary, were the number of women who complained about the shoes they wore, not the risk of STIs. "I would fuck up my feet ['cause of the shoes] and then couldn't work in stilettos," wrote one. "Shoe Reviews" was a popular feature in *$pread* magazine. Sometimes it seems unjust, and plainly sexist, that go-go boys dance on the bar in white socks or wear "sensible" footwear—sneakers and boots—elsewhere in the club.

As a form of intimate labor, sex workers require an extensive set of skills to survive and prosper. No sex worker describes her or his job as a bed of ease. Sociologist Wendy Chapkis argues that the "emotional labor of sex" is similar to the work performed by women in other "smiling" occupations, although the team approach of Starbucks makes these demands of all workers regardless of gender.[50]

Game theory, the strategic manipulation of another person's beliefs and feelings to serve one's own purposes, as Jane Austen's Elizabeth Bennett does in *Pride and Prejudice*, may be a more apt description of sex work.[51] These interactions have been called "performativity," but there's a reason why "the game" is slang for prostitution. Hustling more than a dozen lap dances during a six- or eight-hour shift is tricky, and every dancer devises her or his own rap. Lap dancers must persuade customers to spend their money, but without explicitly agreeing to perform an illegal act.

Dealing with obnoxious customers—who may be male or female— requires experience. A worker isn't allowed to express anger, to shout at a rude client as she might yell at a partner. Management requires her to use her "stripper voice." Johanna Breyer of the Exotic Dancers Alliance explains that voice is "two or three octaves above your real voice," and you're supposed to ask him nicely to change his behavior.[52] Male dancers might be permitted more discretion, though the setting—a predominantly gay bar is quite a different story from ladies' night—also matters.

Angry or unsatisfied customers require another skill set, including the ability to defuse a potentially violent situation. Security in some places can be as flimsy as a negligee, and depends largely on the workers' own assessments of a customer's threat versus his spending potential. Calibrating danger and the need to live in the public world is "a complicated science," observes Carol Leigh.[53] When the customer is spending, sometimes just showing a lot of money, dancers might ignore rough handling, but there are limits. Dancer Gina Gold, one of the founders of

the Exotic Dancers Alliance, slapped a customer who did not behave at
the Market Street Cinema:

> I remember during my first shift there, a customer squeezed my
> breast and I slapped the shit out of him. This other girl saw it and
> said, "Oh, you better tell the day shift guy what happened so you
> won't get in trouble with management." I told the [day shift man-
> ager] what happened, and that I slapped a customer. The guy looked
> at me and said, "I don't care if a customer takes his fist and shoves it
> up your pussy as far as it will go, you sit there and you take it. Then
> you tell me and I'll stick my foot up him." I looked at him and was
> like, you expect me to sit there and take that shit?![54]

If the girl can't take it, or refuses, management will offer the customer another one who will, or who has the skills to handle him.

Game theory accommodates the transactional nature of sexual exchanges and simultaneously integrates the gender performances of each
player; racial and ethnic notions are also put into play. The intimate give-
and-take between gender, sexuality, and color is finessed as a matter of
course by those who make their living in the sex industry. Sex workers,
whether women or men, queer, straight, or anything in between these
categories, are expected to perform both emotionally and sexually. On
the job, they must *act*, performing as "men" or "women" and/or the "exotic other" as the occupation and situation demand.

Brazilian women in Astoria, Queens, and midtown Manhattan consciously deployed gender, sexual, and "exotic" performances in their
work as "go-go girls," the term they prefer to "exotic dancer," notes an-
thropologist Suzana Maia. Middle-class migrant women like herself,
some darker, some lighter, most with college degrees, were "fully modern" global citizens. Familiar with Americans' puritanical ideas about
sexuality, they exploited these ordering mechanisms working in the gentlemen's clubs of New York:

> They had a distinctive view of their bodies, their entitlements, their
> capabilities, and their instrumentality. Such views of their bodies
> translated into a knowledge of how desire functions in the global
> arena ... what kinds of bodily display and performance of national

identity would enable them to make money, and what kinds of people one would be likely to meet or get involved with.[55]

Maia also witnessed the impact of Rudy Giuliani's zoning laws on relations inside the clubs as they dispersed from Times Square to the outer boroughs. The new hierarchy divided upscale Manhattan clubs from neighborhood bars and redistributed patrons and dancers. The new dynamics led to different rules of etiquette bounded by class and citizenship:

> The way the dancers dress, the distance maintained between clients and dancers, the way clients and dancers touch, the exhibition of nude body parts, and types of performance . . . also [came] under government jurisdiction, delineating the kinds of relationships possible among dancers and between dancers and clients.[56]

Transnational border-crossers, some women chose to secure their migration status by agreeing to marry US citizens, while others played and saved, determined to return to Brazil in the future. At what point, or whether, a dancer's "performance" of gender, sexuality, and exoticism became an "enacted" truth can only be determined by the woman herself.

The "girlfriend experience," the "weekend boyfriend," and the "sugar baby" may also balance on a line between continuous role performance and enactment.[57] As sociologist Elizabeth Bernstein notes, "Contemporary 'intimacy providers' (as some in the industry have taken to calling themselves) charge by the hour rather than for specified acts, so their sexual labor is diffuse and expansive, rather than delimited and expedient."[58]

In these arrangements, "bounded authenticity" describes the ability to create a sense of a relationship without the obligations. As television actor Charlie Sheen is widely reported to have said about hiring sex workers, "I don't pay them for sex. I pay them to leave."[59]

Men who are "weekend boyfriends" or companions may perform many roles. Traveling with a client to San Francisco's Folsom Street Fair, the biggest leather/BDSM event in the United States, is an intense job, even more so when the paid companion is a professional dominant. From previous experience, "Master" Conrad knew that his client (who wanted to be treated as his submissive slave) would become fussier as Folsom weekend progressed and negotiated "time-outs" for both of them. Some male clients enact a masculine stereotype and don't permit or even consider cuddling, or the opposite may be true. Rent boys are sent home because they are not butch enough, don't look straight enough, or are too feminine.

The "sugar baby" and the "princess" are other roles, creating a fantasy relationship that may include time apart from each other. Many playing this role are college students who receive money, an "allowance," or tuition money to spend time with her "daddy" or her "prince." During the week, she is expected to correspond by letter, phone, video chat, text, and e-mail.[60] As participants in transactional relationships, these contemporary women are separated only by time and cultural context from the mistresses of the organization men of the 1950s and 1960s. Not every Holly Golightly or Manhattan mistress wanted to become a Greenwich, Connecticut, housewife. Some wanted to pursue intellectual and artistic interests for which they did not have Virginia Woolf's "money and a room of her own."

For club owners and workers, the commercial sex industry is both the most regulated and most unregulated of all US industries. De jure business regulations governing zoning, food and alcoholic beverages, and sales tax, as well as state laws criminalizing prostitution and related activities, are usually enforced; police, followed by liquor control, fire, and building inspectors, drop by regularly. Management sweats out these regulations. Rumors of payoffs are so commonplace that few would believe an investigation that failed to find corruption.

De facto deregulation of occupational health and safety, employment nondiscrimination, and wage and hour laws means that workers do not enjoy the same workplace guarantees and benefits that a McDonald's employee enjoys. Indeed, the government bureaus set up to protect working people engage in benign neglect, and at times are hostile to complaints and requests from employees for assistance.

By design, job security for dancers and related jobs is nil and the benefits nonexistent. The constantly replenishing supply of women applying for these "low-skill" jobs keeps wages at the most minimum level, when workers are paid at all. Workers mention arbitrarily enforced rules, fines, and demerits that reduce their earnings. Workers believe that club owners share the names of dancers who have complained or caused trouble;

certainly, managers have intimated that such blacklists exist. The high turnover, combined with cash tips, creates a mobile workforce. These conditions also make it easy for people with sketchy immigration papers—or none at all—to get work.

Persistent sexual harassment by *management* creates a hostile environment. Auditioning is standard practice for dancers, but job applicants have been asked to perform sexual favors for the manager or hiring agent, even when the work itself does not require intimate contact with customers or other performers. In some clubs, managers and other male staff fondle, pinch, slap, or use other forms of sexual teasing and physical punishment to keep the girls in line. Jennifer Bryce is just one worker who got fed up being "called 'bitches' and 'whores' at company meetings."[61]

Workers complain about conditions that clearly violate basic labor and civil rights laws. What should trouble observers most, however, is the practical impossibility of finding an advocate in government willing to investigate claims. Just as they have failed to punish criminal violence against sex workers, bureaucrats have shown reluctance to investigate complaints about harassment or coercion when they are made by workers in the commercial sex industry.

Johanna Breyer and Dawn Passer filed a sexual harassment complaint against the manager of the Market Street Cinema in 1992. They waited almost a year before an investigator finally contacted them. He tried to persuade them to drop their case, saying it "wasn't that strong." In a clear violation of procedure, he then questioned four other dancers about sexual harassment at the cinema in the presence of the very manager Breyer and Passer had complained about. The investigator shrugged off their complaint, telling another cinema worker with a classic slut-blaming dismissal, "Well, what do these women expect? They're walking around in their underwear."[62]

Strip-club work is legal, but because it is associated with prostitution, workers remain vulnerable to violence and intimidation. Dancers and other female employees have been "outed" by management, endangering their child-custody rights, their housing security, and their access to public services. The common personality trait among strippers, dancers, and other sex workers, however, is their independent streak. It's like herding cats. When they're wronged, and sometimes when they see someone else treated unfairly, they don't stay silent—screw the backfire.

This is what distinguishes sex work—legal, quasi-legal, and illegal— from department store jobs.

"IT'S NOT LIKE YOU WERE AT MACY'S"

In New York City, Macy's Herald Square is a union store. For sex workers in San Francisco, Union Square is the closest thing they have, and it hasn't been part of the stroll since the late 1970s. Union organizing in the commercial sex industry is still a novelty, yet its workers have more in common with waitresses, retail clerks, home health care aides, and counselors than many labor organizers acknowledge.

The sexual service industry is not limited to sex workers, labor historian Dorothy Sue Cobble argues: "Indeed, with the increasing sexualization of work and the heightened emphasis on appearance as well as aesthetic and erotic titillation, few jobs are wholly without a sexual dimension."[63] Working on commission, store clerks flatter customers; upsell more expensive items; encourage additional purchases; and advise on size, color and special features, employing a hustle comparable to dancers working a "live one" from the floor to the VIP room.

The emphasis on "aesthetics" continues to dog female-bodied and transwomen in the workplace. Harrah's Las Vegas fired Darlene Jespersen for refusing to wear lipstick in violation of a company policy requiring women employees to wear makeup; the federal court ruled it was not sex discrimination.[64] But too much makeup, skirt length, heel height, weight gain or loss, "crepey" neck, piercings, tattoos, facial hair, hair color, dreads, weaves, and almost every other aesthetic effect are also firing grounds. Unless it's part of the brand image, managers won't hire workers who are "tacky or garish . . . 'too sexy' so that the wearer looks like a cheap hooker."[65]

The industry's emphasis on youth creates a voracious demand for new faces and keeps the labor force in flux. Experienced workers are routinely pushed out; managers say customers want "new faces" and young and firm flesh, in quantity and variety. "Miss Mary Ann," an organizer at the Lusty Lady, commented,

> Management [insisted it had] the right to fire any dancer who'd been with the company for more than a year and a half. Since customers need "variety," they reasoned, termination of long-term

dancers was a "legitimate business need." In this industry, seniority is a liability; strip joints WANT a high turnover. This was a temporary job, a short-term assignment, the duration of which was determined by a byzantine and arcane set of constantly changing criteria that managers would use to justify firing dancers who got too "old" or too uppity.[66]

The problem is not new. Labor unions representing women have clashed with companies repeatedly over ageist sex discrimination.

Playboy routinely fired waitresses who didn't fit the Bunny image. Union organizers and shop stewards in HERE (Hotel Employees and Restaurant Employees International Union, now UNITE HERE) fought this practice for years, demanding the club provide a definition. Workers complained they were let go at the first sign of "crinkling eyelids, sagging breasts, crepey necks, and drooping derrieres."[67] In Hugh Hefner's opinion, they were women who had aged out of the job; since age discrimination wasn't illegal, HERE's efforts to protect its members were stymied. But HERE made Playboy show more respect to the women who represented the brand.

In 1964, Myra Wolfgang, HERE's legendary organizer, forced Hugh Hefner to the bargaining table at the Detroit Playboy Club, signing a contract for Local 705, the first union contract for sex workers. During the negotiations, they bargained over exact specifications for the uniform, which Wolfgang called "more bare than hare." HERE also wanted a rule that allowed customers to look but not touch.

Wolfgang found out about the problems at the Playboy Clubs from her own seventeen-year-old daughter, Martha, whom she sent in undercover to work as a Bunny. Though underage, Martha was hired. She told her mother about the "no wage" policy: bunnies worked only for tips, they weren't even paid the paltry below-minimum-wage restaurant worker hourly rate. Wolfgang organized a picket of HERE volunteers dressed in Bunny suits and carrying signs that read, "Don't be a bunny, work for money." Reporters liked the barbs she threw at Playboy, "Women should be obscene and not heard."[68] In New York City, the Teamsters jousted with HERE for control over the Playboy Club, supporting the "Bunny Strike" during the blizzard of 1967.[69] By 1969, HERE had organized the Bunnies in every US club. The next time Playboy laid off a group of "defective Bunnies," they filed a grievance with the National Labor Relations Board (NLRB), which ruled in the women's favor. Local shop stewards were known as Bunnies who "bit back."

Contemporary sex-worker activists might complain that Wolfgang chose to organize the Playboy Clubs for HERE; the women, apparently, did not ask for union representation on their own. But Wolfgang's willingness to organize the Detroit club, to send in her own underage daughter as a spy, and HERE's support for women workers over the long run, also shows that some labor organizers were more concerned with working conditions than with sex. The NLRB also focused on labor relations.

In Ann Arbor, Michigan, in the 1970s, the American Massage Parlor was one of the three places that employed most of the town's lesbians. Almost all of them were "very political," had belonged to such organizations as Radical Lesbians and the SDS (Students for a Democratic Society), and were mostly broke, earning $2 an hour at the university bookstore or as maids at the Holiday Inn. Denise T. Turner, who identified as butch and an athlete (the parlor offered a weight-training room for off-duty workers), explained:

> The main criteria for deciding whether or not the job was humiliating, or shameful, was how you were treated, how much control you had on the job. We thought the job should be judged by the same criteria than any job is judged by. Basically what made it not a good job was the fact that you could get busted and that there was a lot of social stigma.[70]

The owner of the American "was a real jerk," though the managers (all men) were "pretty nice guys." When the owner reassigned work hours, the workers went on strike. Then-student Gayle Rubin remembered Carol Ernst, a "visionary" who spearheaded a union drive at the local massage parlor with "hookers with picket signs on the street in front of this dirty book store in downtown Ann Arbor."[71]

The workers also filed a grievance with the NLRB. During the hearing, the "old Commie" assigned as their arbitrator didn't focus on prostitution. He regarded the case as a management-labor dispute. The righteous "girl gang" of twenty-two-year-olds won.

A year later, they had their own place, US Health Spa, built out and owned by a "hippie carpenter." It was "real low-key. Unobtrusive." The police entrapped Turner and four other women in 1977, after the local paper ran an exposé making the typical, lurid—and ultimately unproven—claims about pornography, prostitution, and kiddie porn.

"The local lesbian-feminist community suddenly had to deal with the fact that many of their friends and heroes had been arrested for prostitution," remembered Rubin. Ernst, Turner, and other workers organized PEP, the Prostitution Education Project, to change the local lesbian-feminist community's ideas about sex work, including Rubin's. With all the publicity PEP generated through newspaper coverage, radio, and workshops, they decided to push for decriminalization.[72] Margo St. James came to Ann Arbor, and PEP organized a Hookers' Ball to raise money for future organizing. Though the decriminalization effort didn't go anywhere, Turner "got a girlfriend out the deal," a woman who joined her defense committee and was still her partner twenty years later.[73]

Turner's experience, as well as stories told by women workers elsewhere, suggests an approach to labor organizing that, until recently, traditional labor didn't view as proper and some organizers still don't. Organizations built on intimate relations among workers, based on social networks and shared recreational activities, provide entry into workplaces that are almost never unionized. Workers at Turner's massage parlor were situated primarily in the local lesbian-feminist community but the central struggle focused on working conditions, not identity politics. In the course of organizing, Turner met her longtime partner, which suggests that affection is not always the disruptive influence that traditional organizers perceive it to be.

The proletariat-on-the-factory-floor model of organizing, with an established economic relationship to the means of production, doesn't describe the position of most workers in the sex industry. As a peep show, the Lusty Lady in San Francisco more closely resembled this model, with dancers paid by the hour; this is one small reason for its successful unionization campaign. But in a strip club, dancers' economic relationship to management is inverted: they rely on customers for their "pay," but the club management—along with local bureaucrats—determines the work rules. New models of "intimate organizing," such as the

Domestic Workers Alliance in New York and California, may provide a better example for future union organizing.[74]

Relations among workers in the commercial sex industry tend toward intimacy, though competition among workers can also be fierce. Dressing rooms are natural sites for intimacy; only workers who live collectively experience similar breakdowns of personal barriers.[75] Ties are further strengthened because sex workers fear or have witnessed negative reactions from friends and family members, as well as experienced difficulties renting apartments and finding nonjudgmental health care. In response, some women create new "families," sharing housing when possible, socializing, dating, perhaps even discovering long-term intimate partners who are or have been sex workers. In this context, labor organizing turns intimate relations into workplace bargaining power.

In spring of 1996, 80 percent of the dancers, janitors, and cashiers at the women-managed peep show signed union cards, forcing an NLRB election. Just before Labor Day, workers voted 57 to 15 in favor of unionization. Negotiations dragged over the winter, but in April 1997, Local 790 of the Service Employees International Union (SEIU) signed a contract with Multivue, Inc., doing business as the Lusty Lady in San Francisco.

In reality, the collective-bargaining agreement took much longer than one year to achieve, involved many more people than the seventy-two workers at "the Lusty" and was just one campaign in bigger fight for workplace fairness for sex workers. The Exotic Dancers Alliance, officially formed in May 1993, created the organizing momentum. The San Francisco NOW chapter spearheaded a nonbinding agreement from the Board of Supervisors suspending a policy that used condoms as evidence of prostitution in 1994. The San Francisco Task Force on Prostitution, chartered by the supervisors in 1994, met for almost two years before recommending the city stop enforcing prostitution laws. On the heels of the report in 1996, Margo St. James ran for one of six open seats on the Board of Supervisors with strong support.[76] Though she did not win, she had endorsements from Mayor Willie Brown (an old friend from the early 1960s) and District Attorney Terrence Hallinan (the son of St. James's old ally) and still commanded a large constituency. The rise of "whore power" took place in a city that was rapidly regentrifying during the dot-com bubble of the 1990s and upheaval in the remaining licensed sex establishments.[77]

Fierce competition among San Francisco's prostitutes has been business as usual since the Gold Rush. But in the last decades of the twentieth century, the industry went through an acutely cutthroat phase as clubs struggled with increased city regulation, threats of closure, economic decline, and new technologies that encouraged customers to stay home.

Customers who ventured out wanted "private shows." After the closing of the city's nude, then semi-nude, encounter parlors in 1979, and new licensing restrictions on massage parlors, adult theaters became the only venues left for public sex. Simultaneously, police began a new wave of harassment against street-based sex workers and massage parlor workers, instigated in part by street marches organized by downtown neighborhood groups opposing recommendations that police stop arresting people for soliciting and prostitution.[78]

With few employment options, and budget cuts in housing, education, and social welfare programs that might have assisted a transition out of the sex industry, the women turned to the strip clubs, adult theaters, and peep shows for work. The result, Kerwin Kaye reported, was a new gimmick in which the industry "switched from a strategy of overcharging customers to a policy of under-paying dancers."[79]

Artie and Jim Mitchell, owners of the O'Farrell Theatre, considered the most "elite" club in town, reclassified all their dancers and their dance supervisor as independent contractors in 1988. The Mitchell brothers' move was a first in the sex industry, but companies everywhere were "delayering and re-engineering" to create a permanent workforce of contingent and temporary laborers.[80]

At the O'Farrell, performers were given the option of going into the audience to have "contact" with patrons, but "under no circumstances whatsoever" could they solicit tips or gratuities. And for the first time, all women had to submit proof regularly that they were "free from all venereal diseases"—even though they had no sexual contact with customers.[81]

The new scheme forced performers, now independent contractors, to pay a booking fee of less than $10 for the privilege of being booked by the house agent. Before, they had received minimum wage, overtime, and other employment and social security taxes and had kept all the tips. The paychecks didn't amount to much, but the changes in status and working conditions were enormous. Now performers had only their tips and competed for them against many more girls. It cost nothing to put women on the floor, and customers responded to the greater variety. At the Market Street theaters, one dancer said, there were only eight people working a shift in 1989; by 1992, thirty-five to forty would be on schedule each night.[82]

Performers also found that they had lost all their rights as employees. They had no legal recourse for the notorious sexual harassment they endured from Artie Mitchell because they were contract workers.[83] Owners of other clubs and theaters quickly followed the Mitchell brothers' example.[84]

Debi Sundahl worked for five years as a dancer at the O'Farrell Theatre, and saw how the changes were affecting the workers, especially the lesbian and bisexual women. In her advice column for *On Our Backs*, Ask Fanny (Sundahl's stage name was Fanny Fatale), she was especially bitter after one friend committed suicide, slamming the slut-shaming that lovers and friends of sex workers engage in:

> THAT happens to be the stripper's self-expression and her livelihood. To make a stripper, or anyone, choose between love or her self-integrity, is to destroy her trust in intimacy, her self-esteem, and to play on her fears of abandonment. It's nasty, fucked-up business, and I'm not talking about the sex industry.[85]

Dancers were well aware of the increased demands club managers were making. Some dancers suggested they form a support group for workers in 1991, but a veteran dancer vetoed it, and that was that.[86]

The stage fee scheme began as another trick to squeeze money out of dancers, created by "low-end" theaters on Market Street in March 1992. At first, the amount was small, $10 for day shifts, $15 for night shifts; not that much more than the "booking fee" dancers had been paying earlier. The high-end clubs began to copy the stage-fee scheme; because San Francisco led the industry, clubs across the United States and Canada also began charging stage fees.[87]

The dancers got nothing for their money except "filtered water." The locker rooms were still filthy; at one theater, the women's toilet stalls didn't have doors.[88] If dancers worked a double shift, they paid twice. At the same time, they were allowed to work only when scheduled; if they didn't show up, they were fined. If they complained, they weren't put on the schedule.

If exotic dancers were truly independent contractors, they should have control over their work, their choice of customers, and their earnings.[89] But they don't. That's why Johanna Breyer and Dawn Passar organized the Exotic Dancers Alliance (EDA) in 1993. They told Kamala Kempadoo:

> It's a matter of human rights and making sure that the women who are working in the sex industry are getting the protection that they need. We're all working towards that one obtainable goal, of making sure that we are protected by law.[90]

Two months after it formed, the EDA helped dancers at the Market Street theaters file a complaint against the stage fee scheme with the California Labor Commission (CLC).

In March 1994, the Commission ruled in favor of the dancers, and the club owners, following Willie Brown's advice, appealed. With the decision on appeal, the Market Street theaters retaliated further by doubling the stage fee. The case languished in the state bureaucracy for almost two years, but effective January 1, 1996, the CLC announced stage fees were illegal because dancers were employees who should be paid wages. They awarded the lead plaintiff, Carla Williams, $52,600 in back wages, stage fees, and penalties.[91] However, the order applied only to the Market Street theaters; the other clubs could do as they wished.

Meanwhile, Ellen Vickery and Jennifer Bryce, performers at the O'Farrell Theatre, filed a separate class action sex discrimination suit representing more than five hundred former dancers against the Mitchell brothers in March 1994. Lily Burana, on her "farewell" tour of the United States, was Bryce's initial co-plaintiff. Burana explained, "It's really very simple. You don't pay to work; you are paid to work." After all, what would the O'Farrell Theatre be without the dancers? "A mirrored warehouse with faded carpet and a snack bar attached."[92]

The dancers won a $2.85 million judgment in 1997.[93]

The Market Street theaters continued to resist. They were just two of the businesses in the Bijou Group, of which Sam Conti was half-owner.

Conti had made his name in the 1970s on San Francisco's Broadway with Big Al's Roaring 20's and a string of nude encounter parlors. A large man, he drove his own Cadillac limousine as though he was the chauffeur, an oddity that no one understood. The city forced Conti to close the parlors in 1977; in a deal worked out by his attorney, Willie Brown, he agreed he would never own another.[94]

When Conti's Market Street theaters built booths in 1996 for dancers to "entertain" customers in private, the city should have shut them down. Except that no one, not even the anti-prostitution neighborhood groups, said a word about the reconfiguration. To sex-worker activists and their allies, the collusion between the police, the mayor's office, and the adult theaters seemed clear. Dancer activist Daisy Anarchy charged that the state had ignored "years of labor law and safety violations in San Francisco's strip clubs [owned by Conti]."[95]

After the Labor Commission's order, the Bijou group announced a new policy to underpay its dancers, while continuing to rake in $2 million in annual profits. Playing along with the CLC's ruling, it announced that dancers—oops, employees—no longer owned their tips. A "tip" was simply a polite way to describe the money customers paid for a dancer's individual attention. Therefore dancers had to split those payments with the house 40/60—the same split Conti had used in the encounter parlors in the 1970s. Of course, the house couldn't keep track of all that money, so it imposed a daily $200 minimum.

The combination of new pay structure and private booths transformed the job descriptions of independent contractor-performers. Before then, the work involved stripping to three-song sets, five to six times per shift; between sets, dancers were to sit and mingle with customers or solicit table dances or lap dances. Topless with panties, topless with a G-string, or full nudity depended on the liquor license or the business license. There were variations: some clubs had couches, a few had "beds." Who could touch whom and what could be touched also varied, though that depended more on the performer's decision than club rules or the letter of the law.

The "extras" girls and "dirty dancers" began making money hand over, well, not fist, using the private booths, where management promised it wouldn't watch. As "Isis" explained, they built the "private rooms in the back to go with customers pressuring them to do illegal things to keep their jobs." "What we had to do to make our money changed," said Decadence, aka Katrina. "Girls would be crying that they didn't make their quota." Stage fees climbed to as much as $250 for a five-hour shift. Dancers realized they could go home losing rather than earning money. Those who had begun working before the new pay system was introduced saw it as coercive, even forced prostitution, because they were providing intimate services they would not have provided earlier.

Through EDA, Passar and Breyer tried to provide dancers with all the information and services they might want or need, much like COYOTE had offered in the 1970s. In addition to filing legal complaints with labor agencies to improve working conditions, they combed through city and state regulatory bureaus. They had OSHA issue a citation to one theater forcing managers to replace the doors to the women's toilets. They persuaded the fire department to inspect the buildings. They negotiated with a local drug detoxification center so that members could be referred through the EDA rather than a medical professional. Breyer interned at the San Francisco Commission on the Status of Women, encouraging sex workers to offer comments. Passar became an outreach worker for the Asian AIDS Project and collaborated with the city's public health officials to transfer licensing of massage parlor workers from the police department to the health department.[96] And in 1999, Passar and Breyer were instrumental in pushing through legislation to fund the St. James Infirmary.

"Whore power" in San Francisco in the 1990s encouraged women, men, transwomen, and transmen in the sex industry to come out and organize. COYOTE now had Veronica Monet as its most visible member, but with so many new groups, the sex workers' movement seemed to be taking off almost as fast as dot-com businesses in Folsom Gulch. Two deserve attention.

SEIU 790, organized by dancers and employees of the Lusty Lady, was, famously, the first union to represent peep-show workers. EDA suggested SEIU, which had just begun a national organizing drive that would eventually add more than a million members. Though HERE Local 2 had represented the San Francisco Playboy Club Bunnies, they had not actively supported dancers at the O'Farrell Theatre during an earlier dispute with the Mitchell brothers.

Racism in job assignments and videotaping by customers sparked the protests that led eventually to unionizing.[97] The Lusty alumnae have been especially eager to document their experiences as dancers and activists, among them Carol Queen, Siobhan Brooks, Tawnya Dunash, Debi Sundahl, Elisabeth Eaves, Erika Langley (Seattle), and others known by their dancer names or separate pseudonyms. Vicky Funari and Julia Query's documentary, *Live Nude Girls Unite!*, focuses on the organizing campaign and (spoiler alert) Query's coming out to her mother, Dr. Joyce Wallace, the early advocate for HIV-infected sex workers in New York and founder of FROST'D.[98]

Lusty's workers, just as famously, bought the peep show in February 2003, after the original owners, Multivue Theater, announced they would close it. It became the first *modern* worker-owned cooperative in the US sex industry. SEIU continues to represent Lusty workers; a collective bargaining agreement with SEIU Local 1021 was negotiated in June 2011.[99]

Legal workers, provided they're not independent contractors, may unionize. But illegal sex workers cannot. The criminalization of prostitution and related activities, it could be argued, is the primary obstacle to attaining better working conditions for independent escorts and other sex workers. Criminal conspiracy laws technically prohibit sex workers from meeting to discuss coordinated action. Because prostitution is a crime, planning acts of prostitution or discussing ways to work together constitutes pimping—that is, managing prostitutes. Prostitutes who share their earnings for collective purposes, even if benign in intent, are technically engaging in pandering. These are not theoretical legal arguments. Sex workers have been prosecuted. These laws have had a chilling effect on organizing work in San Francisco.

Teri Goodson founded the Cyprian Guild, a "business and social network for adult entertainers interested in personal and professional improvement," in the early 1990s.[100] She alleged that she became the target of retaliation by the San Francisco Police Department (SFPD) after finishing her term on the city's prostitution task force. Police raided her home in 1999, confiscating her computer, and then began a "witch-hunt" to entrap and arrest other guild members, including Jill Nagle, editor of *Whores and Other Feminists* (1997), who was dressed in her pajamas when the police executed a search warrant.

Terrence Hallinan told the press he would prosecute Goodson for felony pandering, arguing that the Cyprian Guild illegally promoted prostitution. Goodson told *Out* magazine columnist Pat Califia,

> I know I was targeted because of what the police said to me while I was in jail. . . . They wanted information about the [Cyprian] guild and told me they saw me as a community leader and organizer. Waves of arrests like this tend to scare people and make them less likely to come together, which is exactly what the police want. And I think that's a mistake because there is power and strength in numbers.[101]

Califia questioned why Goodson and guild members were arrested while larger escort agencies, some with over one hundred workers on call, had been left alone.

Public sex would be tolerated and, in a sense, "deregulated" as long as it was commercially licensed. This seemed to be the message, if not the explicit policy, of Mayor Brown, District Attorney Hallinan, and police officials. On the surface, it appeared a roundabout method for implementing the recommendations of the 1996 San Francisco Task Force on Prostitution, which had called on "[c]ity departments [to] stop enforcing and prosecuting prostitution crimes."

The Task Force recommendations were never officially adopted but prostitution and solicitation arrests declined by almost half between 1994 and 2003. Meanwhile, arrests for disorderly conduct rose from 166 to 929, making up for the decline, noted sociologist Elizabeth Bernstein, who served as a consultant to the task force. Who, exactly, the police arrested is unknown, and it is likely that some of these "DO" arrests were for "drunk and disorderly" not prostitution-related. But public arrests, the Task Force noted, revealed inconsistent enforcement focused on "the most visible, those working on the street, and those most vulnerable, including African American, transgender, and immigrant women."[102]

The commercial sex businesses of San Francisco, in contrast, were deregulated, contrary to the task force's explicit recommendations for protecting the safety and well-being of workers. Deregulation meant that licensed theater owners could conduct business with little oversight from law enforcement and government agencies, including the state Labor

Commission, the state Occupational Health and Safety Administration, and the Department of Fair Employment and Housing. Even fire and building inspectors took a noninterventionist approach. Only when Passar, Breyer, and other sex-worker activists pressured city officials into doing their jobs were business and employment practices investigated and owners ordered to comply.

Self-employed sex workers and independent contractors in off-street "de facto legalized" businesses, such as escort agencies, outcall services, alternative sex/BDSM, and fantasy fulfillment/cross-dressing had almost never been subjected to regulation. Police had not investigated them until Goodson and members of the Cyprian Guild were rounded up. Those arrests had a chilling effect on efforts to improve working conditions for independent and other "middle-class" sex workers.

CHAPTER 6

"FUCK THE PIGS!"

Public Sex and Police Violence

*Police violence against sex workers is not perceived
as either police brutality or violence against women,
when it is clearly a manifestation of both.*[1]

—INCITE! Women of Color Against Violence

IN THE FINAL DAYS of the George W. Bush administration, more than one hundred sex-worker activists from around the United States gathered in Franklin Square, in Washington, DC, armed with red umbrellas (symbolizing sex-worker solidarity), signs, and banners to prepare for the National March for Sex Worker Rights. By national standards, by most protest standards, it was a small event. Yet so too were the 1965 protests of Gay Activists Alliance (GAA) members who stood in front of the White House. And similar to that earlier picket line, sex workers, like homosexuals, were outing themselves to demand their rights. They outed themselves as lawbreakers, allowing their identities to be known to police, to demand human rights and to claim their rights as citizens.

"Respect Sex Workers": SWAAY (Sex Work Activists, Allies, and You) sticker, designed by Furry Girl.

"Vive!" Franklin E. Kameny, founder of the GAA, would have shouted to the marchers. Then, like the storyteller he was, Frank would have shared his happy memories of the infamous Fourteenth Street Strip that began at the square and ran down to H Street, a line of topless dance clubs, adult bookstores, and massage parlors that, from the 1950s into the 1980s, "were alive, vibrant and full of people." GAA had supported licensing nude dancing in the District, to keep the Strip hopping as barkers and girls invited customers into the Butterfly Room, This Is It, Benny's Home of the Porno Stars, Cocoon, El Ceazar's Palace, the Golden Eagle, the Californian Steak House, Adam & Eve Model Studio, Paradise Escort and Model Service, the Gold Rush, and Casino Royal. "Let the people frolic!" Kameny wrote, chastising "the Puritans" from the *Washington Post* and the Franklin Square Association of developers who bragged about their success in shutting off the neon lights.

Hundreds of people once worked those blocks of the Strip, and further north, up the hill to U Street and east toward Union Station, running into the streets to talk to drivers, stopping the cars cruising from Virginia and Maryland. "Boy-whores" hustled a block east on Thirteenth and New York Avenue.[2]

To the cheers of developers and gentrifiers in Logan Circle, the cops and the courts started cracking down in the early 1980s and some women began to disappear. "Serious about combating prostitution," in 1981 a judge sentenced a thirty-year-old woman with a string of arrests and eight convictions for soliciting in five years to a fifteen-month sentence for violating conditions of her bond. Police and residents said that prostitutes brought crime to the neighborhood, which police said wasn't often reported because "male victims don't want it known where they've been."[3]

Waves of crackdowns on the Fourteenth Street stroll had been going on for decades, but on the last weekend in July 1989, at 1:30 a.m., five police officers, stressed out perhaps by their inability to stop violent crime in the District, decided to round up two dozen street-based workers and march them 1.4 miles to Arlington, effectively deporting them to Virginia. Republican congressman Stan Parris said it was another example of the city sending its "sewer sludge, garbage and convicted felons" to his district.[4] Police sold T-shirts proclaiming "I Survived the March to Virginia"; the commanding sergeant had his wrist slapped and was honored the next month by a local neighborhood association.

The women and transwomen strolling the track knew the police wouldn't protect them, just harass, arrest, and even blackmail them. Chrystal K., her arm "an embroidery rug of long, wiry scars that criss-cross down her wrist," was sliced by a customer with the edge of a can. She told a reporter, "What am I going to say, 'Mr. Police Officer, a john cut me?' God help you if you get in worse trouble. Nobody is going to think twice if you don't come home the next morning."[5] Against criminals who might rob, rape, maim, or threaten their safety, they chose to fight. Some carried "scissors, pocket knives, straight edge razors and letter openers" to defend themselves.[6]

Murders of sex workers were once less common, police said, but starting in the mid-1980s, the District's rate climbed; DC became the nation's murder capital in the early 1990s, when drugs, particularly crack, took over many streets. Street-based workers near the old Strip and elsewhere began turning up dead in greater numbers, though "many more deaths may go unreported," said Cyndee Clay, executive director of HIPS (Helping Individual Prostitutes Survive).[7]

"I've never seen these girls so paranoid," local activist Prissy Williams-Godfrey of COYOTE told the *Post* (in the same article, the reporter described COYOTE as "an organization that promotes prostitution"). In June 1990, District police speculated about a possible serial killer after seven women who worked the "high track" (as the K Street stroll of high-class streetwalkers was known) were found dead, all of them white, blonde, and in their twenties. Their deaths amplified public fears, just two months after five "wilding" young men were railroaded into falsely confessing to raping a jogger in New York's Central Park. They also helped to distract newspaper readers from the 465 other murder victims in the District that year, almost all of them young African American men who would be branded "superpredators."

Between 1985 and 1995, District police found as many as twenty women, most of them black and in their twenties and thirties, described as "prostitutes, transients and drug addicts," whose deaths may have been related. Only a fluke led a homicide detective to turn over forensic evidence to the FBI at that point, but no one has ever been charged.[8] A year later, police didn't connect the murders of four sex workers until a fifth and then a sixth body turned up on Georgia Avenue NW, far away from the Strip, an area largely unpoliced and with many abandoned crack houses.

"Something else . . . just drove" twenty-one-year-old Chander Matta on Memorial Day Weekend in 1990, and he knew where to go: to the track at Fourteenth and K Streets, where he picked up three women and then murdered them in the basement of his family's Arlington, Virginia, home in thirty-six hours of mayhem. One of his victims, Sherry K. Larman, age twenty-six, was the daughter of a retired District police officer. A few years later, her mother, Sandra Johnson, started volunteering at HIPS, spending "almost every Saturday night in a van" handing out safer-sex supplies and candy and lending an ear to street-based workers.

It was in Larman's memory in 1997 that local groups held what was probably the first US vigil for murdered and missing sex workers. Sixty people, among them a "half-dozen streetwalkers" and some former sex workers, gathered to read the names of the twenty-two known victims killed in the Washington area since 1982. Johnson said her daughter's "life meant just as much as any doctor's daughter."[9] The following year, the organizers—HIPS; Positive Force DC, a "punk collective committed to radical social change"; the Magdalene Community, an activist Catholic feminist group; and other churches—held a street walk, lit candles, and read the names of eight more murdered women.[10]

If homicide detectives were slow, vice detective John Mehalic III "played by no known rules." He "demanded sexual favors in return for leniency, not always giving [sex workers] a choice." Two women testified against him, leading to Mehalic's conviction in 1998 for ten felony counts of kidnapping, sexual assault, extortion, and stalking.[11] Sergeant Frank Morgan, head of the prostitution unit, admitted, "Everybody messes over the prostitutes."[12]

Ten years later, on December 17, 2008, a day of activism globally dedicated to ending violence against sex workers, protesters walked down Fourteenth Street again, this time toward the US Department of Justice on Pennsylvania Avenue, chanting "Sex Workers' Rights Are Human Rights."[13] The Strip was long gone, replaced by high-rise office buildings and expensive restaurants, but murders and violence have not ended in the District or anywhere else. Organized by Robyn Few, founder of the SWOP-USA, the marchers demanded that police investigate crimes against street workers as zealously as they did others.[14]

The Green River Killer, Gary Leon Ridgway, who confessed to murdering at least forty-eight women—and perhaps as many as seventy—had finally been arrested on December 17, 2003, in Seattle. For twenty years, this "respectable family man" had been stalking, assaulting, and killing street-based sex workers and other women on Seattle's Strip. He said the murders were his personal crusade to rid the streets of "scum." Robyn Few and performance artist and sex worker Annie Sprinkle wanted to remember and honor those victims, many of them fifteen to twenty years old, and all other victims. They chose the day of his arrest to hold vigils, organize speak-outs, or march through the streets. In DC, before the closed doors of Justice, Few and others read aloud the names of those who had been killed in 2008; sometimes there wasn't a name, just a date, a place, and sometimes an approximate age.

Sex workers are fighters, and they have been fighting against the police and predators for a long, long time. Though the victims of some gruesome crimes, they also tell stories about building community and organizing protests about individual acts of resistance—sometimes their survival *is* resistance. When weapons and entrenched power abound; no one is invincible. Survival means actively resisting the many forms of victimization that lurk in dark corners and on sunny streets. It means developing the psychological resiliency to fight back and heal.[15] Organized resistance means sharing information with others, profiling clients and cops, knowing when and how to physically defend oneself, when to use "street justice," and when, if ever, to go to the police.[16]

The confrontations at Compton's and Stonewall in the 1960s and the recent candlelight vigils and marches are not their only tactics. Girl Army dojo teaches self-defense classes at the St. James Infirmary in San Francisco.[17] In Seattle, "grrrlarmy" paints slogans across the red-light district where Ridgway once preyed: "Human, Not Just a Ho," "Keep Sex Workers Safe," "Do What You Wanna Do, Just Know You're Not Alone," with contact information for three sex-worker support groups.[18] More informally, Street Transvestite Action Revolutionaries (STAR), founded by Sylvia Rivera and Marsha P. Johnson, continues to inspire trans/queer/sex trader anarchists to resist violence and "pig power."

Fighting back in every way imaginable, sex workers have demonstrated individual resiliency and tenacity, and shared community values of social justice and the right to personhood. Street-based sex traders, party girls, transwomen, male hustlers, and sexual outlaws of every color deal with violence that can seem immeasurable and, like all human relations, complex.[19] The abuse that sex workers experience and their collective and individual efforts to avoid victimization, are gutsy examples of resistance and resilience.

For years, sex workers have heard their stories distorted by academics, policy experts, and courtroom attorneys. In the last decade, sex workers have refused to be silenced by prohibitionist researchers who deny speech to "the subaltern," a practice that reifies victimization and whore stigma.[20] The historical exclusion of sex workers from discussions about policy and politics has been challenged by groups such as the Young Women's Empowerment Project in Chicago, the Best Practices Policy Project, Washington's DC Trans Coalition, New York's FIERCE (Fabulous Independent Educated Radicals for Community Empowerment), and Queers for Economic Justice, which have engaged in participatory action research to survey their communities, record people's stories, and present proposals to policymakers directly. Their studies and persistent engagement in the discourse on sex work and sex trades have changed police procedures, changed the law, and shown a canny ability for wielding power.

POLICING THE PUBLIC SQUARE

Police are tasked with the duty to keep the public square clean. Sex "crimes" between consenting heterosexuals such as prostitution, adultery, and fornication, are punishable when they are "open and notorious," disrupting public order. Until 1917, prostitution and brothel-keeping were not crimes in New Orleans; proprietors were charged only with keeping a *disorderly* bawdyhouse. "What was illegal," legal historian Lawrence Friedman writes, "was not the sin itself—and certainly not secret sin— but sin that offended *public* morality."[21] In this sense, decriminalizing prostitution on the grounds it is a victimless crime doesn't apply, because the consent of the private parties is immaterial. Rather, society is victimized because citizens must contend with other people's flagrant sexual behavior in the streets, or on public display.

Street harassment and slut-shaming are very old ways to punish "open and notorious" gender nonconformity. Historically, prostitutes, hustlers, transwomen, and sex traders were viewed as models of female dishonor, a social-political class united by its members' disregard for traditional gender roles and sexual behavior. They had to be kept apart from "good" society, especially honorable women, with laws to ensure their subjugation and customs to maintain their marginalization. For freeborn women, rape and fornication meant death by stoning, the punishment prescribed by religious authorities. Enslaved people and other second-class persons had no civil rights because their "prostituted" status was evident; modernity altered, but did not abolish, those laws. By custom, citizens could use physical violence and verbal abuse to remind them of their dishonorable status. Everyone could abuse them: clients, managers, fellow workers, family, friends, domestic partners, neighbors, and strangers on the street; such bullying was considered almost a civic duty.[22]

"Open and notorious" violations of gender roles are also policed with myths about rape and whorephobia, which are used to explain away the sexual abuse and murder of sexually active public women.[23] One myth about rape says a woman is asking for it because she is out in public at the wrong time, in the wrong place, wearing the wrong clothes, displaying the wrong attitude, behaving badly. Asking "What's a nice girl like you doing in a place like this?" isn't about the place "like this," it's about the woman's honor. "Nice girls" don't go to bars alone, so they must be prostitutes or loose women. They are fair game, "public property [whose] bodies are open territory for assault."[24] Angela Davis observed that rape is regarded as a serious crime only when the woman is "owned" by a "powerful" man.[25] And it is precisely because sex workers are not owned by any honorable "man" that they can be raped with impunity.

Putting the blame on "sluts" and "whores" excuses the criminal justice system when it fails to arrest or to convict the perpetrator. When Susan Brownmiller interviewed a police sergeant about rape in New York's Greenwich Village precinct in 1971, he claimed that every one of the thirty-five complaints filed that month originated with "prostitutes who didn't get paid."[26]

Whore stigma is another, more pernicious, version of the rape myth.[27] Female dishonor, combined with criminalization, allows the police to ignore violence against sex workers because they have no civil rights. Many question whether a crime has occurred; detectives and district attorneys tell the victim she should "just expect that in your line of work." Some doubt whether the victim suffered; after all, "rough sex" is a part of the game. Drug users were probably too strung out to have felt anything at all. Forced sodomy of transwomen is dismissed: they are "unrapeable," yet violence is justified on the grounds that "that's what you get for trying to fool a man." These too-predictable defamations of character and practical disregard for bodily integrity are designed to disempower the victim, to stop them complaining, to get them to just go away.

Whore stigma leads some feminist researchers to ignore sex workers' experiences with sexual assault or to blame abuse on men as clients, pimps, and traffickers without factoring in other forms of violence. Brownmiller cited a 1974 Memphis study in which the investigator claimed "only 1.02% of all rape victims were prostitutes."[28] The researcher may have thought she needed to defend women's honor, but should have considered the structural violence that potentially skewed the data. In all likelihood, "whores" knew they wouldn't get protection or respect from the notoriously racist Memphis police and never attempted to report crimes committed against them. If the study and attitude seem outdated, a 1991 investigation discovered that police in Oakland, California, had failed to investigate 203 reports of sexual assault, most made by sex workers and by women who traded sex for crack or other drugs.[29]

Whether they are the victims of crimes or are charged with violent crimes, the moral character of sex workers is scrutinized by both the police and district attorneys. While police guidelines instruct investigators to treat rape victims with care and respect, these instructions are frequently ignored when the person is not white, not "straight," uses drugs, or has an arrest record. Prosecutors can be reluctant to rely on "sluts" as witnesses; defense attorneys will introduce prior arrests and past relationships to demonstrate a sex worker's pattern of sexual consent.

The 1974 case of Joan Little tells us what happens when a young African American woman who liked to party fights back to save her life. Raised in Beaufort, North Carolina, local police profiled Little as a truant and incorrigible "party girl" as a teenager. A few years later, she was in the county jail, serving a seven-to-ten-year sentence for trying to steal a television.[30]

Her trial for the murder of warden Clarence Alligood became an international cause célèbre at the beginning of the anti-rape movement. The small, twenty-year-old black woman did not deny she stabbed the two-hundred-pound white warden. The question was why. Did she stab him in self-defense when he entered her cell with the intent of sexual assault, or did she intend to commit the murder to escape the jail? The prosecution released her criminal record, which included charges for breaking and entering, passing bad checks, and prostitution; it alleged that Little offered Alligood sex in exchange for favorable treatment in jail. Knowing the conditions women endured in prison, Angela Davis came to Little's defense, focusing on systemic sexual violence against black women, especially the institutionalized and incarcerated. In a *Ms.* magazine article, she rejected the prostitution charges as "unfounded and malicious." Davis and Little's defense attorneys drew attention to the long legal and social history of racism, sexism, and classism that oppressed black people. The institutionalized rape of African American women supposedly arose from the "natural" lasciviousness of the "African race." A white man could not be convicted of fornication with a slave woman, the North Carolina Supreme Court ruled, because she had no rights to her body.[31]

The other "truth" about "whores," the prosecution implied, is that they'll cock-tease or screw to get what they want. The prosecutor tried to frame Joan Little as a "known prostitute" who had no scruples about enticing Alligood. Lacking morality or integrity, he claimed, she would commit perjury to save herself from the death penalty.[32]

Nationally syndicated Chicago columnist Mike Royko agreed: "It was just as easy to believe she had set up the old geezer for murder and escape as it was to believe that he forced her to defend herself."[33] Like other commentators, Royko believed the prosecutor's description of Little as an incorrigible "party girl" who sometimes traded sex for favors or money.

A racially balanced jury acquitted Joan Little of murder in August 1975. But her lawyers, Jerry Paul and William Kunstler, did not attempt to explain that a "party girl" could say no to sex. In fact, they used a very old story whose truth had become acknowledged: the historical plight of black people under Southern justice. They even had Little carry *To Kill a Mockingbird* into the courtroom.[34]

Harper Lee's novel, as well as the Southern Poverty Law Center's appeals for donations to her defense committee, focused on racism and the lynching of blacks. Little was a black person who happened to be female; intersectional analysis was for a future generation of scholars. The defense lawyers compared the case against Little to an act of mob violence, arguing the prosecutor presented no physical evidence linking her to the crime scene. A murder conviction would be equivalent to a legal lynching.

Little's case provided an opportunity to reconsider British jurist Sir Matthew Hale's rule that a woman must "resist to the utmost" to prove rape. Little fought back. But by covering up her sexual history, her lawyers denied women a heroine who exercised both her right to have sex *and* her right to say no. Popular culture of the 1970s reflected widespread fears about the sexual emancipation of women and of African Americans, a fear that was not restricted to conservatives but shared by many feminists.[35]

These fears complicated calls for states to pass new laws that protected rape victims from having their sexual pasts introduced as evidence of consent. In Little's trial, her reputation as a party girl was brought up against her, but under a "rape shield," her past could not have been used in court. Theoretically, these laws turn all rape victims, including sex workers, into honorable women and justify the state's efforts to protect public safety. In practice, they do not.

Crimes of murder, rape, and violence are prosecuted to ensure public safety, not to win justice for those who suffered.[36] This aspect of trying a criminal case often eludes observers; the heroic image of prosecutors (sometimes exaggerated by their campaign literature, and certainly by television) makes it appear as if they are defending someone who has suffered from a horrible crime. But in actuality, a victim is simply a witness for the state, the same as a medical expert or mere bystander. The testimony of the victim—like that of others called by the prosecutor—is intended "to protect the security of the community rather than represent [themselves] or police interests."[37]

As a prosecutor in the Manhattan District Attorney's office, Linda Fairstein argued that protecting "special victims" was in New York's interest. Criminals who broke laws against rape, domestic violence, incest, stalking, pandering, pimping, and other sex crimes endangered the public. She recognized that (female) sex workers were particularly vulnerable to crime, but she did not believe their every complaint represented a threat to the state's security. Sex workers, she implied, chose their dangerous and illegal occupations; as a prosecutor, it was not her responsibility to defend every crime committed against them.

Fairstein dismissed sex workers who complained about "theft of services," comparing them to fare-beaters, people who jump subway turnstiles in order to avoid paying the fare. These cases, she wrote, happened when "inexperienced" street-based workers "forgot" to get their money up front and the client refused to pay. "No rape has occurred" because there had been "no force, no threat, no violence."[38]

However, Fairstein's argument ignores the woman's lack of consent: she did *not* agree to free sex, she agreed to *paid* sex. By refusing to even investigate such cases, this "Special Victims Unit" pioneer suggested that sex workers are "public property"—people who can be used or abused because doing so is somehow in the state's interest.[39] By the logic of her argument, sex workers pose as much danger to public safety as rapists.

The real rapists, according to Fairstein, are those whose motives were eerily similar to serial killers, "degradation and humiliation, control and possession, anger and hatred, intimidation and terrorization." Inarguably, crimes committed with motives this odious should be prosecuted, but this is a very high standard of proof, even in New York, where the law has long blamed victims for inviting the crime.[40]

Former congresswoman Elizabeth Holtzman, who served as district attorney in Brooklyn in the 1980s, explained the difficulty of prosecuting someone accused of rape when the victim did sex work. New York State offered no protection, she said.

> [Sex workers] are viewed as the dregs of this earth. You can try to prosecute . . . but the defense can bring in every single prior sexual act she's ever had, on the theory that if she's ever said "yes" once, she'll say "yes" again.[41]

Changes in the city's rape shield laws have limited introduction of a victim's prostitution convictions to three years, and only if they are "relevant" to the case.[42] Yet the accused's past rape convictions are inadmissible at trial because the law regards them as irrelevant. When sex workers and queer and transgender people are accused of crimes, their sexual histories always seem to matter, even when they are fighting for their lives.[43]

FIGHTING BACK

Serial killers have preyed on sex workers and sexual outlaws for a very long time. From Jack the Ripper in Victorian London to the "Craigslist

Killer" in contemporary Boston, victim blaming, whorephobia, homo/ transphobia, and racism encourage violence against sex workers. But predators choose their victims not simply because they are pathetic or careless, or because they happen to be in the wrong place at the wrong time. Weakness, ignorance, or bad luck alone don't make them targets. Ripper Jack and "Killer" Philip Markoff can rob, kidnap, maim, rape, and murder because few people care what happens to sex workers, whether they're female, transwomen, youth, or males. Systemic violence against sex workers cannot be blamed on criminal psychopaths alone. The police are also violent.

The women of Downtown Eastside in Vancouver, BC, have marched through the streets every Valentine's Day since 1991, to demand justice for their missing and murdered sisters. Local and federal law enforcement agencies had done little to investigate the reports of women missing from DTES until 1998, when Aboriginal activists sent a list of forty names and demanded answers. Four years later, the bodies of forty-nine women were discovered buried on Robert Pickton's pig farm. Sex workers, drug users, Aboriginal women, and anti-violence activists organized many more marches before the Missing Women Commission of Inquiry convened in 2012.

For the first month, "hundreds of marginalized women" protested the hearings every morning; to them, as well as to civil liberties and human rights groups, "the Inquiry was an absolute failure." They were shut out of the hearings, their stories of "the callous sexism and racism of the police" were systematically ignored. The truth of the matter was captured in the title of a dissenting commission member's report about police conduct: "Wouldn't Piss on Them If They Were on Fire: How Discrimination Against Sex Workers, Drug Users and Aboriginal Women Enabled a Serial Killer."[44]

Government commissions and their reports represent the least official effort; all too rarely are they given the mandate, investigatory power, and resources to substantially change public policy. But the disappointing final report was not accepted: continued public protests, combined years of community organizing by marginalized women, and a lawsuit filed by Sex Workers United Against Violence forced Vancouver police to adopt new guidelines. The policies, which went into effect in January 2013, require that sex workers' safety take precedence; police are to treat all reports of violence as serious criminal matters rather than interrogating victims on the suspicion they have broken prostitution laws.

Even in cities with large commercial sex industries, for those who lack job skills, self-discipline, or the "correct" genitalia, highway hustling and street work are two of the few ways to earn a living. But by working in public, they violate the unspoken rule that sex and sex work should be done in private.

Vancouver, like other North American cities, has its skid row and "lower track," public reminders of its local street-based economy where people hustle to survive. These designated areas, whether in Los Angeles, San Francisco, the Bronx, Chicago, Washington, DC, or elsewhere, are part of the urban geography of prostitution, affected by the larger economic disruptions, migration and gentrification, and strategies of police surveillance. Starting in the 1980s, these neighborhoods have experienced the full force of the war on drugs, the criminalization/commercialization of the sex industry, deindustrialization, the abolition of the social safety net, and "Negro removal" in the guise of urban "renewal."

When Washington's Strip closed down, local sex workers had few legitimate work opportunities available. Some went private or online, advertising in area magazines and weekly alternative newspapers, using pagers and answering services. Others joined the women and transwomen on the stroll, leading to tension, harassment, and violence. In the summer of 1981, Logan Circle residents slapped hot pink stickers on cruising cars that read: "Disease Warning: Occupants of this car have been seen cruising street ladies along 14th Street."[45]

In the late 1980s, street-based sex workers in Washington and many other North American cities started disappearing from their known strolls. Many went "underground," chased from downtown areas, away from the public view of political leaders and gentrifying voters. Some sex workers migrated with the drug market as it moved, while others began trading sex for crack cocaine and crystal methamphetamine where drug dealers controlled the streets. Buyers followed them to the far reaches of the city, especially after 1992 when DC copied a Portland, Oregon, law that allowed police to seize the cars of johns who cruised the downtown stroll, even when the owner was innocent.[46]

"You keep talking about prostitution," Rosa Lee Cunningham observed to *Washington Post* reporter Leon Dash. "I saw it as survival."

Married at sixteen in 1952 to an abusive husband she soon left, Rosa Lee had hustled every way possible to support herself and her eight children. "Mama Rose," in her late fifties, still hustled dope and crack on Fourteenth and W Streets, a mile north of the old Strip, to support her daughter Patty and her transgender child "Ducky." They, too, hustled and traded sex for drugs and necessities when they came of age, working in other areas of the District. In 1988, all three were diagnosed with HIV, but only Rosa Lee was eligible for methadone and HIV medications—which she often split with Patty. "She fought all the way to the end," another son said when she died in 1995 from pneumonia. "She didn't give up trying."[47] HIV was another reason why some street traders disappeared.

Wherever sex workers loiter, they have been subjected to random police harassment and sweeps, but in less-populated and less-traveled neighborhoods and deindustrialized zones, under bridges, near freeways, and at truck rest stops, they have lost the meager protection offered by downtown streets. In these desolate areas, they must negotiate dates quickly, at a speed that prevents "going with their gut" about the potential client and making them more vulnerable to violent criminals and cops.

In December 1989, Richard Mallory, a business owner with an old conviction for attempted rape, sexually assaulted a sex worker he picked up on the side of a Florida highway. She fought back, killing him with a gun she had acquired after several previous attacks.

Over the next eleven months, Aileen Wuornos killed another six men; she was arrested in January 1991. Prosecutor John Tanner called her a "predatory prostitute who turned robber to killer." Documentary filmmaker Nick Broomfield thought Wuornos "had a lot of awful encounters on the roads. And I think this anger just spilled out from inside her." She "finally exploded into incredible violence. That was her way of surviving."[48]

All of Wuornos's victims presumably agreed to pay her for sex. Walter J. Antonio, the fifth victim, was a truck driver and reserve police officer. After they parked in a remote wooded area,

> Antonio pulled out a false police badge and said he could arrest her but would not do so if she had sex with him for free. Wuornos said she challenged him, contending he was not a law officer. He kept on making his demand for sex, she said, and she then pulled a gun.[49]

Wuornos confessed to shooting him and then took his ring, pocket-knife, handcuffs, police baton, and flashlight before fleeing. Charles "Dick" Humphreys, the sixth victim, was a retired Air Force major with two careers in law enforcement. He'd been a police chief in Alabama before moving to Florida and taking work as a state investigator, specializing in child-abuse cases.

Wuornos had reason to distrust police and youth services. Her father was a convicted child molester; the grandfather who raised her was also abusive. Pregnant at thirteen, she was sent to a home for unwed mothers; the baby was taken for adoption. Neighbors repeated a rumor that her grandfather's friend was the father. No state official appears to have investigated the abuse. Wuornos spent time in a girls' training school; when she was released, her grandfather kicked her out of the house. Homeless at fifteen, she hitchhiked to Florida; in 1981, she served a thirteen-month prison sentence. During the nearly ten years she spent on death row, she regularly lashed out at prison guards, complaining of harassment and brutality.

Prison activists called for justice for Wuornos, arguing she acted in self-defense. Out of Control, a San Francisco Bay–area lesbian political collective, argued that women incarcerated for defending themselves against sexual abuse were political prisoners. The Spear & Shield Collective of the New Afrikan Independence Movement editorialized that sex workers were often victims of rape and institutional violence.[50] Other men, including clients, testified that Wuornos did not threaten them; in fact, they said, "she was worried that they would attack her." Her defenders also disputed the serial killer label, because she did not stalk her victims, nor did she "kill in moments of fear or passion."[51] Wuornos did not acknowledge the efforts of prison abolitionists; for a time, she allowed a "famous feminist" to help her but later accused her of selling her out.[52]

"Famous feminist" psychologist Phyllis Chesler asserted that Wuornos acted in self-defense, striking out against patriarchal violence and highlighting her multiple oppressions as a woman, a lesbian, a "prostituted woman," a member of the working class, unemployed and undereducated, and an older woman.[53] The legal system's double standard judged battered women more harshly than men, Chesler argued, citing a study of gender bias conducted in 1990 by the Florida Supreme Court that women were more likely to serve time, and serve longer sentences, than men convicted of similar crimes.

Though Chesler and other carceral feminists indict the justice system for its patriarchal attitudes, they fail to question the ways police and prisons instigate violence against sexual outlaws and gender nonconformists, perpetuating the very wrongs they believe can be fixed through liberal reforms. In Chesler's view, Wuornos was a prostituted woman who fought back because she had been thoroughly victimized by men; she was a battered woman whom men turned into a "bad girl"—even a "predator."[54] Chesler later admitted her "pitiless politics": "I wanted to educate the jury about the extreme level of violence that prostitutes routinely absorb, the danger they always face."[55] In coming to Wuornos's defense, she wrote:

> Prostituted women have long been considered "fair game" for sexual harassment, rape, gang-rape, "kinky" sex, robbery, and beatings. Their homes have been destroyed, and they have been taunted, even killed, for "sport."[56]

Chesler ignored Wuornos' testimony that Antonio tried to coerce her by showing his badge, preying on her as a sexual criminal. Wuornos may have also reacted violently upon learning that Humphreys was a retired police officer and a state investigator. Wournos could be called a "cop killer," though no commentator connected her crimes to the simultaneous controversies over hip hop anthems such as N.W.A.'s "Fuck tha Police" (1989), Tupac Shakur's "2Pacalypse Now" (1991), or Ice-T's "Cop Killer" (1992).[57]

Wuornos didn't fit the profile of "typical" serial killers, but in the early 1990s there were many who did. The number seemed to rise sharply; certainly the press seemed to pay more attention. Criminologist Kenna Quinet identified 502 male serial murderers active in the United States between 1970 and 2009; she also identified 3,228 of their female victims. Nearly one-third (32 percent) had been engaged in sex work or street-based trades. In the 1970s, police solved only 16 percent of cases involving sex workers; in the last decade, between 2000 and 2009, 69 percent of known cases have been solved.[58] Though the number of killers and victims had declined over the years, Quinet found that "victims [were] increasingly likely to be prostitutes, particularly female prostitutes." More alarmingly, when the victims are engaged in sex trades, the killers "amass a greater average number of victims than do non-prostitute killers" and kill "for slightly longer periods of time." Reading this another way, homicide detectives work less diligently when sex workers go missing or turn up dead. Police slang for murder cases involving prostitutes, noted Linda Fairstein, is "No Human Involved."[59]

Though Quinet tracked only female victims, boys and young men involved in street-based sex trades are also prey, and police also ignore their pleas for help. In 1991, Milwaukee police returned fourteen-year-old Konerak Sinthasomphone, drugged, naked, and bleeding, to Jeffrey Dahmer's apartment, believing the serial killer's claim that they'd had a lovers' fight.[60] Dahmer's first victim had disappeared in 1978; another four died after Sinthasomphone's attempted escape. Most of his seventeen victims, *$pread* magazine editor Will Rockwell reminds readers, were "hustlers lured by promises of cash in exchange for nude photographs"; almost all of them were young African American and Asian men.[61]

Sex workers and the families of murdered sex workers in the United States have begun to take action against brutality and the indifference of law enforcement agencies. Sinthasomphone's family successfully sued, not because of "police inaction, but of police action," because the police had failed to return him to his family as police procedure requires for minors.[62] In Spokane, Washington, families and friends began reporting the disappearances of street-based sex workers in 1990, but according to an outside investigator, there were "witnesses who were never questioned and leads that were never followed," delaying the indictment of Robert Yates, believed to have murdered eighteen women, until October 2000.[63]

Seattle police claim they were unable to connect Gary Leon Ridgway to the murders of forty-eight sex workers until DNA testing became available.[64] His first six victims were found in August 1982; by December 1983, there were eighteen bodies. Many of the murdered women knew each other from "the Strip" where they worked.[65] Sex workers gave reports about various men who had abducted and raped them, sometimes at gunpoint, to the special task force. Others did not come forward because they didn't trust the police. "Diantha G." wrote to Ann Rule, former Seattle police officer turned true crime author, that she had been forced to fellate Ridgway at gunpoint in 1982 or 1983:

I didn't call the police because I didn't trust them. One time I got arrested for prostitution and this one cop opened up my shirt and just looked down at my breasts, and there was no reason for him to do that. So when this happened to me, I decided I wasn't going to tell them anything. I wasn't hurt and I wasn't dead . . . I found out [early] that nobody believes you when you tell the truth. Especially the cops. I just kept it myself all these years.[66]

The police task force identified, questioned, and even tailed several of the men the sex workers had identified, including Ridgway. None were arrested, not even men linked to other kidnappings, sexual assaults, and crimes against sex workers. Ridgway got away with killing women for years because he knew police wouldn't investigate.[67]

I picked prostitutes as my victims because I hate most prostitutes and I did not want to pay them for sex. I also picked prostitutes as victims because they were easy to pick up without being noticed. I knew they would not be reported missing right away and might never be reported missing. I picked prostitutes because I thought I could kill as many of them as I wanted without getting caught.[68]

Indeed, as the reports from women who came forward show, many violent criminals recognize they could attack sex workers and other marginalized people without fear of arrest.

When beat cops prioritize violent crime over prostitution and minor offenses, people and neighborhoods feel they are safer. This finding runs counter to the "broken windows" approach used by New York City police during Rudolph Giuliani's administration. But in 1998, Patricia A. Hurt, Essex County's first black female prosecutor, accomplished this feat in Newark, New Jersey. Fourteen African American women, all street-based sex workers and most drug users, were thought to have been murdered by a serial killer, but despite warnings from state police, the city's homicide squad had done little. Hurt established a special investigative task force, and beat cops started talking to, rather than arresting, women on the streets. A special hotline allowed others to report information or if "they are abused by a john." (It received more calls than the drug hotline.) The more cooperative relationship led "directly to the arrests of seven men for crimes against prostitutes that range from an unrelated murder to sexual assault."[69] One, a serial rapist identified by at least eight women, was arrested on seventy-nine counts, including kidnapping, aggravated sexual assault, robbery, and "making terroristic threats."[70]

The "Merseyside model" launched by police in Suffolk, England, takes a similar approach. Sex workers' organizations in Liverpool strategized how they wanted police to respond when Anne Marie Foy died after sustaining over sixty injuries; six other sex workers had been killed in the previous five years. The toll-free hotline led to the identification and quick arrest of Steve Wright, the "Ipswich Murderer," who was convicted of killing five sex workers in the winter of 2006. Police took reports from any sex worker with information to share or who needed to report another crime, and promised all callers amnesty. The call center became permanent. Like the Newark experiment, police take reports of other violent crimes committed against sex workers, leading to more arrests. Conviction rates "rose dramatically to 83%, whereas the national average of such convictions in the UK is only 6.5%."[71]

Sex-worker activists have generally praised this model, and a Conservative member of parliament now wants to make it a national program. One factor is amnesty, giving sex workers a safe space to talk openly about violence against them, without worrying that they may incriminate themselves for other minor offenses. It also coordinates with the "Ugly Mugs Project," run by the UK Network of Sex Work Projects. Ugly Mugs, like Bad Date Sheets in US cities, distribute notices about people who threaten, hurt, rob, or assault sex workers; clients, street thugs, pimps, and others may be reported.

Most importantly, the Merseyside model recognizes that violence against sex workers is an expression of whorephobia, a hate crime that singles out members of a stigmatized group. The change in procedure allows police to prioritize the more serious crime; it does not exact additional penalties in the case of conviction, but it sends "a message to society at large that the unique oppression faced by sex workers is not acceptable."[72]

Long Island, New York, police discovered the bodies of eight female sex workers on a seaside parkway in 2010.[73] Police speculate that they are the victims of a serial killer, and the murders remain unsolved. Sex Workers Action New York (SWANK), SWOP-NYC, and Audacia Ray of the Red Umbrella Project, a sex worker–run media advocacy group, launched a campaign asking the Suffolk County district attorney to grant amnesty to anyone who might have information but feared arrest on prostitution or related charges. In 2012, the county police announced a non-prosecution policy; it "took a very long time," but Ray believes "it is a powerful testament to our advocacy efforts."[74]

Sex workers and their allies may never fundamentally redirect or abolish the carceral system. But they have altered some police practices, moving toward harm reduction approaches and a human rights framework. Independent research, investigative journalism, and scholarly studies designed to maximize the participation of sex workers have exposed systemic incompetence and brutality. As *Tits & Sass* reporter Katie Zen observes:

> In the end, what matters most is evidence-based research of the effects on the ground; the way a policy is implemented can be more important than the policy itself, and it will be our responsibility, in the sex worker movement, to continually monitor the impact of these policy projects.[75]

WE KNOW WE ARE OUR OWN HEROINES

Thirty-five years after Susan Brownmiller claimed that sex workers were only 1.02 percent of rape victims in Memphis, Duanna Johnson, an African American transwoman, was beaten by two officers while she was in custody on prostitution charges. After her release, she was shot to death as she worked a street corner, the target of three men. Her family and transgender activists across the United States demanded that the Memphis police be held accountable for their brutal disregard of her human rights and civil liberties.[76]

In Eugene, Oregon, the repeated "grumblings of prostitutes and junkies," as department supervisors characterized their complaints, finally led to the arrest and conviction of two police officers in 2004 for abusing at least fifteen women over a period of six years. On the street, sex workers called Officer Roger Magaña "Officer Blow Job," but the crimes they reported went beyond forced oral sodomy.[77]

One witness, a thirty-nine-year-old sex worker who had been repeatedly victimized by him, asked, "Why the hell didn't they listen to me? That's gravely offensive."[78] When she filed a complaint, he retaliated, threatening an investigation of her home by child protective services. He then raped her using his city-issued gun. "If you tell anyone anything about me," he threatened, "I'll blow you up from the inside out." Magaña received a ninety-four-year sentence, and the city paid $5 million to settle victims' lawsuits. His supervisor, Pete Kerns, was named Eugene's chief of police in September 2009.[79]

Victim-blaming is routine, noted Jessica Xavier, who surveyed violence against transwomen of color in the District. "The implication is that it's your fault for being beaten or killed," especially when the transgender victim is linked to sex work. "But a lack of privilege means you don't have a choice."[80]

In March 2011, a forty-year-old sex worker sat in a New Orleans courtroom while a defense attorney repeatedly "called the woman a 'whore' and 'trash.'" She had testified that veteran police officer Henry Hollins had picked her up and suggested she could have sex with him in exchange for her release on drug-possession charges. Hollins took her to an abandoned warehouse, where he raped the handcuffed woman at gunpoint. Nearby were his Taser gun and a "collection of sex toys" that he kept in the trunk of his squad car along with "unused condoms and a bag of used condoms."[81] Another sex worker testified that Hollins had made the same offer to her; she chose arrest.

The New Orleans assistant district attorneys argued that Hollins had profiled the woman as a street-based hustler with a probable criminal drug record and sexual history. Hollins and his partner picked her up on a public nuisance charge but never logged the pickup nor called it in to the command center as procedure required.[82] According to one ADA, "He sized her up as fit prey. . . . He knew that at the moment he ran her name."[83] The jury convicted Hollins of second-degree kidnapping and attempted aggravated rape, and he received a forty-five-year prison sentence.

Hollins's conviction was unusual, *but his crimes were not.*[84] Hollins should not be dismissed as a rogue cop or a bad apple, nor should his disregard for citizens' constitutional rights be written off as just another example of the systemic pattern of the city's corrupt policing, as the US Department of Justice concluded that same month.[85] Indeed, Hollins's conviction is perhaps remarkable in light of the federal report: New Orleans Police Department (NOPD) investigations "seemed to focus on the trustworthiness of the victim herself, rather than on the alleged crime." Officers said they did not fully investigate "many complaints of sexual assault" based on "the victim's criminal . . . history of prostitution."[86]

The jury convicted Hollins. Politics played a part: a new mayor, a newly appointed chief of police, and a recently elected district attorney had all vowed to clean house, and the NOPD was under federal scrutiny. Hollins could be held up as a bad apple, letting other officers escape public scrutiny. More harmfully, high-profile convictions shift public attention away from the structural violence of policing, whose values and rules remain unchallenged.

Women With A Vision, an African American grassroots organizing and advocacy group, worked closely with the victim, providing support and making sure the court and the public heard her story. That story connected violence against street-based workers to systemic police brutality and the expanding criminalization of socially marginalized people.[87] Hollins was not the only predator cop.

Hollins's attorney called his victim a "whore" and "trash," insinuating that her decision to engage in street work seduced him. Similarly, when the federal government cites the NOPD for misconduct and its failure to uphold the Constitution, people are led to believe that with better training and greater supervision, the police will protect both New Orleans residents and tourists. But this form of distancing wishes away the institutionalized police brutality—which is not mere misconduct—and the abuse of sex workers occurring in communities everywhere.[88]

While not every person who engages in street sex trades experiences police brutality, reports and studies from around the world indicate that law enforcement is the "Big Daddy" of perpetrators. Profiling and police violence against civilians, the US Commission on Civil Rights reminds us, "are morally reprehensible and an ineffective way to enforce the law."[89] Profiling and violence also encourage modern-day vigilantism, creating a climate for ordinary citizens to stalk, threaten, and harass sex workers on the street.

"You'd be surprised how many policemen I had sex with," said Toni Collins, cofounder of Washington, DC's Transgender Health Empowerment. "They'd say, 'You do it with me, or I'm going to arrest you for prostitution.' Then they'd tell me to go home and I better not tell anybody."[90] Systemic violence remains a particular risk for transgender people, whether or not they engage in sex work. HIPS outreach worker GiGi Thomas said police sometimes simply "arrest all transgender women in certain areas on suspicion of their engagement in prostitution."[91]

Ryhannah Combs, an African American transwoman profiled by the NYPD, told her story to an investigative reporter for Jezebel.com. Combs claimed the arresting officer said:

> "I've seen girls like you come around here all the time. Just because you're dressed differently doesn't mean you're not a prostitute." [Combs] says other officers later lied to make her look like a prostitute, claiming she was carrying 9 condoms when she was actually carrying zero . . .

Eventually all criminal charges against her were dropped.[92]

Profiling is based on stereotypes, location, and status; the NYPD *Patrol Guide* advises officers to observe "the suspect's activity and perceived conversations with passersby . . . as well as the suspect's location, conversations, clothing, conduct, associates and status as a 'known prostitute.'"[93]

The intent of profiling, like the NYPD's controversial stop-and-frisk policies, is not simply to harass people on the streets, which in itself is a democracy-chilling tactic. The New York Civil Liberties Union discovered that the names and personal information of every person stopped are placed in police databases, even when there was no evidence of wrongdoing. Frisking, which routinely includes a demand to inspect purses, backpacks, and other items in the person's possession, invades personal space, so that nothing is private.

Carrying three or more unopened condoms can be probable cause for prostitution, a deeply troubling view that outrages human rights advocates. San Francisco police used to follow CAL-PEP outreach workers as they distributed condoms in the Tenderloin and arrest the people who took them, said codirector Priscilla Alexander. Teri Goodson, the San Francisco NOW member of the city's prostitution task force, led the campaign to end using possession of condoms as evidence of prostitution. City Supervisor Terrence Hallinan cheered passage of the nonbinding resolution in October 1994. However, the city did not permanently abolish its policy until May 2013.[94] In Washington, HIPS, the Women's Collective, the DC Trans Coalition, and other local activists forced the

Metropolitan Police Department to clarify its policies. In March 2013 it issued a palm card informing the public that police cannot stop or search anyone based on condom possession.

Though there is no law against the possession of condoms, it was used as proof to convict at least thirty-nine people on prostitution-related charges in Brooklyn alone in 2008 and 2009. Even when no one is arrested, police "confiscate and/or destroy condoms from people they believe to be involved in the sex trade."[95] Human Rights Watch reports that police in New York, Los Angeles, and Washington, DC, still confiscate condoms from sex workers and transwomen. "These cities gave out 50 million condoms [in 2011]," said Megan McLemore, the report's author. "But the police are taking them out of the hands of those who need them the most."[96]

In New York, a coalition of sex-worker groups, led by the PROS Network (Providers and Resources Offering Services to sex workers) and the Sex Workers' Project, determined it was past time for this practice to be abolished and began organizing in 2011. Collaborating with the Open Society Institute, PROS volunteers queried people in the sex trades, harm reduction advocates, service users, and outreach workers; SWP attorneys and the Brooklyn Defenders Office investigated prosecutions. New York City Department of Health and Mental Hygiene, which distributes three million "NYC branded" condoms every month, commandeered NYPD data on condom confiscations.

For over a decade, a bill had been floundering in Albany without enough committee support to go to the House or Senate floor. To create new momentum, PROS, SWP, and the Red Umbrella Project organized a "broad coalition of public health and reproductive rights advocates, civil and human rights organizations, LGBT groups, and sex workers' rights organizers." They have gone to Albany two years in a row, meeting with dozens of legislators to ask their support of a bill that would prohibit using condoms as evidence. One twenty-two-year-old transgender citizen told her Harlem representative, "I'm damned if I do, I'm damned if I don't. I don't want to get any disease but I do want to make my money. Why do they take our condoms, do they want us to die, do they want us to get something?"[97]

Even as US activists seek to abolish condoms as evidence, they are watching developments internationally. Police in Kenya, Namibia, Russia,

South Africa, and Zimbabwe use condom possession as evidence of prostitution.[98] Other medical advances may be used to further target and criminalize HIV-positive status. Rapid oral HIV-testing, for all it may promise, also poses a threat. In Macedonia and Malawi, police have tested sex workers for HIV and hepatitis C without their consent; "sex workers who tested positive for hepatitis C were charged with intentionally spreading infectious diseases," according to Heather Doyle, director of the Sexual Health and Rights Project at Open Society.[99]

The stories told by Toni Collins, GiGi Thomas, Ryhannah Combs, and Duanna Johnson's family document individual experiences of injustice and acts of violence. Considered separately, they make good copy, drawing public attention with their tragic drama. They can also inspire people to offer help: to sign an Internet petition demanding justice for Duanna Johnson, to send letters supporting passage of legislation, to rescue young prostitutes from the streets and suspected brothels. Scholars can be motivated to document "violence against sex workers," contributing to the already overloaded shelves of scholarly articles and books.

Empathetic tallies recording the frequency of threats, thefts, beatings, sexual assaults, and murders, cross-tabulated by the types of perpetrators, are as useful as FBI crime statistics. The numbers calculate the individual acts, and some may suggest "who" poses the most frequent threat: clients, managers, landlords, intimate partners, family members, human traffickers, adults, and so on. Data tends to reinforce persistent stereotypes and encourages police to profile particular men as abusers and criminals.

Such statistics do not capture unquantifiable institutional violence. Interviewing sex workers in jail about the violence they have experienced fails to contextualize the coercive setting or the policies that put them there. Their informants are there because they are serving sentences or awaiting trial because they couldn't make bail.[100]

When scholars "fail to conceptualize the state as a perpetrator of violence," INCITE! founder Andrea Smith argues, "they often minimize the harms done to women by the criminal justice system."[101] Qualitative research makes numbers real.[102] Black women are victimized by violence, scholar-advocate Gail Garfield argues, stigmatizing conditions and practices of race, gender, and sexual morality that "threaten, jeopardize and compromise their sense of personhood [in] violation to women's humanity."[103] When former sex workers apply for jobs, housing, or assistance programs that require a criminal background check, revelations of their "scarlet letter" are used against them.[104] "Embarrassment, humiliation, shame, and fear" are a form of violence that can't be calculated; their effect is truly "immeasurable."[105]

Some researchers use terms that consciously contextualize experiences of "violence" and "resilience." The experiences of "prostituted women" must be violent; the means of survival used by "girls in the sex trade and street economy" demonstrate their resilience.[106] Two groups of researchers used these two terms to discuss the experiences of the same Chicago population, which they each surveyed several times between 2000 and 2012.

"Prostituted women" were interviewed by other "prostituted women" for an academic study about violence. The conclusion was foregone: Jody Raphael and Deborah Shapiro defined "prostitution as a form of violence against women," creating a tautology that is "neither verifiable nor falsifiable," sociologist Ronald Weitzer notes.[107] Their report employed a victimization model that saw "survivors as clients who required services" saving women from themselves.

Their abolitionist recommendations included increasing criminal penalties against pimps and johns to "end demand"; incarcerating minors in youth facilities and placing adult women in coercive diversion programs; and greater surveillance by police and social welfare agents. Their reports "obscure[d] the complex reality on the ground" for girls and women. They also ignored the neoliberal political motives of local and state government, and the profits Illinois's private prison system would earn should their recommendations be adopted.[108]

"Girls, including transgender girls, in the sex trade and street economy" is not an elegant phrase, but it was coined to convey the resiliency of youth who have been kicked out and left out. Research about violence in their lives reveals strategies for resisting individual perpetrators as well as challenging institutional conditions that attempt to disempower them. Resistance acknowledges there are many forms of harm, validating the experiences of sex workers in contexts that outsiders may interpret as abuse or exploitative. Girls from the Young Women's Empowerment Project (YWEP) write, "Resistance is any way you fight back and resilience is any way you heal from violence. We value the rebellion of girls impacted by the system."[109]

"The world may call us victims—but we know differently," concluded the YWEP. These young women were infuriated by the systematic dismissal of their views and misrepresentation of their experiences by "adults," the academics who called them "prostituted." "No matter what we said" to Raphael and Shapiro, they wrote, "their reports always said the same thing: we were victims who needed police and social workers to save us."[110]

Jazeera Iman, Naima Paz, Daphne W., Shira Hassan, and C. Angel Torres of YWEP conducted their own research. As insiders, they wanted to record the "knowing what we know" experiences of marginalized people, particularly the young, poor, undocumented, or people of color. Their work took into account the ways that "cultural and social arrangements place constraints on [women's] needs, interests, and aspirations as human beings."[111]

The YWEP research concluded, "Girls face as much institutional violence (like from the police or DCFS [Department of Children and Family Services]) as they do individual violence (like from parents, pimps, or boyfriends)."[112] Their report documented the strategies girls used to survive and to help others, suggesting ways adults could assist in developing stronger, workable, and accessible support systems.

Troubled by their finding that "institutional violence made individual violence worse," YWEP conducted a follow-up study. They gathered documentation of what they had experienced on the street: Chicago police, immigration officers, and the FBI's anti-trafficking task force didn't take their complaints seriously.

But the most "upsetting" findings were the actions of nonprofit agencies and health-care providers that turned away youth seeking treatment or, worse, held some transgender minors against their will in psychiatric units.[113] Institutions denied help "both passively and actively." Complicated systems "are set up to fail us." At others, "we are simply told that we cannot access help because we are involved in the sex trade or street economy."[114] Security at agencies turned them away even before they talked to social workers or sexually harassed, abused, and solicited girls and transgender girls seeking services from "shelters, clinics, drop-in programs and community centers."[115]

The YWEP recommendations focused on frontline issues—the difficulties girls encountered in their daily lives. Chicago Street Youth in Motion, a YWEP task force, met and discussed ideas with over two hundred participants, creating a "Street Youth Bill of Rights" to alleviate institutional violence. Similar to earlier work of Sista II Sista, their allies in Brooklyn, New York, YWEP saw survivors as "potential organizers on their own behalf."[116] They have done workshops with youth service providers to rethink the ways they interact with street traders, and set up a "Bad Encounter Line" encouraging people to report good or bad experiences with agencies and services.

Knowing that many avoided the health-care system because of bad previous encounters, YWEP outreach workers developed self-care 'zines, enabling youth to recognize health warning signs, strategies for healing, and even instructions for stitching and caring for deep wounds. The personal "will[power] it takes to give yourself stitches is so bad ass," said Vea Cleary from the Broadway Youth Center in Chicago, "you don't want people to have that [kind of] courage."[117]

YWEP represents a model of organizing that shifts from liberal citizenship models focused on legal reforms and punishment to a human rights model focused on transformative justice. Changing public policy is slow and ineffective; the law cannot "bring fast and positive change to ALL girls" in their community. YWEP chose to organize community-based programs and develop harm reduction materials to meet peoples' needs.[118]

Prohibitionists in the Chicago metro area used Raphael and Shapiro's research to enact "end demand" laws that focused on arresting customers and expanding anti-trafficking measures to include any adult who provides assistance or material support to sex traders. Such "remedies" YWEP counters, cause more harm to girls, including transgender girls, women, and their allies. They want to shift the focus away from sexual morality and public security that marginalize and stigmatize young people of color, creating the social conditions for sexual exploitation and trafficking.

Systemic changes that foster empowerment are a better means for ending violence against individuals created by institutional neglect and indifference. Figuring out how to end the criminalization and sexual abuse of women of color, YWEP members believe, could also address violence in all families. Transformative justice, YWEP and its INCITE! allies believe, places women and girls of color at the center of analysis, asking, "What would it take *to end violence against women of color?*"[119]

"I was raped and used [drugs] myself a lot of times, I never hurt anyone. Why am I on the registry as a sex offender?" one Louisiana women wondered.[120] Why does the system make her register but not her rapist? Her experiences trading sex, as a hustler, and as a grandmother who cannot evacuate with her family during a hurricane because she is a registered sex offender, suggest what it would take to end violence against women of color, against sex workers, and against other marginalized people.

Deon Haywood, executive director of Women With A Vision (WWAV), didn't need research to prove the unfairness of Louisiana's criminal justice system. The state made "crimes against nature" a felony in 1805. Female prostitution became a crime in 1942; the ACLU challenged the law in 1974, arguing that only women were arrested, but lost in the state supreme court.[121] But it was not until 1982 that soliciting "a crime against nature" became a felony, after New Orleans police convinced legislators they needed stronger laws to go after male prostitution. In 1991, the state added people convicted of a felonious "crime against nature" to the state sexual-offender registry.

The law imposed prison sentences of up "to five years, with or without hard labor, and/or a fine of not more than $2,000.00" on anyone convicted of soliciting oral or anal sodomy. In contrast, soliciting for "indiscriminate sexual intercourse"—that is, for prostitution—is merely a misdemeanor; "known prostitutes" are not required to register. The maximum fine is $500, with a potential jail sentence of no more than six months.[122]

For decades, people had unsuccessfully challenged the crimes against nature statute, arguing it violated citizens' right to privacy or that police used it selectively to criminalize gays and lesbians. But most troubling, the law made solicitation into "a talking crime." Customers were not charged. As a result, "at least two of every five people" registered as sex offenders in Orleans Parish had been convicted for soliciting. "Of the approximately 400 offenders in the region, 43.6 percent probably are prostitutes," the *Times-Picayune* reported.[123]

In New Orleans, three out of four offenders were women, and nearly four out of five (79 percent) were African Americans. The police were responsible for this racial disparity, activists claimed, because they charged black women with felony solicitation while white women arrested in the French Quarter and downtown hotels were booked on misdemeanor prostitution charges.[124] Among male offenders, the registry does not make a distinction for transwomen.[125]

Despite the nonviolent nature of the "crime," Louisiana was the only state that required people convicted of the unconstitutional sodomy statute to register as sex offenders and to suffer "civil death." Sex workers were convicted just for talking about it, not for actually doing it.[126]

Sex offender registries, which the federal "Megan's Law" requires all states to maintain, essentially impose a sentence of "civil death" on every registrant. The disabilities that result include driver's licenses with "SEX OFFENDER" in bright orange letters.[127] Their names, addresses, and identification photos are available online and searchable by anyone; indeed, a mobile telephone application uses GPS to identify people registered in any vicinity.[128] In Louisiana, registrants must also print and mail postcards to their neighbors, at their own considerable expense. Failure to do so is a separate crime. One offense requires registration for fifteen years; a second offense results in lifetime registration.

In other states, registration is mandatory only for offenses that include an element of force, coercion, use of a weapon, lack of consent, or if the victim is a minor. Sex workers understood that this could be a laudable goal; it was the inclusion of them, as adults, that was unfair. As "Hiroke Doe" said, "There are children getting raped every day, but you want to go after me, and go after the transsexuals out there. It just vex my spirit."

Stalking, harassment, and violence are not uncommon consequences for registrants. Neighbors physically threatened "Audrey Doe," a fifty-year-old grandmother, when they learned she was registered; a group of boys threw rocks and yelled for her to "suck [their] dicks." "Eve Doe," a forty-year-old transwoman living in rural southern Louisiana attempted to enroll in a residential drug treatment but was turned away because the program didn't permit sex offenders to participate. "When I present my ID for anything," said Eve, "the assumption is that you're a child molester or a rapist. The discrimination is just ongoing and ongoing."[129]

WWAV organized the "NO Justice" campaign to overturn the law. Its first victory, in August 2010, amended the 1805 statute so that first-time offenders would be guilty only of a misdemeanor. But everyone convicted between 1982 and 2010 had to maintain their registrations; in Orleans Parish alone that meant more than five hundred people.[130]

The Center for Constitutional Rights and Loyola University's Center for Social Justice prepared a federal civil rights suit against the state while Haywood and WWAV lobbied the legislature to abolish the law altogether.[131] In June 2011, legislators amended the centuries-old statute, but, in a compromise, only abolished registration for future convictions.[132] Everyone convicted under the old statute remained on the register.

Audrey, Becca, Carla, Diane, Eve, Fiona, Georgia, Hiroke, and Ian "Doe," all African American women and transwomen who had been convicted of a "crime against nature by solicitation" and were required to register, sued Louisiana governor Bobby Jindal and other officials to have their names, and others convicted under the law, removed from the register retroactively and their criminal records expunged. They were "largely poor Black women, including transwomen, and gay men who have themselves experienced violence and discrimination their whole lives," said Haywood. "They deserve a second chance."[133] On March 30, 2012, the federal judge hearing the case issued a cease and desist order, effective immediately.[134]

The campaign was remarkably swift. None of the earlier lawsuits succeeded, nor had Louisiana Equality or other gay rights changed it despite years of lobbying. The one-two punch of a federal lawsuit and legislation, as well as support from African American representatives in the state's House and Senate, demonstrates the usefulness of a "both/and" strategy.

But the moral power of this strategy doesn't rest with elected, confirmed, or appointed officials. Its power was in "storytelling," in the "story circles" held at WWAV, where "the people most affected spoke their truths—not some abstract 'speak truth to power,' but their truths from their hearts—and that is what made the difference," said Haywood. WWAV kept its focus on the stories people told, including people afraid to be other "Does" in the lawsuit. The group had to fend off efforts to hijack the decriminalization campaign by more powerful interest groups who "didn't believe that poor, uneducated women could win a victory on this scale, [who] didn't think that our women were important enough, or that they had the ability to change their own lives." In a letter explaining what the victory meant, Haywood wrote,

> This was not a legal fight or a legislative fight. This was a fight for women's lives and well-being. This was a fight, simply put, about everything. This was about the freedom of people to make choices for themselves. This was about public health. This was about sex worker rights. This was about human rights. This was and is about everything. [This] is why we cannot pick apart injustice. . . . For once, women and men won. And we believe that this is not just a win for us. This is a win for every group that has ever been criminalized.[135]

And in that spirit, WWAV launched the Louisiana Women's Advocacy Alliance to take the grassroots fight against injustice statewide.

Whether they work by choice, circumstance, or coercion, sex workers demand and deserve justice. Ending violence against sex workers cannot be addressed through decriminalization alone; abolishing slavery did not end racial discrimination. Investigating crimes committed against sex workers by civilians would affirm their civil rights. Police officers abuse sex workers and other vulnerable citizens through entrapment schemes, sexual coercion, and other means. Challenging these practices may require a more vigorous definition of rights. The SWOP slogan, "Sex workers' rights are human rights," pushes all of us to globalize our definition of rights.

CHAPTER 7

SLUTS UNITE!

Disrupting Whorephobia and Slut-Shaming

THE POSTER SAID: "I'M A SLUT. And I vote. So does everyone I sleep with." Favianna Rodriguez is not a sex worker; she is an Oakland-based artist, a printmaker, and an activist ally who works with INCITE! Women of Color Against Violence and other resistance groups. The posters she made for International Women's Day 2012 came because "I was fed up. Patriarchy is destructive to society, it's a form of violence against women, and there is no place for it in contemporary culture." Conservative talk show host Rush Limbaugh had just called Sandra Fluke a "slut" because she wanted Congress to preserve funding for Planned Parenthood: "I decided it was time for some slut positivity and some major ass-kicking of these conservative, woman-hating men."[1]

"Politicians out of my poontang!" chants and signs about sluts who vote weren't the polite messages observers expected at the Democratic National Convention in Charlotte, North Carolina, in August 2012, especially when they were delivered by immigrant women protestors telling the United States, "Keep your government off my pussy." The message

---

"Slut (r)evolution": Button for Cameryn Moore's original production *Phone Whore*.

was culturally and politically disruptive. "Straight" people don't think of "sluts" as voters, much less as a bloc of citizens who would cast their ballots based on issues of sexual liberty and gender-based violence. The message "Politicians out . . . " could also be read as mocking: sex scandals involving public officials and sex workers (or someone other than their spouse) stopped the political rise of more than a few men and women on both sides of the aisle. Why shouldn't politicians be called out for their hypocritical slut negativity?

Tied intricately to politics, cultural activism seeks to redirect peoples' attitudes to change public opinion and then policy. For sex-worker activists, years of working to decriminalize prostitution have brought only a handful of legislative and courtroom victories, and many of those were often reversed later. Despite slow progress, negative opinions against sex work and sex workers have lessened, especially among the younger classes of American society. It was perhaps predictable, given the vicious war against sex waged by religious conservatives and anti-porn feminists in the 1980s and 1990s, that some people wanted to find out for themselves what was so bad about sex, porn, and queer politics.

What they found was that "bad" could be a lot of fun. Adult-film stars like Nina Hartley, Candida Royalle, and Veronica Vera were making their own feminist porn, Betty Dodson was still teaching women about masturbation, and there was Joani Blank's Good Vibrations in San Francisco. Many sex workers had access to new technology, giving them greater power over their working conditions and freeing them from the middlemen who, in earlier times, had demanded large shares of their earnings. Working as a stripper or a go-go boy could be liberating; even if club management sucked, the dressing-room camaraderie was better than any women's studies class. Performing gender became another means of self-expression, redefining the meanings of camp and drag. The rediscovery of fifties underground icon Bettie Page led to the re-creation of the pinup girl, with Dita Von Teese as the leading new star. Young women revived burlesque and the striptease, erotic dance arts on the verge of dying, generating another vibrant subculture with several varieties within it. Cultural shifts are years in the making, spread over generations. The 1980s were by no means an easy decade for sex; conservative fear-mongering about porn, queer and alternative sex, AIDS, urban crime, crack, and black male violence challenged the creative efforts of sex workers and other sex activists to shift the narrative. Proclaiming "No More Nice Girls!" radicals decided to embrace the stigma, refusing to drink the Kool-Aid of the Reagan Revolution. Susie Bright and Debi Sundahl began publishing *On Our Backs* in 1984, thumbing (or was it fisting?) their noses at the "politically correct" *off our backs* and financing it, in part, with Sundahl's earnings as a dancer.[2] Though some commercial presses, art galleries, and theaters wanted to exploit outlaw representations created by artists such as Robert Mapplethorpe, Karen Finley, and Holly Hughes, Bright remembers that "because we were women, printing sex . . . [we] ended up paying what amounted to enormous bribes to be printed at all."[3] There were neither federal grants nor fairy godmothers for most creators.

Working Girls (1987) was an independent, unrated film by director Lizzie Borden, shot in her own Manhattan loft. It focused on Molly's eighteen-hour shift in a Manhattan brothel, showing the people she worked with and her clients, conveying the banal, "daily realities of the job" without judgment or titillation, said Borden.[4] It is still regarded as "the gold standard for realism in prostitute pictures," writes former *$pread* editor Monica Shores, in large part because Borden based the characters on women she met—Ivy League–educated, smart humanities majors who were shut out of the yuppie jobs their classmates had.[5] Film historian Mark O'Brien observed that the sex workers' "marginality is not a function of their otherness but of their ordinariness. They're too disturbingly like us to be acknowledged."[6]

Books by sex workers that disrupted what "straight" people thought they knew are one kind of cultural activism. The voices of French *putes* were heard in Claude Jaget's *Prostitutes, Our Lives*, published in English in 1980, including the women who went on strike in Marseilles in 1973 and in Lyons in 1975 to protest their oppression by the police and the Catholic Church.[7] The memory of that strike inspired Frederique Delacoste, the head of Cleis Press, to issue a call for stories and essays documenting "women's resistance on issues that have previously been either invisible or distorted by sexist ideology." That book became *Sex Work: Writings by Women in the Sex Industry* (1987) and introduced the term "sex work" into public discourse.[8]

When the former president of the Screen Actors' Guild became president of the United States, the culture wars, the sex wars, and the porn wars split the producers of commercial culture. Sex-negative political rhetoric and government policies that institutionalized "straight" family values often seemed overwhelming in the 1980s. Distrust in electoral politics eroded while conservative Republicans and "greed is good" capitalists controlled government; the confirmation of Supreme Court Justice Clarence Thomas and new restrictions on abortion, sexual privacy, and sexual-harassment claims undermined the belief that the Supreme Court would uphold justice and equality. Activists turned to culture—to "meme warfare"—to restore, and even reinvent, the radicalism needed to change the system. "Critical engagement with popular culture" became "a political strategy" for attacking the status quo.[9] The sexually repressive culture and politics of the Reagan-Bush years became an obvious target.

Popular culture included graphic and textual depictions of people performing sex or working their bodies; critical engagement picked apart the images and stories of pornography to "acknowledge what excites us, and support women who make their living providing that excitement to men and to ourselves."[10] Porn was "designed to titillate or excite"; what was wrong with that? "Girls just want to have fun," Cyndi Lauper sang, even if "Money changes everything," from her platinum album *She's So Unusual* (1983). Cultural work reoriented the feminist war against porn, framing it as "a sexual story to tell," writes Susie Bright in her memoir.[11]

"Whores and strippers and butches" were the working-class activists telling sexual stories in the women's pro-porn movement; they weren't academics "so eloquent and rational it would have made Rousseau swoon."[12] The scholars and lawyers from the Feminist Anti-Censorship Taskforce (FACT) debated Catharine MacKinnon, Andrea Dworkin, and the women's studies crowd in academic journals and in court; sex workers and sex radicals made their own films, wrote their own books, and published their own magazines. FACT, formed in 1984, spoke about the *theory* of pornography, with its focus on censorship and freedom of expression as constitutional rights. But while anti-porn activists tried to shame FACT members by calling them "pimps," the group didn't address the *fact* of sex work, with the women and men who work in the sex industry.

FACT's successor, Feminists for Free Expression (FFE) formed in 1992 to resist new attempts at censoring sexually explicit materials, and articulating a feminism that was not anti-sexual. Since the beginning, Candida Royalle, Veronica Vera, Annie Sprinkle, and other adult film performers have been board members and speakers. Yet it was two decades before "sex-positive" FFE came out in favor of decriminalizing sex work, as a result of Vera and Royalle's intense efforts.[13] Whores and strippers and a handful of butches and porn stars took on whorephobia using cultural activism.

When former stripper and Bikini Kill singer Kathleen Hanna lipsticked SLUT on her stomach in 1992, she inspired "grrrls" around the world to "start a fucking riot."[14] Riot grrrls were committed to creating their own media, to control their own representations. Younger, third wave activists questioned the anti-porn, anti-sex rhetoric of mainstream feminism and women's studies scholarship. As Lusty Lady organizer and comedienne Julia Query joked, women's studies majors employed in the commercial sex industry were the new stereotype. The sex-positive feminism of the 1990s had pop culture appeal for ironic Gen-Xers; it could also be packaged, marketed, and commercialized. In 1995, MAC cosmetics contracted RuPaul as its spokesmodel for VIVA GLAM lipstick, with "every cent of the selling price" going to the MAC AIDS Fund, monies that help the St. James Infirmary and other sex workers' groups do harm reduction work. Sex workers also cashed in, penning autobiographies, novels, and advice books, often with mainstream presses—Norma Jean Almodovar, Carol Queen, Tracy Quan, Ericka Langley, Shawna Kennedy, Lily Burana. Even the unemployed workers in Sheffield, England, did *The Full Monty*. The 1990s made pro-sex feminism cool.

Lipstick feminism, even VIVA GLAM, requires constant reapplication to stay bright. Women in Toronto organized the first SlutWalk in April 2011 because they were tired of slut-shaming and victim-blaming. The police, the media, and everyone else needed reminding that rapists were the criminals; victims did not ask to be sexually assaulted. London organizers declared, "Rape is never, ever OK. Not if she was wearing a miniskirt. Not if she was naked. Not if she was your wife, girlfriend or friend. Not if she was a prostitute."[15]

Sex-positive feminists might party all night with the "sluts," but some folks couldn't abide the "whores" from the other side of privilege town. "A prostitute," commented a "17 year old girl," "will do anything for sex and . . . have no standards."[16]

Despite the acceptance of "sluts," the "prostitute" remains a deeply embedded symbolic marker between decency and disrespect. The "ethical slut" engages in sex of her or his own "free" will, while the "dirty whore" insists on getting paid for sex. Sex-positive feminists and other "sluts" believe there is nothing morally wrong with consensual sex between two (or more) people in private, or for adults, in a semi-public setting such as a sex club, dungeon, or swingers' retreat. But money changes everything.

Whorephobia remains pervasive in the social psyche, showing its ugliness even in sex-positive communities. The positive emphasis on sex work confuses "straights" into thinking that sex work is about sex, not work. That cognitive dissonance—the deep chasm filled with stereotypes and prejudices—interferes with the capacity of civilians to hear sex workers speak about their experiences. Stories that don't conform to the "superhappyfunsexysexwork!" narrative tend to flummox pro-sex feminists; they can identify with privileged exotic dancers, porn performers, and professional dominants (even fantasize about being one) but think "junkie whores" need to be rescued and should be prevented from working in their gentrifying neighborhoods. Such disrespectful treatment leads to silencing, ignoring, or rewriting what sex workers have to say.[17]

Writing in the blogosphere recently, sex workers say they're frustrated with the uncritical acceptance of sex-positive feminism. Furry Girl, the Seattle-based founder of SWAAY, is also the blogger behind *Feminisnt* because she "got tired of trying to shoehorn my life into a useless ideology like a pair of ill-fitting high heels."[18] The habit of always trying to put a "good" face on sex work leaves little room for those who have had not-so-good experiences. They fear talking about the bad stuff because "straight" audiences, whether pro-sex feminists, prohibitionists, or the media, tend to stuff those stories into established morality tales about sex, violence, and bodily integrity. But the truth is that by telling stories with all the gory details and delicious specifics, we can get to the revolution that sex workers are creating right now.

INVENTING "SEX WORK"

Sex workers are not as voiceless as civilians assume. It's the white noise—the stigma and stereotypes—that makes hearing something else difficult. The static from prohibitionists who claim that sex workers' stories are compromised by "false consciousness" or "Stockholm syndrome" interferes too. Even sympathetic, early sex-positive feminists like Kate Millett and Germaine Greer couldn't seem to tune in. In the 1970s, Xaviera Hollander, the "Happy Hooker," sold millions of her books, as did Iceberg

Slim and John Rechy. All were involved in the sex trades, yet as authors, they also struggled with ghostwriters, editors, publishers, and book reviewers who had their own agendas and profits in mind. They were also stereotyped as "upper class libertine and foreigner" (Hollander), exploitative black ghetto pimp of runaway white girls (Slim), and gay street hustler drug addict (Rechy), making it easier for "straights" to dismiss them as deviant others rather than see them as people like themselves.

Sex Work, along with Laurie Bell's *Good Girls/Bad Girls: Sex Trade Workers Confront Feminists*, presented a fresh, alternative narrative, correcting the errors and disputing the allegations made by Kathleen Barry in *Female Sexual Slavery* (1979).[19] As in Borden's *Working Girls*, the people in *Sex Work* were sometimes too disturbingly like "us." New scholarly monographs by feminist historians Carroll Smith-Rosenberg, Judith Walkowitz, and Ruth Rosen and sociologist Barbara Meil Hobson reexamined the anti-prostitution morality campaigns waged by nineteenth-century female crusaders, drawing portraits of bourgeois lady "do-goodism" that had horrendous consequences for working-class women.

These books made sex work "a difficult issue for feminists" and for anti-porn activists and homophobes. It was the mid-1980s, and the culture wars were being fought on several fronts. The news was not good. The number of AIDS diagnoses had jumped among white women, presumably heterosexual, while the Meese Commission recommended "violent pornography" be censored, the Supreme Court ruled that gay people didn't have a right to sexual privacy, Reagan's first public speech on AIDS called for mandatory testing of immigrants and prisoners, and Senator Jesse Helms had added a "no promo homo" amendment to federal law. The voices of people in the sex industry could barely be heard over the din.

But they were heard, if just barely. Slut-shaming was still widespread; some people were too embarrassed to buy *Sex Work*, but would risk shoplifting to get a copy. For a few months, it was one of the most frequently stolen books at Kramerbooks & Afterwords in Washington, DC. The locally produced women's newspaper *off our backs*, by then the voice of radical anti-porn feminists, published two positive side-by-side reviews of *Sex Work*. In the *Women's Review of Books* (*WRB*), lesbian AIDS activist and filmmaker Amber Hollibaugh "came out" as a former sex worker in solidarity in her review of Gail Pheterson's *A Vindication of the Rights of Whores* (1989), based on the proceedings of the first and second World Whores' Congresses.[20]

Concern about backlash wasn't unreasonable. In the trenches, the culture wars were playing out as a nasty war of words. In 1984, sex workers and their feminist allies in Berkeley, California, had organized a march in support of a local adult theater, where they were heckled by anti-porn activists screaming "Fucking whores!" and "Sluts!"[21] "Sisterhood" indeed. President Reagan turned affirmative action into "reverse racism" and Attorney General Meese declared *Playboy* "violent pornography," while prohibitionists Kathleen Barry and Catharine MacKinnon continued their campaigns against prostitution, calling it "female sexual slavery" and "institutionalized rape."

Barry, MacKinnon, and their allies soon responded to sex worker–produced books. Evelina [Kahe] Giobbe, the founder of WHISPER (Women Hurt in Systems of Prostitution Engaged in Revolt) and, as "Sarah Wynter," a contributor to *Sex Work*, attacked Amber Hollibaugh's *WRB* review of *Vindication*, challenging the author's "attempts to decontextualize prostitution from the social system (male supremacy)." Giobbe saw herself as a victim, a woman forced to work for ten years in the sex industry. "Prostitution wasn't something *I* had done, it was something that was done *to* me." Another letter disputed the authenticity of *Vindication* and *Sex Work*, claiming the articles in them did not "derive primarily from prostitutes' voices," because one contributor was merely a "part-time hooker."[22] They even questioned the authenticity of *The Maimie Papers*, Ruth Rosen's edited collection of letters between a former prostitute and a sympathetic Bostonian matron, published by the Feminist Press in 1977, because Maimie Pinzer had "never actually lived in a brothel."[23]

The systematic campaign conducted by prohibitionists to prevent the participation of sex workers (including adult-film performers) was soon clear: first, prohibitionists asserted that "prostituted women" were the victims of patriarchy and discounted alternative critiques of capitalism, the war on drugs, political disenfranchisement, and other systems of oppression. Second, they dismissed sex workers' stories as fakes, denying they were written by "real" sex workers: a "part-time hooker" and non-brothel worker could not have experienced the true victimization of prostitutes. Third, positive claims made by sex workers must have been false because "prostituted women" were enslaved by pimps and pornographers who controlled their bodies, their thoughts, and their speech.

Anti-porn feminists—the "antis"—made these same claims when sex workers attempted to engage in face-to-face dialogue. Dolores French, the founder of Atlanta's HIRE (Hooking Is Real Employment), tells a story about trying to attend the 1983 Global Feminist Workshop to Organize Against Traffic in Women, in Rotterdam, only to discover she had been barred from entering. Prohibitionist and convener Kathleen Barry had refused her admission because "prostitutes were too brainwashed and oppressed to represent themselves, that we were all slaves to our pimps."[24]

When sex workers were allowed to participate, they were treated with disrespect. Dottie Meyer, a *Penthouse* Pet (November 1977), politely answered numerous hostile questions posed by the Meese Commission on pornography in 1986, explaining her work, her happy family life, and the satisfaction she derived as a "working woman" by advancing up the company's management ladder. Afterward, she complained it "was degrading to me. I walked out of there feeling . . . horrible. I think I felt more insulted about the questions they asked me than anything I've ever done in my life."[25] As a final insult, the report twisted the words of Meyer, Candida Royalle, Veronica Vera, Priscilla Alexander, and other sex-worker activists in favor of testimony given by Andrea Dworkin, Wynter (aka Giobbe), and WAVPM founder Laura Lederer, concluding "models live with highly abusive husbands or boyfriends, whose relationship to them is that of pimp to prostitute."[26]

The Meese Commission consciously used "prostitute" and "prostitution" throughout its report on pornography. Though Carol Vance and other FACT feminists have commented on the troubling conflation of pornography with violence, the report's conflation of pornography with prostitution was equally problematic. In her testimony before the Commission, Priscilla Alexander, director of the National Task Force on Prostitution, used "sex work" and "sex worker" to detail labor issues in the porn industry.

Anti-porn forces, not surprisingly, rejected the labor framework of "sex work," but they liked the suggestion that the porn industry was a form of "prostitution." Thus, throughout the report, female models and actresses are referred to as "prostitutes," the men who produce porn as "pimps," and the men who buy it as "johns." By implying that legally employed adult film performers are exploited in the same ways as people who engage in criminalized forms of sex work, the Commission report gave government prosecutors permission to begin grand jury investigations of the porn industry, and to tie it to "sexual slavery."

As a linguistic strategy, Carol Leigh's invention of "sex work" disassociated people in the sex industry from the negative representations of immoral, uncontrollable, nymphomaniacs who indulged in their psychoses, and got paid too. Margo St. James wanted to reclaim the word "whore" to eradicate the stigma of whoring around, just as lesbians were reclaiming "dyke" to end the stigma against butch, boot-wearing females. St. James and Gail Pheterson argued, "The whore as prostitute or sex worker is the prototype of the stigmatized woman or feminized man."[27] At the 1985 and 1986 World Whores' Congresses convened by St. James, activists from outside the United States rejected the suggestion. "Whore" had equivalents in every other language (including British English), but like "the oldest profession," "hooker" and "harlot" were too culturally specific for globalization. It was also difficult to imagine "straight" people ever using the word "whore" neutrally.

The term "sex worker" was more inclusive of the commercial sex industry and underscored labor issues; it soon became the politically correct way to refer to people who engaged in sexual commerce. It also translated easily into other languages; when the Global Network of Sex Work Projects informally organized in 1990, members pushed HIV/AIDS workers to replace "prostitute" with "sex worker." "This shift in language had the important effect of moving global understandings of sex work toward a labour framework . . . and represents greater recognition of sex workers as rights bearers, with the capacity to make a difference."[28] The UNAIDS *Terminology Guidelines*, issued in October 2011, instructs staff and members to use "sex worker," not "prostitute," because the term is "[nonjudgmental] and focuses on the working conditions under which sexual services are sold." If only the AP and *New York Times* stylebooks would do the same.[29]

Way back in the second wave, feminists challenged the term "girls" as a synonym for adult females. But "rent girls" and "rent boys" are still used in the sex industry, though more often by employers than by workers. Toronto activist Wendy Babcock complained, "Using the term 'girls' to refer to sex workers also makes [a client] sound like a pedophile ('I just fucked the sweetest girl')." The word *women*, she argued, has greater cultural value: "[A]cknowledging that female sex workers are autonomous, capable, independent adults . . . would be a significant step on the way towards granting them the rights that all women deserve."[30]

Prohibitionists don't think that "prostituted women" have the capacity to make a difference or to make decisions about their own lives. In company with media elites like *New York Times* columnist Nicholas Kristof, they employ emotional terms that explicitly or contextually demean sex workers. The Coalition Against Trafficking in Women (CATW) insists on using the term "prostituted persons" in order to emphasize "the physical, psychological, and sexual violence inflicted" on people in the sex trades. Most recently, CATW pushed hard for an international treaty defining sex for pay as "sexual exploitation."[31] It's a term as fuzzy as "violent pornography." "Sex exploitation" doesn't provide a legal test similar to the "force, fraud, or coercion" test used for trafficking, but rather encourages a person to apply her or his individual viewpoint to define a sexually exploitative situation. Marriage, anyone?

"Sex slavery" is another emotional term. Kelli Dorsey of Different Avenues in Washington, DC, rejects the implication that the contemporary sex industry is as methodically genocidal as five centuries of Vatican-sanctioned Western imperialism in Africa and the Global South. "Sex-trafficking" places undue emphasis on women and girls while ignoring the 14,500 to 17,500 people each year who, through force, coercion, or fraud, come to the United States under labor contracts that violate international treaties.[32]

Sex workers complain that prohibitionists' terms are disempowering, deliberately denying women and men agency and choice, casting them as "victims" in need of "help" and "rescue" rather than as people who have had to make conscious, if difficult, decisions. The terms "conflate victims of trafficking with sex workers, which is an insult to both groups," writes Lori Adorable.[33] She and Maggie McNeill reject the idea that sex workers "sell their bodies." The wording "reinforces the same notions that undergird the violence against us: that we maintain no control over our physical selves and, therefore, anything and everything can be done to us." McNeill continues:

The claim . . . is not only logically absurd (I was a prostitute for years, but my body is still right here with me), but totally sexist because it is based on the notion that a woman's sexuality is her entire worth. The belief behind this expression is that since a woman has nothing of value to offer except her sexuality, if she "sells" that she has "sold herself" and there is nothing left. The fact that anti-sex worker activists use this expression so often says a lot about them.[34]

"Use" is an equally dehumanizing verb, as in "to use a prostitute," as though he or she is disposable. A member of Empower Thailand, a sex workers' group, complained that CATW founder Melissa Farley "called us terrible names and accused us of being like toilets!"[35]

ON OUR BACKS

The feminist sex wars over pornography, sex work, and sexual expression started as mostly self-inflicted, internecine campus affairs between women's studies faculty and feminist activists from the community, but the peripatetic lives of academics made them international. In Canada, the 1985 Fraser Report accepted Catharine MacKinnon's argument against pornography and recommended "criminalization of violent and sexually explicit material . . . [because it] harmed women's right to equality." In spring 1992, Canada's highest court cited the MacKinnon harm standard to reinterpret its national obscenity law in the *R. v. Butler* decision, which gave the government the right to censor pornographic materials. The prohibitions primarily affected lesbian-produced erotic materials, including the Boston sex magazine *Bad Attitude*, *On Our Backs*, and other independent and small-press women's publications. Also in the fallout, Matthew McGowan, a street-based male sex worker in Toronto, was charged with obscenity for making a safer-sex video with two friends.[36]

In recognition of *Butler*, the University of Michigan Law School, where MacKinnon is a tenured professor, inaugurated the *Michigan Journal of Gender and Law* and organized a national conference, "Prostitution: From Academia to Activism," in October 1992. In the spring of 1993, the University of Chicago Law School held a conference to explore connections between "woman-hating" pornography and "racist" hate speech.[37] In Ann Arbor and in Hyde Park, conference organizers barred sex-worker activists from participating, but they fought back in court and in courtyards.

At first, Michigan law students honestly attempted to consider "both sides" of the prostitution question by asking Detroit artist Carol Jacobsen to curate an exhibit on sex work. *PORN'IM'AGE'RY: Picturing Prostitutes* included "seven noncommercial, socially motivated, feminist art works," documentary videos, in which a spectrum of sex workers talked about their lives, including homelessness and run-ins with police, the courts, and government censors.[38] The video/installation was intended to counterbalance the law school's conference, which featured MacKinnon, Andrea Dworkin, Evelina Giobbe, and other anti-porn heavies.

But on the day the exhibit opened in the Michigan Student Union, the law students objected to it, going so far as to remove a compilation video that they said contained "medium and hard-core" pornography and "threatened" the safety of conference participants. Yet no one would say exactly what material they found objectionable. Each film observed sex workers' resilience and resistance working as strippers, porn stars, escorts, on the street and as activists. Jacobsen speculated that students were discombobulated by Veronica Vera's film, which included footage from her porn films (spliced with her Congressional testimony against censorship), but it may have been that most of videos featured sex workers who looked like ordinary women.[39]

"The more frightening truth," Carol Leigh observed, "is that there is an entire generation of young people/students who are more than willing to continue the marginalization, censorship and stigmatization of those sex workers who will not climb on the anti-porn bandwagon."[40] As undergraduates, the feminist law students had been taught by the first generation of women's studies faculty, schooled in the anti-violence paradigm that saw rape, wife-battering, pornography, and prostitution as prime examples of patriarchy's subjugation of women. While they may have begun to question that orthodoxy, they were MacKinnon's students; "coming out" as pro-sex feminists could have had serious consequences for their legal careers.

"No one seems to understand that sex workers might have real reasons to be afraid of pornography," said Laura Berger, one of the law students involved.[41] Speaking for "sex workers," she claimed that they removed the tape to protect the sex workers attending the conference. Two speakers were former "prostituted women." "Anonymous" had been a "Call Girl" who spoke briefly in favor of legalization.[42] The other was Evelina Giobbe, who had moved into international activism in founding CATW.[43] None of the students dared question their authenticity, yet that was exactly what Leigh's film, *Outlaw Poverty, Not Prostitution*, and Jacobsen's *Street Sex* did.[44]

A year of legal threats and campus debates ensued, all focused on censorship and sex panics, rather than honest discussions about sex work with the people who did it. When the exhibit reopened in October 1993, Jacobsen reported it was "accompanied by a hugely successful speak-out that included acts of sexual civil disobedience."[45]

Ann Arbor's disobedient students weren't going to let "politically correct" feminists police their sex. *P.C. Casualties*, a local queer punk 'zine, criticized:

> As if *bullying* prank phone calls from those young Republican shit-heads weren't enough now we have half-assed, pseudo-radical academics playing the same old power games as well. Hey, you and your "analysis" can fuck off. . . . Sex is great fun, but like right-wing Puritanical anti-sex crusaders, these boring people think sex . . . should be a guilt-ridden affair. Yeah, you've got all the "correct" answers, and even a little power in your corner of this political ghetto. But you're all fake. . . . All you've managed to do is torture and maim those you really ought to be caring for—your own brothers and sisters. The bodies of P.C. Casualties lay strewn all over, ghosts of dreams too afraid to materialize, and whispers too fearful to make a sound.[46]

Radical sex activists and pro-sex feminists, on campus and off, used a do-it-yourself approach to cultural politics, creating their own media and opting for political independence from the university.

Rejection of the status quo by the "politically incorrect" came, almost ironically, just as the far right geared up its attacks on the "politically correct" multicultural curriculum mounted by Dinesh D'Souza's *Illiberal Education* (1991), William Bennett's defense of "dead white men" and America's virtues, and others. Younger women wrote an entire shelfful

of books dismissing "victim feminism." Kate Roiphe's *The Morning After* (1993) and Naomi Wolf's *Fire with Fire* (1994) sold well, though they
competed with Robert Bly's *Iron John* (1991) and Madonna's *Sex* (1992).
Sexual dissenters and other queers challenged identity-based politics
and second-wave feminist orthodoxy. The "project," as Queer Nation
historian Lisa Duggan noted, consisted of "denaturalizing categories of
sexual identity and mobilizing various critiques of the political practices
referred to under the rubric 'identity politics.'"[47]

The affiliation of sex workers with the feminist movement dis-
integrated as lesbian separatism and the anti-porn movement gained
strength, and coalitions with AIDS activists and the prison abolition
movement became more fruitful in opposing the criminalization of
radical and queer sexual cultures. For the Sex Workers' Action Coalition (SWAC) and other activists, however, identity politics remained
appealing because they offered an organizing meme and a label for the
prejudices prostitutes and other women employed in the sex industry
continued to confront.

Sex workers were not asked to participate in the University of Chicago
conference "Speech, Equality, and Harm: Feminist Legal Perspectives on
Pornography and Hate Propaganda," held on International Women's
Day in 1993. While the *PORN'IM'AGE'RY* fight continued, MacKinnon,
Dworkin, Giobbe, and others reaffirmed their policy to not appear at
any conference where prostitutes or pornographers would also speak. So
Carol Leigh and two dozen other activists staged "a piece of political performance art" for the public to air their views. The site they chose was a
courtyard, visible through the large lunchroom windows where several
law professors—including future Supreme Court justice Elena Kagan—
held a roundtable discussion, "On Freedom of Expression."[48]

The crux of the conflict, as Kagan noted, was a matter of "viewpoint
discrimination." The Indianapolis anti-pornography ordinance, based
on MacKinnon's legal theory, allowed individuals, who could reasonably
have vastly different views, to declare certain materials "harmful and
degrading." To the audience, where Patricia Williams, who wrote the *Nation*'s Mad Law Professor column, sat, viewpoint very much mattered.
As a white male professor pontificated on "the purpose and principles
of interpretation" in the *Butler* decision, another scenario began outside.
"Against a window I saw file behind him a group of women costumed as

bright harlots bearing signs that said 'Whore Power' and 'Sluts Unite'—
back and forth, back and forth, and I was instantly lost."[49]

It was Scarlot Harlot (Carol Leigh) and the Sex Workers' Action
Coalition. Questions inside the conference flew: Who were they? What
did they want? Williams heard "the people involved were not actually
prostitutes but young women, students, who were dressed up like prostitutes." Another opined they were "people with a self-esteem problem,"
because in her view, no psychologically whole woman could be a proud
prostitute. Williams saw "the self-proclaimed sluts and whores parade by
tossing their hair, rolling their hips," exhibiting themselves to the police,
the cameramen, and the conference people watching from inside: "No
self-esteem problems here, it all seems to say."

Judges view obscenity like the smell of a "foul cigar," Williams heard
another panelist say, as she watched Carol Leigh, with all the cameras on
her, climb on a bench. "The woman with the American flag . . . looks like
a glaringly colorized version of the Statue of Liberty, the reigning goddess
of liberty. She is . . . higher than the rest, wearing a red wig and a feather
boa."[50] Leigh told reporters she should be inside too: "The strategies developed at this conference will serve to punish prostitutes (and) adult
entertainers." Collette, another protestor, proclaimed, "Targeting us is a
little wacko. . . . They should attack poverty, not prostitution." Conference attendee and UC student Ann Reinhold dismissed their complaints;
in her view, men couldn't respect "real women" because "they are bom-
barded with images of women as sexual objects."[51]

The performance of the "sexual objects" effectively disrupted Williams. In the "wider sphere," the harms were structural: the "colonies
of despair" in the nearby Robert Taylor Homes, where girls grew up in
high-rise ghettos of poverty that led to prostitution. Milwaukee police
continually ignored the complaints of Jeffrey Dahmer's Asian and African American neighbors, and refused to investigate as seventeen men
and boys disappeared.[52] Williams concluded that attitudes and actions
perpetuated a more frightening structural violence, a "spirit murder" of
the disenfranchised that outweighed the words and pictures MacKinnon
sought to suppress. To Williams, prostitution was a form of "spirit murder," but "sexual objects" were also living, thinking "real women" whose
impoverishment should not deny them human rights and dignity.[53] It
was a bleeding-heart start.

BOUND, NOT GAGGED

"Girls Rule" underwear and "Girls Kick Ass" T-shirts weren't the typical uniform for the revolution until riot grrrls took the stage. A movement with roots in punk music, sex work, and feminist-oriented anti-violence services, the cultural activism of the riot grrrls appeared completely contradictory to "straight" second-wave feminists: "girls" wearing lipstick and baby-doll dresses growling lyrics denouncing rape and sexual abuse, but believing sexuality was a way for women to express themselves and their power.

Olympia, Washington, and Washington, DC, were the bicoastal centers for "Revolution Girl Style Now." In high school in the late 1980s, Kathleen Hanna made "flyers about the politics of calling women sluts." By the time she turned twenty-one, she'd worked as a stripper; been a women's studies student at Evergreen State College; run Rekomuse, an art gallery and punk performance space (Nirvana did fund-raisers for it); worked as a domestic-violence shelter counselor; founded Bikini Kill; and issued the Riot Grrrl manifesto "BECAUSE I believe with my whole-heartmindbody that girls constitute a revolutionary soul force that can, and will change the world for real."

Hanna arrived in Washington, DC, in 1991 with her Bikini Kill bandmates and hooked up with members of Bratmobile, another all-female punk group. The movement gelled into "something like a cultural underground railroad for young girls" when the band members called a meeting at "Positive Whore House" and decided to put out a 'zine they called *Riot Grrrl*.[54] Hanna said, "The meetings were exciting because a lot of us had never been in the same room with only women. I had, because I had been a stripper. That was a big thing that stripping gave me: an all-female atmosphere and a sort of camaraderie, like in a locker room, that I really craved."[55] Bikini Kill band member Tobi Vail had been making "angry girl 'zines" that called for resistance and revolution in the post-feminist era.[56]

Lyrics announced their action strategy, taking on rape culture, thrashing against sexual violence that band members and their female audience knew too well. Inspired by performance artist Karen Finley, Hanna used punk to "make feminism cool for younger girls." Bikini Kill taunted the boys, "Us punk rock whores/We don't need you." Dressed in a black bra, miniskirt, and Doc Martens boots, Hanna and band members Vail, Kathi Wilcox, and Billy Karren confronted audiences with such songs as "Daddy's Little Girl" (on incest) and "I Like Fucking" (on date rape). They had nothing to prove; what they needed, what they wanted, was "action/strategy," believing in the "radical possibilities of pleasure, babe."[57]

In DC, Positive Force (PF) organized numerous fundraisers for feminist and women's groups, including HIPS, founded in 1993. A day-glow pink poster announcing that Bikini Kill would play a benefit for HIPS attracted the attention of feminist/Mormon/women's studies major Cyndee Clay in 1995. With PF's Mark Andersen, a HIPS board member, Clay helped organize the first memorial action in the United States for murdered sex workers in 1996.

Out in Olympia, "whore activist" Annie Oakley organized the first *Sex Workers' Art Show (SWAS)* in 1997 as a benefit for nonprofit sex work organizations. She wanted to "humanize" sex workers. The "bleeding hearts' tedious reactions" to her work as a stripper, were "part condescending pity-trip, part feminist 'you're taking us back to the time of wire coat-hanger abortion' tedium." A sex worker at night and "lefty-organizer by day," she convinced the Liberation Café to make one of "their regular infotainment events a forum for people who worked in the sex trade."[58]

Popular demand moved the show to the eight-hundred-seat Olympia Theater, and the annual performances didn't attempt to make the sex industry glamorous, fun, and happy. Instead, "a parade of once and future hookers, professional spankers, lap grinders, and clothes-shedders" talked about "what it's really like to work in the industry."[59] At conferences before the show, sex workers got the chance "to hobnob with others in their business," often about labor issues. For many, it was a space outside of work where *SWAS* performers and local sex workers met and were "inspired by each other."

SWAS was an all-in-one cabaret, burlesque, drag, multimedia, and art show. No other show, not even the biennial Sex Workers' Film Festival in San Francisco, boasted the diversity of performers and performances of *SWAS* when it started to tour nationally in 2002. Among the performers were *Rent Girl* author Michelle Tea; writer Jayson Marston of LA's Adult Industry Medical Center; blues artist Candye Kane; Scarlot Harlot (Carol Leigh); Lusty Lady alums Gina Gold, *Real Live Nude Girl* author

Carol Queen, and cartoonist and muralist Isis Rodriguez; Emi Koyama of the Intersex Society of North America; Miss Dirty Martini (Linda Martinelli); Ducky DooLittle; Kirk Read; Jo Weldon; Amber Dawn; Stephen Elliott; the World Famous Bob; and "Krylon, a tall slender black man in his early 30s, [who] walks onstage in white tutu and magenta wig and proceeds to sing an original song about the Iraq War acapella [*sic*]."[60]

For David Henry Sterry, author of *Chicken: Self-Portrait of a Young Man for Rent* (2002), *SWAS* was life-changing:

> I had never spoken about being a prostitute publicly, and the humiliation, mortification and disgraced shame-faced terror of it was paralyzing me. . . . But when I saw all those beautiful freaks standing in line with their freak flags flying . . . I had to get up and tell America that, yes, I too was once a whore. . . . My first time . . . was one of the greatest nights of my life. I came out as a prostitute, claimed my scarlet letter and never looked back.[61]

Empowerment came from "owning" membership in the sex workers' movement, and reduced the shame performers and perhaps some of the audience felt.

For audiences, *SWAS* was an evening of "entertainment, arousal, and education." It was spoken word, stagecraft, dance, music, and storytelling that didn't try for "balance" because there is no other "side" to the stereotype that all sex workers are "stupid, drug-addicted, or abuse survivors."[62] Instead Oakley sought "a fuller articulation of the complicated ways sex workers experience their jobs and their lives."[63] With ten thousand tickets sold every year in six years of national tours, it was more than "a small blip on the national radar of dialogue about feminism, workers' rights, capitalism, and sexuality."

The live performances created their own community standards of what was "decent" or "obscene," a radical idea that the Portland, Oregon–based *Bike Porn* travelling shows adopted in their performances around the country. In 2008, Jennifer Whorley created *Sex on Wheels*, a bike tour of sex workers in San Francisco, featuring "guerrilla street-theater performances that re-tell one city's history from the point of view of its most sensational, but often forgotten residents."

TELLING STORIES, MAKING POLICY

For those who have never attended the *Sex Workers' Art Show*, a *Sex on Wheels* tour, or a *Bike Porn* show, performers continue to produce amazing stories and make them available to the public. Each month at Happy Endings Lounge, a former massage parlor on the Lower East Side of Manhattan, the Red Umbrella Diaries produces a new live show, coordinated by Audacia Ray and a cast of guest hosts. More than six dozen podcasts of the show are available free on iTunes. Kirk Read hosts a similar show regularly in San Francisco, and Carol Leigh produces the weeklong Sex Worker Film Festival and Carnival biennially. Podcasts of *Sex Worker Literati: Stories of Dirt, Danger and Debauchery*, drawn from David Henry Sterry's *Hos, Hookers, Call Girls and Rent Boys*, are available free on iTunes, as well as several other sex worker–produced videos and Internet radio shows.

This sophisticated work goes far beyond the old do-it-yourself projects, and remains strictly noncommercial by design. Sterry and Ray are both former sex workers who have developed writing classes and media training workshops and provide a safe space for people to make their voices heard. The writing is "unpolished, unpretentious and riveting," wrote a *New York Times* reviewer, "but don't worry, their tales are also graphic, politically incorrect and mostly unquotable in this newspaper."[64] Workshop members bring a range and diversity of experiences in the sex industry and sex trades that make one-dimensional stereotypes of "fallen women" obsolete.

The Red Umbrella Project (RedUP) believes, "Everyone has a story, and the people who are best equipped to tell the stories of people in the sex trade are the people who have personal experiences in the industry." By allowing stories to be long and complicated, this type of cultural activism supports new voices and in the process reveals public-policy issues that haven't been addressed. "Not everyone is an activist," Ray says, and it's okay for sex workers to "show up at the Diaries or participate in one of our creative programs and feel awesome."

The storytelling encouraged by RedUP and other creative projects counters the observational and anecdote-based research of outsiders and journalists. The voices of sex workers favor empowerment and human rights, not patronizing rescue schemes and patriarchal protection. Stories can do that, but for Ray, "the creative work cannot be an end point or a stand-alone thing; it has to be linked to greater social change. I want to validate art for arts' sake, but we've got a revolution to do here, and it's important to link personal storytelling to cultural and policy change."[65]

In RedUP workshops held in conjunction with Streetwise & Safe, members started to share their experiences with being arrested for prostitution when New York City cops found a couple of condoms in their possession. Those stories spurred the Sex Workers Project of the Urban Justice Center to investigate police practices and the policies of borough district attorneys. They found that dozens of people, many of them transwomen of color, had been convicted of prostitution on the basis of condom possession alone. With their stories and hand-drawn pictures, sex workers have lobbied representatives in the state capitol to enact a bill that would abolish condoms as evidence.[66]

Private corporations have rejected, altered, and censored sex worker–produced educational advertisements. In 2011, two billboard companies refused to accept public awareness ads for the St. James Infirmary created by Rachel Schreiber because, by including the term "sex worker," they failed to meet "community standards." The twenty-seven designs featured photographs of people associated with SJI, including allies, supporters, family members, and their pets with the tagline, "Someone you know is a sex worker." Like the provocative campaign "Kissing Doesn't Kill: Greed and Indifference Do," created by Gran Fury of ACT UP in 1989, the SJI ads challenged stigma by humanizing sex workers as ordinary people.[67] The original SJI ads finally appeared on local transit buses in November 2011. Similarly "every major (and many minor) outdoor advertising company in LA rejected the pro–sex worker billboard" that SWAAY wanted to mount; Furry Girl finally had to settle for mobile signs attached to a truck.[68]

Private companies are permitted to engage in viewpoint discrimination, and CBS Outdoor and Clear Channel discriminate routinely, willingly accepting signs from anti-abortion, anti-immigrant, and anti–gay rights groups. Shared Hope International, an anti-prostitution organization, helps local groups to fund their deceptive "Do You Know Lacey?" billboards against "child sex-trafficking." Twenty-one were posted in eight states (including California) in 2012; they apparently conformed to "community standards" even though sex workers complained about them.[69]

The *Sex Workers' Art Show* and other public storytelling—in 'zines, music, video, live performances, podcasts, comic books, illustrated novels, wheat-pasted signs, commercial billboards, and the graphic arts—provide anyone willing to listen with a complicated picture of the sex industry and the sex trades. This work defiantly rejects prohibitionists' demand that sex workers "'perform' stereotypical tragedy porn," in the words of Australian activist Elena Jeffreys of Scarlet Alliance. She tells feminists, "We shouldn't have to use arenas . . . as a public counselling or debrief space for the difficulties of our lives just so that you will believe us when we say we want human rights."[70]

Looking at sex work in the wider sphere, the obstacles to securing rights—human, labor, sexual, or civil rights—don't look the same. *Feministe* blogger Renegade Evolution, returning from the 2008 Desiree Alliance conference, called on other sex-worker activists to pay attention to differences in occupations and their associated problems:

> *In the here and now, while there is sex industry, treating it or the people in it in a monolithic fashion does nothing to help anyone.* The needs of a porn performer are not the needs of an erotic masseur are not the needs of an independent escort are not the needs of a street-based worker are not the needs of a stripper are not the needs of a trafficked person forced into an illegal brothel.[71] (Italics in original)

The sex workers' movement could no longer focus only on women; a human rights–based movement needed everyone in the sex trades.

Though the term "sex worker" is gender neutral and industrywide, the movement didn't really diversify until the late 1990s. In 1998, Shane Luitjens created *Hook*, a xeroxed 'zine with "great stories and interviews." HookOnline went live in 1999, "created by, for, and about male sex workers," adding resources, tips, and a twenty-four-hour one-on-one hotline when there were fewer than ten such programs in the United States.[72] In San Francisco, Kirk Read started volunteering at the St. James Infirmary when it opened in 1999 and later, with transgender activist Mattilda Bernstein Sycamore, participated in Gay Shame, a protest against assimilation and the commercialization of gay politics. Other activists were angered by the "safety in monogamy" trend in AIDS/HIV-prevention messaging. For queer and transgendered sex workers, the Millennium March on

Washington, with its conservative "faith and family" theme, proved that "gay rights" no longer meant sexual freedom, the fundamental demand of the Gay Liberation Front.[73]

Queer theory and intersectional analysis challenged the essentialism of a fixed and gendered "prostitute" identity; postmodernism also reconfigured the "grievous flaw" in the movement's political agenda.[74] The very diverse lot of workers in the sex industry meant that focusing on winning citizenship rights by decriminalizing prostitution skimmed over the complexities of peoples' lives. Decriminalization grew both less urgent and more complicated in the 1990s because of changes in employment: for workers in the legal sex industry and for independent, Internet-based escorts, decriminalization was not a priority. Pro-sex feminism had also reduced some of the stigma attached to sex work, making it easier for some people to work a few years and then move on to other occupations.

But the ability to transition to jobs outside the sex industry depends on whether a sex worker has a criminal record. Systemic sex, gender, racial, and class discrimination means that privileged workers are more likely to enjoy this new freedom, while others do not. For those with police records of any sort, the USA PATRIOT Act, passed in the aftermath of the September 11 attacks and the rise of the "surveillance industrial complex," has closed off many other job opportunities. Decriminalization can no longer be focused only on prostitution-related laws, but must consider the larger prison-industrial complex.

In this millennium, activists in the sex workers' movement are involved in many issues: harm reduction, the defense of public sex venues, the prison-industrial complex, police violence, immigration, homelessness, welfare "reform," the war on drugs, labor organizing, feminist porn, HIV criminalization, hate crimes against gays and transgender people, and anarchist and "lavender left" politics. Their work consistently crosses over the not-so-neat, identity-based categorizations that once dominated Cold War civil rights struggles.

SLUTWALKS AND HO STROLLS

In January 2011, a Toronto police sergeant told a class at York University what law enforcement officers from Helsinki to Halifax, from Paris to Pretoria, from San Francisco to Santiago, from Petrograd to Perth, have been telling women for decades: if you don't want be a victim, don't dress like a slut. Though some weren't surprised by the patronizing comment, others were appalled at the "slut" stereotype and outraged that police would blame women for inviting sexual assault. The Toronto police had never been on good terms with queers, dykes, sex workers, and street people, but this remark sparked protest.

In July 2010, Sasha Van Bon Bon, a sex-advice columnist and burlesque performer, called for an unpermitted "Take Back the Dyke" march that brought out one thousand people to "break from the hot apolitical mess" that Toronto Pride had become.[75] In September, the Toronto police had demonstrated overwhelming brutality against protestors during the G-20 summit meetings, and people were still fighting charges. For Toronto's anti-violence activists, queers, progressives, and leftists, Slut-Walk, a protest against the police, was born.

SlutWalk organizers fired off an angry and dramatic "NO!" They had "ENOUGH of victim-blaming, slut-shaming, sexual profiling, and gender policing. With a feminist analysis filtered through Spice Girls and Buffy the Vampire Slayer and organizing practices that combined new social media, radical street performance, DIY cos-play, and old-school rights-based marches, they began organizing. On Facebook, Twitter, Pinterest, Instagram, and the blogosphere, their campaign went viral.

In the next six weeks, activists Heather Jarvis and Sonya JF Barnett made three separate attempts to meet with Toronto's chief of police but failed. They thought they could educate constables, officers, and detectives about sexual violence and make them stop using their "bad cop" tactics against victims. They believed that whether dressed like sluts or like soldiers, women deserved the human right to "security of person," as guaranteed in the Canadian constitution and in international human rights conventions. They wanted law enforcement to respect the civil rights of sexual assault victims; police needed to investigate their complaints, not interrogate the complainants.

Nearly five decades after the sex workers' movement began and almost as many years since the anti-rape movement, "sluts" (female or male) are accepted in some circles, but prostitutes, whores, and hustlers continue to "represent a cultural bogeyman." "They are sin, immorality, indulgence," according to a reporter on Salon.com.[76] Putting sex workers into a news story about a scandal, violent crime, murder, or trafficking makes it sexy. In "dead hooker" stories, the bogeyman's true function becomes clear: the victim's "deviant lifestyle" serves as the explanation for her or his death.

Police and "straight" civilians imagine that women who look like "prostitutes" are loose women "whose dress means yes." This is the slut that Toronto Constable Michael Sanguinetti likely had in mind when he said, "Women should avoid dressing like sluts in order not to be victimized."[77] His obtuse comment reminded activists once again that the police were equally responsible for perpetuating violence.

In a flurry of texts, Jarvis and Barnett decided it was time to "reclaim the word slut." There were no long, fingernail-biting meetings about the name "SlutWalk," no polls before they sat down on the bus. It was a pure gut, on-the-spot decision, made by two women who decided to do something. On Sunday, April 3, 2011, three thousand or more people, mostly white, mostly young, mostly female, wearing "comfortable attire suited to the weather" gathered.[78] They rallied in Queen's Park and marched one kilometer to Toronto Police Services' headquarters "demanding better from an institution that is supposed to support victims, not scrutinize them."[79]

Only a few of the marchers dressed like stereotypical "sluts." Photojournalists in Toronto focused especially on two young white women at the start of the walk of thousands: Sierra "Chevy" Harris in knee-high black boots and Magdalena "Maggie" Ivasecko, wearing "see-through, waist-high net stockings over white panties," carrying the signs "Proud Slut" and "Sluts Say Yes."[80] As cities around the world organized Slut-Walks of their own—during the days of the Arab Spring and Occupy Wall Street—slut costumes and the word "slut" became the central theme in mainstream news stories. Aware of media attention, many marchers went the extra mile with their "slut" costumes.

Anti-porn feminist Gail Dines quickly chastised the organizers' strategy, calling it misguided and claiming that "slut" could never be reclaimed. With hundreds of signatures, Black Women's Blueprint, an anti-violence group based in Brooklyn, New York, sent out an "open letter" saying they too were "deeply concerned." As women of color, they stood in solidarity with coordinated actions against sexual assault, street harassment, and law enforcement indifference, but words also mattered: "slut," like "ho," "bitch," and racial slurs, could never be reappropriated.

In the ensuing debate, the original message about victim-blaming disappeared. SlutWalk was reduced to epithets and fishnets; the culpability of police in their failure to protect citizens, even the hate mail and flame wars organizers dealt with daily, were mostly lost in the blogosphere quarrel.

SlutWalk participants and observers alike remarked that the people who dressed in baggy sweatpants and hoodies carrying signs that said "This is what I was wearing when I was raped" delivered the most effective costume message. It shouldn't matter what a person wore, it shouldn't matter where a person was, and it shouldn't matter what kind of work a person did; sexual assault was a crime. Victims, as citizens and as human beings, deserved respect from government officials, regardless of gender, race, class, or clothing.

Respect for women and gender self-determination were the core issues of SlutWalk. Clearly, a felonious assault is a crime. But what about the hostile environment women and gender-nonconforming people experience when they are out in public? Constable Sanguinetti's patronizing advice suggested that the way a woman was dressed could be interpreted as an invitation for both physical and verbal assault. Street harassment is violence too: catcalls, sexual commentary, leering, rude gestures, bullying, and unwanted touching are evidence of society's fundamental disrespect for women and transgender people. SlutWalk, Black Women's Blueprint, Hollaback!, indigenous women's organizations, Sista II Sista (an INCITE! member group), Take Back the Night, anti-porn feminists, as well as sex workers' groups all agree that street harassment is offensive and makes them feel unsafe. It was the core issue for SlutWalk participants around the world.

International Porn Superstar Stoya™ is as repulsed by street harassment as Gail Dines, though she would rather punch harassers "in the balls." She can remember every time some man acted inappropriately at a porn convention or trade show, and there aren't many. But that "is absolutely nothing, NOTHING, compared to what it's like to be a girl or woman walking around in public in broad daylight. With dirty hair up in a ponytail or bun, no makeup, and baggy clothing on." Men will grab, poke, corner, follow, block, stop their cars, solicit, and harangue, and "pretty frequently they get mean, slipping into a loud Tourette's-like chant of bitch-whore-cunt-slut."

Like almost every other female, Stoya™ has experienced street harassment since she was a teenager, and her stalkers don't know she takes her clothes off for a living: "Let me remind you that in a room of pornography fans, who have actually seen me with a dick in my mouth and who can buy a replica of my vagina in a can or box, I am treated with far more respect than I am walking down the street."[81]

Despite the typecasting, sex workers rarely dress like "sluts" in public. In a strip club or other indoor job site, appropriate work clothing might include sexy panties, fishnets, and six-inch platform heels, but being out in public requires urban armor. Entering a hotel or another public place alone, escorts know they can't be "obvious" because security will keep them out. Just "WWT"—walking while transgender—is probable grounds for arrest for soliciting, even if she's running to the convenience store for a soft drink and isn't carrying condoms.[82] *$pread* magazine readers' favorite features were the "work" and "off-work" photographs contributed by sex workers of themselves.[83] More than once, it was the same "street" picture.

SlutWalk Toronto deliberately included sex workers in their original call for action. Activist and York student Wendy Babcock, along with sex workers from the Bad Date Line and the Safer Stroll Project, joined the first SlutWalk, and sex workers have participated in other walks, though rarely as a visible contingent. Early on, the Toronto group realized they couldn't and shouldn't control how women in other communities organized or how they analyzed the issue and released them to work as they needed. As a result, the leadership of groups in Las Vegas, Los Angeles, and Vancouver were—perhaps unsurprisingly—pro–sex work, while in other cities, such as London and Pittsburgh, Pennsylvania, the protests were led by prohibitionists and veteran "Take Back the Night" organizers.

"Slut isn't a look, it's an attitude. And whether you enjoy sex for pleasure or work, it's never an invitation to violence," says SlutWalk Las Vegas on Facebook. S**tWalk LA (which chose to change its name because of objections to *slut*) was "very explicit [in its] inclusion of the sex worker community," local organizer Hugo Schwyzer wrote, and it worked to include women engaged in survival sex trades. "Sex workers deserve the same legal and cultural protections against rape as everyone else," he argued. "And getting them those protections requires bringing their work out of the shadows without stigma."[84] SlutWalk Vancouver declared its support for sex workers who "face extensive historical and current victim-blaming and slut-shaming due to their work." Through the PACE (Providing Alternatives Counselling & Education) Society, street-based sex traders in Vancouver's Downtown Eastside neighborhood added their support, reminding people that "these are issues that sex workers face with staggering frequency."[85]

"If the word 'slut' bugs you then focus on the WALK part of Slut-Walk and stop attacking political allies who are working to prevent sexual assault," political scientist Shira Tarrant of S**tWalk LA responded to Dines on *Ms.* magazine's blog.[86] SlutWalk Toronto organizers identify themselves as queer, sex-positive feminists. To them, the word *slut* represented a transgressive form of grrrl sexuality and femme-gender performativity; they believed it should not have negative consequences for anyone's rights.

Black feminists in the United States slammed the Toronto organizers' very Canadian belief in human rights and social justice as privileged white girl outrage, and the criticisms piled up. The Crunk Feminist Collective proposed and rejected the idea of a "ho stroll" because "Black female sexuality has always been understood from without to be deviant, hyper, and excessive."[87]

African American and anarchist feminists dismissed Jarvis and Barnett's initial efforts to meet with the police as liberal feminism, potentially even carceral feminism, that failed to consider the prison-industrial complex. Chicago activist Yasmin Nair warned the movement: "SlutWalk is in danger of becoming the Halloween of feminism: the one day of the year when women feel empowered to dress in scanty clothes and call themselves sluts, but which leaves them without the power with which to actually make and create the kind of change that goes beyond an Obama slogan."[88]

In the blogosphere, opining about the racially specific historical experiences of gender and sexuality in the United States took on a life of its own, becoming a flame war that severely undermined organizing in some communities, and was amped further by a racially obtuse sign carried in the New York City SlutWalk. Perhaps most frustrating for Jarvis and Barnett in Toronto, however, was the rampant chauvinism: Canada is not the fifty-first state of "America," and the history of Canadian women of color, especially Aboriginal women, is different from that of US black women.[89]

For activists committed to ending violence and empowering women, the spring of 2011 was quite busy in Toronto and elsewhere in the Dominion. Nationally, progressives were trying to stop a third term of Prime Minister Stephen Harper and his Conservative Party. The Tory government had almost halved funding for women's advocacy programs and women's legal services, tightened regulations that had given immigrant women asylum from abusive spouses and partners, and stopped funding safe abortion services abroad. Maggie's: The Toronto Sex Workers' Action Project took part in the "No One is Illegal/Status for All" rally on May Day, one day before national elections.

In March, the body of twenty-year-old Kera Freeland was found in a ditch in Ontario; the press lewdly connected her death with "her escort lifestyle." The Sex Workers' Action Project condemned the media hype as "sexist victim-blaming and discrimination against sex workers."[90] (In January 2013, police charged Freeland's male roommate with her murder and admitted her work had nothing to do with it.)

Meanwhile, the deaths and disappearances of at least 582 native women in Canada, many of them substance users and street-based sex traders, were mostly unremarked in the media and uninvestigated by the Royal Canadian Mounted Police. Since at least 1990, over 70 women with "high risk lifestyles" in the Edmonton, Alberta, area had gone missing; the local police policy of "no body, no investigation," meant nothing had been done.

Research by the Native Women's Association of Canada (NWAC) Sisters In Spirit Project found that perhaps one-quarter of missing and murdered women were involved peripherally or substantially in the sex trades, emphasizing that sex trading was *not* the "cause" of their deaths. Structural violence, drugs, and lack of care gave women and girls "limited options . . . after experiencing multiple forms of trauma or victimization."[91]

For their efforts, the Tory government took away NWAC's research funds in May 2011 and transferred the monies to the Mounties—the very same federal investigation agency that had done almost nothing in the past. Maggie's, POWER (Prostitutes of Ottawa/Gatineau Work, Educate and Resist), and other Canadian sex workers' groups joined the solidarity march in support of missing and murdered Aboriginal women, held in Ottawa in July 2011.

POWER and Vancouver's Downtown Eastside Sex Workers United Against Violence (SWUAV) each filed lawsuits in 2007 to fully decriminalize prostitution; three years later, in September 2010, a Toronto judge ruled in POWER's favor. Activists Terri-Jean Bedford, Valerie Scott, and Amy Lebovitch argued that, while "it is not unlawful to work as a sex worker [in Canada, other] criminal laws make it virtually impossible for a sex worker to work in a safe and secure environment." In *Bedford v. Canada*, the statutes against "communicating" with a client, working in a "bawdy house," or hiring a driver or a taxi in order to meet a client, were declared unconstitutional under the Canadian Charter of Rights and Freedoms, which guaranteed all people the "right to liberty and security of the person" and the "right to freedom of expression."[92] POWER chair Chris Bruckert "actually squealed with delight" when she heard the judge's decision.[93]

Just before the second SlutWalk Toronto, however, the Court of Appeal for Ontario reversed the communications decision, holding that restrictions against negotiating with a client in a public place was not a free speech issue. Lux, an experienced street-based worker, told Maggie's, "I reject the conclusion that street work is so bad for neighborhoods that stopping it is more important than protecting women's lives."[94]

Jarvis, Barnett, and SlutWalk Toronto 2012 organizers recognized that these developments were interrelated. The globalization of SlutWalk was an opportunity to make clear the role of government and the police in perpetuating violence against women. The following spring, the character and content of SlutWalk Toronto fundamentally changed. Transqueer activist Morgan M. Page spoke, remembering "a girl who changed my life at the corner of Homewood and Maitland, Toronto's trans sex worker stroll." Morgan memorialized Wendy Babcock, who had committed suicide the previous August, but her legacy of activism, including the Bad Date Line and the Safer Stroll Project, had inspired sex workers all over the metropolitan area and beyond to fight for human rights, respect, and justice.

ACKNOWLEDGMENTS

AT LEAST TWENTY DOZEN people have helped with this project over many years of friendship, support, e-mails, and difficult discussions, as well as good times. Priscilla Alexander, Carol Leigh, Cyndee Clay, Deon Haywood, Laura McTighe, Melissa Ditmore, Naomi Akers, Penney Saunders, Kirk Read, Serpent Libertine, Darby Hickey, Midori, "Conrad," Elizabeth Stewart, Monica Shores, Tanya Gulliver, Gayle Rubin, Wendy Chapkis, Anne Gray Fischer, Alisa Swindell, Alix Lutnick, Amber Hollibaugh, Anna Gavanas, Audacia Ray, Ayah Wilson, Barbara Brents, Bhavana Nancherla, Bliss Frontiere, Byllye Avery and Ngina Lythcott, the baristas at Café Envie, Benjamin Shepard, Camryn Moore, Carl Klaus, Carroll Smith-Rosenberg and Alvia Golden, Christina Handhardt, Chuck Renslow, Corey Westover, Crystal Jackson, David Kramer, Emily Tynes, Eric Rofes, Eve Minax, Greg and Erin Scott, George Wong, Gert Hekma, GiGi Thomas, Graylin Thornton, Heather Jarvis, Ilana Tarr, Irina Alexander, James Tracey and Amy Sonnie, Janette Norrington, Jannelle Martin, Jenny Whorley, Jessica Halem, Jessica Gordon Nembhard, Jill Dabrowski, Joe Gallagher, John Richmond and Leila Roberts, Johonna McCants, Judy Guerin, Julie Ost, Kalan Sherrard, Kate Larkin, Kelli Dorsey, Kelly Quinn, Alex Warner, Kitten Infinite, Larry Barat, Lia Scholl, Linda Faye Williams, Liz Highleyman, Lyndsey Marsak, Marci DeLoatch, Margot Weiss, Marika Maypop, Mariko Passion, Marilee Lindemann, Marilyn J. Perry, Mark Andersen, Melanie Braverman, Melanie Graham, Melissa Broudo, Michael Cunningham, Myra Gold, Nancy Irwin, Nick Flynn, Pat McCarty, Pele Woods, Peggy Sioux, Philip Jean-Pierre, Qimmah Najeeullah, Rachel Aimee, Robyn Few, Ron Meschanko, Ronnie Djoukeng, Rozelle Worrell, Ryan Shanahan, Sam Williamson, Sarah Jenny Bleviss, Sarah Sloane, Sean and Gilbey Strub, Shaquita Borden, Sharmus Stewart,

Sharon Harley, Sherdina Randolph, Sonya Michel, Stacey Swimme, Susan Stryker, Susan Wright, Suzan Abebe, Tanarra Schneider, Taja Ambush, Thembi McWhite Butler, Theresa Kolish, Teresa Reed, Tracy Quan, Tukufu Zuberi, Urvashi Vaid, Veneita Porter, Victoria Gayton, Vinnie Cancellerie, V. P. Franklin, Will Rockwell, Wilhelmina Perry, William Falk, Yael Zekai Cannon, Mary Lipe Chateauvert, Jackie Blank, Jocelyn Chateauvert, and, most especially, Mary Frances Berry.

NOTES

INTRODUCTION

1. Carmen and Moody, *Working Women*, 8.

2. Stacey Mulick, "Ridgway's Victims," *Tacoma (WA) News Tribune*, November 6, 2003; Quinet, "Prostitutes as Victims of Serial Homicide," 74–100; Stacey Swimme and Sienna Baskin, "Breaking: US Acknowledges Human Rights Needs of Sex Workers," SWOP-USA and Urban Justice Center, March 15, 2011, http://www.swopusa.org.

3. Carol Leigh, "The Invention of Sex Work," in Leigh, *Unrepentant Whore*, 66–69.

4. Cohen and Alexander, "Female Sex Workers," 195–219.

5. US Bureau of Labor Statistics, *Occupational Outlook Handbook*, 2010–11 (Washington: Government Printing Office, 2010); State of California Employment Development Department, http://www.labormarketinfo.edd.ca.gov.

6. Danny Hakim and William Rashbaum, "Spitzer Is Linked to Prostitution Ring," *New York Times*, March 10, 2008; Paul Duggan, "Trial Starts in Case of Upscale Escort Service," *Washington Post*, April 8, 2008.

7. Young Women's Empowerment Project, *Girls Do What They Have to Do*; Kristen Hinman, "Lost Boys: New Research Demolishes the Stereotypes of the Underage Sex Workers," *Village Voice*, November 2, 2011.

8. Almodovar, "For Their Own Good," 132.

9. "SWOP Founder Robyn Few," http://www.swopusa.org/about-us/founder -robyn-few/.

10. Priscilla Alexander, "Sex Workers Fight Against AIDS: An International Perspective," in Schneider and Stoller, *Women Resisting AIDS*, 99–123; Maggie McNeill, "Confined and Controlled," May 25, 2012, http://maggiemcneill.wordpress.com.

11. Almodovar, "For Their Own Good," 132; Carol Leigh, "On the Frontline of Sex Wars," *On the Issues*, Summer 2008, http://www.ontheissuesmagazine.org.

12. ProCon.org, "100 Countries and Their Prostitution Policies," updated December 22, 2011, http://prostitution.procon.org/view.resource.php?resourceID=000772.

13. Amnesty International USA, *Stonewalled*.

14. International Committee for the Rights of Sex Workers in Europe, "Red Umbrella Campaigns" and "The Declaration of the Rights of Sex Workers in Europe," October 17, 2005, Brussels, http://www.sexworkeurope.org.

CHAPTER 1

1. Sylvia Rivera, interview by Leslie Feinberg, *The Workers World*, 1998, http://www .workers.org/ww/1998/sylvia0702.php.

2. Hobson, *Uneasy Virtue*; Hegarty, *Victory Girls*.

3. Susan Stryker, "(De)Subjugated Knowledges: An Introduction to Transgender Studies," in *The Transgender Studies Reader*, Susan Stryker and Stephen Whittle, ed. (New York: Routledge, 2006), 1–2; Susan Stryker, Victor Silverman, and Jack Walsh, dirs., *Screaming Queens: The Riot at Compton's Cafeteria*, DVD, 2005.

4. Benjamin, *Transsexual Phenomenon*.

5. Tamara Ching endorsed San Francisco's Proposition K in 2008, stopping the district attorney from prosecuting misdemeanor solicitation and prostitution cases (http://yesonpropk.org/tamara_endorse.html); Kiki Whitlock, Sex Workers' Issues Testimony Meeting, City Hall, November 29, 1994, San Francisco Task Force on Prostitution, http://www.bayswan.org/Testkw.html.

6. Duberman, *Stonewall*, 224.

7. Ibid., 204; Ehn Nothing, "Introduction: Queens against Society," *Street Transvestite Action Revolutionaries: Survival, Revolt, and Queer Antagonist Struggle* (n.p., Untorrelli Press, n.d.), 3–9;

8. Elizabeth Armstrong and Suzanna Crage, "Movements and Memory: The Making of the Stonewall Myth," *American Sociological Review* 71 (2006): 7241–51; Duberman, *Stonewall*, 203.

9. "Rapping with a Street Transvestite Revolutionary," in Jay and Allen, *Out of the Closets*, 113.

10. Jeffrey Schwartz, dir., *Vito* (Automat Pictures/HBO Documentaries, 2012), DVD; Duberman, *Stonewall*, 308–9; Terrence McKissack, "Freaking Fag Revolutionaries: New York's Gay Liberation Front, 1969–1971," *Radical History Review* 62 (1995): 123.

11. Pheterson, "Whore Stigma"; Ward, *Respectably Queer*.

12. Michael Warner, *The Trouble with Normal: Sex, Politics, and the Ethics of Queer Life* (Cambridge, MA: Harvard University Press, 1999).

13. David K. Johnson, *The Lavender Scare: The Cold War Persecution of Gays and Lesbians in the Federal Government* (Chicago: University of Chicago Press, 2004); Stryker et al., *Screaming Queens*.

14. Susan Stryker, "It's Your History—Use It! Talking Points for Tran-Inclusive ENDA Activists," Transgender Law & Policy Institute, September 2007, http://www.transgenderlaw.org/HistoryLessons.html.

15. Armstrong, *Forging Gay Identities*.

16. Nestle, "Lesbians and Prostitutes"; Meyerowitz, *How Sex Changed*, 192–207, 235–38.

17. Rita Mae Brown, "Reflections of a Lavender Menace," *Ms.*, July 1995, 40–47.

18. Weitzer, "Prostitutes' Rights in the United States," 23–41; Jenness, *Making It Work*; Gall, *Sex Worker Union Organizing*.

19. Colter and Glenn, *Policing Public Sex*; Califia, *Public Sex*; Siobhan Brooks, "Working the Streets: Gloria Lockett's Story," http://www.scapa-lv.org/Resources/aboutsexwork/people/glorialockett.htm; Lutnick, "St. James Infirmary," 56–75.

20. Cindy Patton, "A Sexual Community Learns New Games: Claiming the History of Safe Sex Organizing," *Gay Community News* (Boston), June 14–20, 1987; Cindy Patton, "Over-Professionalization of Safer Sex Education," *Radical America* (1987): 69; Nancy Stoller Shaw, "Preventing AIDS Among Women: The Role of Community Organizing," *Socialist Review* 100 (1988): 76–92.

21. Lutnick, "St. James Infirmary."

22. Jo Doezema, "Who Gets to Choose? Coercion, Consent and the UN Trafficking Protocol," *Gender and Development* 10, no. 1 (2002).

23. Gall, *Sex Worker Union Organizing*; Dewey and Kelly, *Policing Pleasure*.

24. Van Smith, "Around the Block: The Colorful Past, Controversial Present, and Uncertain Future of Baltimore's Red-Light District," *Baltimore City Paper*, February 2, 2000.

25. Heather Worth, Cindy Patton, and Diane Goldstein, "Introduction to Special Issue, Reckless Vectors: The Infecting 'Other' in HIV/AIDS Law," *Sexuality Research & Social Policy, Journal of NSRC* 2, no. 2 (2005): 7.

26. Alliance for a Safe and Diverse Washington, *Move Along.*

27. Young Women's Empowerment Project, *Denied Help.*

28. "Brazil: Lula Rejects US 'Aid' for AIDS," *Green Left Weekly*, May 11, 2005, http://www.greenleft.org.au/node/32543; Best Practices Policy Project et al., *Report on the United States of America.*

29. Melissa Gira, "Whore Culture Rising," San Francisco Bay Area Independent Media Center, http://www.indybay.org/newsitems/2005/06/09/17467151.php, September 10, 2006; Gene Sharp, "198 Methods of Non-Violent Direction Action," *The Politics of Nonviolent Action* (Boston: Porter Sargent Publishers, 1973).

30. Rachel Kramer Bussel, "Whore Pride: Young Empowered Sex Workers Want Respect Along with Your Dollars," *Village Voice*, January 19–25, 2005.

CHAPTER 2

1. Friedan, *Feminine Mystique.*

2. Millett, *Prostitution Papers.*

3. Haft, "Hustling for Rights," 9.

4. Pamela Roby, "Politics and Criminal Law: Revision of the New York State Penal Law on Prostitution," *Social Problems* 17 (1969): 83–109; Moira K. Griffin, "Wives, Hookers and the Law: The Case for Decriminalizing Prostitution," *Student Lawyer* 10 (1981–82): 18.

5. Millett, *Prostitution Papers*, 154, 17.

6. James et al., *Politics of Prostitution*, 77; Allyn, *Make Love, Not War*, 240; Jenness, *Making It Work*, 42.

7. Ruth Milkman, "Women Workers, Feminism and the Labor Movement Since the 1960s," in Ruth Milkman, *Women, Work and Protest: A Century of US Women's Labor History* (Boston: Routledge & Kegan Paul), 300–322.

8. Kimberly Springer, *Living for the Revolution* (Durham, NC: Duke University Press, 2005).

9. Combahee River Collective, "Twelve Black Women: Why Did They Die?" in *Fight Back! Feminist Resistance to Male Violence* (Minneapolis: Cleis, 1981), 68.

10. Nancy Hulse, "Valerie Solanas"; Valerie Solanas, *The SCUM Manifesto*, http://www.womynkind.org/valbio.htm; Masters and Johnson, *Human Sexual Response*; Anne Koedt, "The Myth of the Vaginal Orgasm," in *Radical Feminism*, Anne Koedt et al., eds. (New York: Quadrangle Books, 1973), 198–207.

11. Eliot Fremont-Smith, "Beyond Revulsion," *New York Times*, November 8, 1964; Wini Breines, "The 'Other' Fifties: Beats and Bad Girls," in *Not June Cleaver: Women and Gender in Postwar America, 1945–1960*, ed. Joanne Meyerowitz (Philadelphia: Temple University Press, 1994), 382–408; Marcel Martin, review, "Last Exit to Brooklyn," *ONE* 13, no. 3 (March 1965): 20.

12. Cannato, *Ungovernable City*, 537; Charles Grutzner, "Prostitute Drive Pressed by Police; Midtown Campaign Follows Mugging and Stabbing," *New York Times*, March 17, 1971.

13. Roby and Kerr, "Politics of Prostitution," 463–66; Haft, "Hustling for Rights," 15.

14. Cannato, *Ungovernable City*, 537–38; Grutzner, "Prostitute Drive"; Sheehy, "Wide Open City," 24.

15. Grutzner, "Prostitute Drive."

16. Roby and Kerr, "Politics of Prostitution"; David A. Andelman, "New Tricks in the Oldest Profession," *New York Times*, March 28, 1971.

17. Xaviera Hollander, *The Happy Hooker: My Own Story* (New York: Harper Collins, 1972); Barrows, *Mayflower Madam*; Andelman, "New Tricks"; Gail Sheehy, *Hustling: Prostitution in Our Wide Open Society* (New York: Delacorte Press, 1973); Lesley Oelsner, "Prostitute Neighbors Vexing Tenants; Especially in Those Luxury Units," *New York Times*, August 22, 1971.

18. Murray Schumach, "City Plans Drive on Prostitution; Will Also Move to Control Pornography in Midtown," *New York Times*, July 8, 1971; Sheehy, "Wide Open City," 22.

19. Carmen and Moody, *Working Women*, 79–80.

20. Schumach, "City Plans"; John A. Hamilton, "Prostitution: The Story of 'I'—Or, A Sensuous Man Pursued," *New York Times*, July 11, 1971.

21. Martin Arnold, "How Raids to Continue Here; Times Square Drive against Pornography Expanding," *New York Times*, July 16, 1971.

22. Oelsner, "Prostitute Neighbors Vexing Tenants."

23. Murray Schumach: "Mayor Stepping Up Drive On Prostitutes and Smut," *New York Times*, July 30, 1971; "Sex Exploitation Spreading Here," *New York Times*, July 11, 1971; "Police Unit Aims at Curbing Pimps," *New York Times*, July 12, 1971; "9 Peep Shows Are Raided in Times Square Area," *New York Times,* August 11, 1971.

24. Louis Zurcher Jr. et al, "The Anti-Pornography Campaign: A Symbolic Crusade," *Social Problems* 19, no. 2 (1971): 217–38.

25. Lockhart and Wagman, *Report of the Commission on Obscenity and Pornography*; Whitney Strub, *Perversion for Profit: The Politics of Pornography and the Rise of the New Right* (New York: Columbia University Press, 2011).

26. Schumach, "Police Unit Aims at Curbing Pimps."

28. Ibid.; Richard Severo, "Whitman Knapp, 95, Dies; Exposed Police Corruption," obituary, *New York Times*, June 15, 2004.

29. "Sad Reflections on the Oldest Profession," *Time*, August 23, 1971, http://www.time.com/time/magazine/article/0,9171,877272,00.html; James Markham, "Judge Supported on Prostitution," *New York Times*, August 1, 1971.

30. Roby and Kerr, "Politics of Prostitution," 463–66.

31. Eric Pace, "Feminists Halt Session on Prostitution, Demanding to Be Heard," *New York Times*, September 15, 1971.

32. Brownmiller, *Against Our Will*, 279.

33. Pace, "Feminists Halt Session"; Sheehy, "Wide Open City," 26.

34. Millett, *Prostitution Papers*, 13.

35. Ellen Strong, "The Hooker," in *Sisterhood Is Powerful: An Anthology of Writings from the Women's Liberation Movement*, ed. Robin Morgan (New York: Vintage Books, 1970), 329.

36. Reisig, "Sisterhood & Prostitution."

37. Ibid.

38. Ibid.

39. Millett, *Prostitution Papers*, 18.

40. Handwritten notes by Kate Millett on the prostitution conference program, December 1971, Box S17, "Prostitution, 1971–1973 and Undated" file, Kate Millett Papers, Special Collections Library, Duke University, Durham, North Carolina (hereafter, "Millett, program notes").

41. Reisig, "Sisterhood & Prostitution."

42. Karen Durbin, "Casualties of the Sex Wars," *Village Voice*, April 6, 1972.

43. Resources for Community Change, *Women Behind Bars: An Organizing Tool* (Washington: RCC, 1975), 26; Strong, "The Hooker," 329.

44. Millett, *Prostitution Papers*, 18.

45. Ibid., 19.

46. Reisig, "Sisterhood & Prostitution."

47. Millett, *Prostitution Papers.*

48. Millett, program notes.

49. Catharine MacKinnon, *The Sexual Harassment of Working Women: A Case of Sex Discrimination* (New Haven, CT: Yale University Press, 1979).

50. Reisig, "Sisterhood & Prostitution."

51. Ibid.

52. Millett, *Prostitution Papers*, 19.

53. "Gay for Gain: A Talk with a Lesbian Prostitute," *off our backs*, January 31, 1972, 18; Roger Blake, *Lesbian for Hire: A Study of the Female Homosexual Prostitute* (Cleveland, OH: K.D.S., Century Books, 1967); Nestle, "Lesbians and Prostitutes"; Boyd, *Wide-Open Town*, 85–91.

54. The following account, including quotations, has been drawn from Reisig, "Sisterhood & Prostitution."

55. Millett, *Prostitution Papers*, 20–21.

56. Ibid.

57. Ibid., 19.

58. Ibid., 24.

59. Ibid.; Reisig, "Sisterhood & Prostitution."

60. Carmen and Moody, *Working Women*, 23; Barnes, *Report of the Commission on Obscenity and Pornography.*

61. Sarah Bromberg, "Feminist Issues in Prostitution," in *Prostitution: On Whores, Hustlers, and Johns*, eds. James Elias et al. (Amherst, NY: Prometheus, 1998). California State Assemblyman Leroy Greene introduced legislation to legalize prostitution that closely resembled Canadian decriminalization and limited advertising for commercial sex; Box 24, Folders 1–13, Leroy F. Greene papers, MSS 1998/02, Department of Special Collections and University Archives, California State University, Sacramento.

62. George Vescey, "'I've Had a Wonderful Time. And I Feel Like I've Helped a Lot of People,'" *New York Times*, December 27, 1971, 32.

63. Alexandre-Jean-Baptiste Parent-Duchâtelet, *Prostitution in Paris* (Boston: C. H. Brainard, 1845), http://www.hathitrust.org.

64. Sara Davidson, "An Oppressed Majority Demands its Rights," *Life*, December 12, 1969, 68; Margo St. James, "The Reclamation of Whores," in *Good Girls/Bad Girls: Sex Trade Workers & Feminists*, ed. Laurie Bell (Seattle: Seal Press, 1987), 81; Cheryl Overs and Paulo Longo, *Making Sex Work Safe* (London: Network of Sex Work Projects, 1997), 332.

65. Alice Echols, *Daring to Be Bad: Radical Feminism in America, 1967–1975* (Minneapolis: University of Minnesota, 1989).

66. Millett, *Prostitution Papers*, 97–98.

67. Jane Gerhard, "Revisiting 'The Myth of the Vaginal Orgasm': The Female Orgasm in American Sexual Thought and Second Wave Feminism," *Feminist Studies* 26, no. 2 (2000): 449–76.

68. Robin Morgan, "Goodbye to All That," *Rat*, 1970.

69. Allyn, *Make Love, Not War*, 196–205; Erica Jong, *Fear of Flying* (Boston: Holt, Rinehart, and Winston, 1973); Judith Rossner, *Looking for Mr. Goodbar* (New York:

Simon and Schuster, 1975); Marge Piercy, *Small Changes* (New York: Ballantine Books, 1973); and Marilyn French, *The Women's Room* (New York: Summit Books, 1977), explore the possibilities of female self-reliance.

70. Kate Coleman, "Carnal Knowledge: Profile of Four Hookers," *Ramparts* 10 (December 1971) 16–28; Tiefer, *Sex Is Not a Natural Act*, 56.

71. Masters and Johnson, *Human Sexual Response*.

72. Tiefer, *Sex Is Not a Natural Act*, 47–49, 58–59.

73. Millett, *Prostitution Papers*, 17.

74. Meredith Ralston and Edna Keeble, *Reluctant Bedfellows: Feminism, Activism and Prostitution in the Philippines* (Sterling, VA: Kumarian Press, 2009), 25.

CHAPTER 3

1. Susan Brownmiller, *In Our Time: Memoir of a Revolution* (New York: Random House, 2000), 64; Millett, *Prostitution Papers*, 27

2. James et al., *Politics of Prostitution*.

3. Jenness, *Making It Work*, 59.

4. Kathy MacKay, "Bay Area Benefit: Who's Afraid of Anita Bryant?" *Los Angeles Times*, June 2, 1977, H14

5. Allyn, *Make Love, Not War*, 49.

6. Jenness, *Making It Work*, 49–50.

7. Paul Krassner, "The COYOTE Convention: Organizing the Oldest Profession," *Rolling Stone*, August 15, 1974, 12–13.

8. Mary Frances Berry, *Why ERA Failed: Politics, Women's Rights, and the Amending Process of the Constitution* (Bloomington: Indiana University Press, 1986); Weitzer, "Prostitutes' Rights."

9. Jenness, *Making It Work*, 109; Weeks, *Sexuality and Its Discontents*; Boyd, *Wide-Open Town*; Margot [*sic*] St. James, "Summer of Love: 40 Years Later," *San Francisco Chronicle*, May 20, 2007, http://www.sfgate.com/.

10. Leff and Haft, *Time Without Work*, 184.

11. Ibid.

12. Ibid., 185.

13. Rosenbleet and Pariente, "Prostitution of Criminal Law," 373.

14. Ibid.

15. Amanda H. Littauer, "The B-Girl Evil: Bureaucracy, Sexuality, and the Menace of Barroom Vice in Postwar California," *Journal of the History of Sexuality* 12 (2003): 171–204; John D'Emilio, *Sexual Politics, Sexual Communities: The Making of a Homosexual Minority in the United States, 1940–1970* (Chicago: University of Chicago Press, 1983); Boyd, *Wide-Open Town*, 200–236.

16. Robert L. Jacobson, "'Megan's Laws': Reinforcing Old Patterns of Anti-Gay Police Harassment," *Georgetown Law Journal* 87 (1998): 2341.

17. Leff and Haft, *Time Without Work*, 185.

18. Ibid.

19. Ibid., 186.

20. Sylvia Rubin, "COYOTE's New Leadership—An Ex-Teacher and an Ex-Hooker Will Be at the Helm of the Advocacy Group," *San Francisco Chronicle*, February 25, 1986; Vincent Hallinan, *A Lion in Court* (New York: Putnam's, 1963).

21. Leff and Haft, *Time Without Work*, 185–86.

22. Jennifer James, "Two Domains of Streetwalker Argot," *Anthropological Linguistics* 14, no. 5 (1972): 172–81; Kitsuse, "Coming Out All Over."

23. Michel Foucault, *History of Sexuality* (New York: Pantheon, 1978).

24. Howard K. Becker, *Outsiders: Studies in the Sociology of Deviance* (New York: Free Press of Glencoe, 1963).

25. Weeks, *Sexuality and Its Discontents*, 185–86.

26. Betty Liddick, "Hefner Hosts Fund Raiser," *Los Angeles Times*, March 21, 1978.

27. Morgan, *North Beach Leathers*.

28. Leff and Haft, *Time Without Work*, 186; ibid.

29. James et al., *Politics of Prostitution*, 77.

30. Susan Sward, "Richard Hongisto: 1936–2004," *San Francisco Chronicle*, November 5, 2004.

31. Leff and Haft, *Time Without Work*, 185.

32. Kitsuse, "Coming Out All Over."

33. Margo St. James, keynote address, Desiree Conference, Chicago, July 2008.

34. Jenness, *Making It Work*, 41.

35. Leff and Haft, *Time Without Work*, 185.

36. Margo St. James, testimony, Sex Workers' Issues Meeting, City Hall, November 29, 1994, San Francisco Task Force on Prostitution, http://www.bayswan.org/Testms.html.

37. James et al., *Politics of Prostitution*.

38. Dave Smith, "Re-exploring the Whole Earth," *Los Angeles Times*, September 22, 1975; Liddick, "Hefner Hosts Fund Raiser."

39. Saul Alinsky, *Rules for Radicals: A Pragmatic Primer for Realistic Radicals* (New York: Vintage Books, 1971); Marilyn L. Booth, "New Tricks in the Labor Zone," *Harvard Crimson*, February 18, 1976.

40. Valerie Jenness, "From Sex as Sin to Sex as Work: COYOTE and the Reorganization of Prostitution as a Social Problem," *Social Problems* 37 (1990): 403–20.

41. Booth, "New Tricks"; "Fund Raiser for Bail Bonds: Hookers Have a Ball in S.F." *Los Angeles Times*, October 29, 1974.

42. Rickie Solinger, *Wake Up Little Susie: Single Pregnancy and Race Before Roe v. Wade* (New York: Routledge, 1992), 103–46; Sherrill Cohen, *The Evolution of Women's Asylums Since 1500: From Refuges for Ex-Prostitutes to Shelters for Battered Women* (New York: Oxford University Press, 1992).

43. Leff and Haft, *Time Without Work*, 186.

44. Ibid.

45. Priscilla Alexander, author interview, November 7, 2009.

46. Ronald Weitzer's article "Prostitutes' Rights" erroneously declared the movement a failure, based on the argument that COYOTE could not overcome its label as a deviant group and compared it to the "success" of the homosexual rights movement. At the time of publication (1991), sodomy laws were still in effect in more than half the states; four years later, in *Bowers v. Hardwick* (1995), the Supreme Court would uphold state regulation of private sexual behavior. More problematically, Weitzer equated a waged activity (sex work) to "homosexuality," which was variously described as "a lifestyle," "a particular type of sexual practice," and "a biologically determined identity" but without distinguishing what, exactly, constitutes the "homosexual." Finally, he inflated a single, primarily local organization, COYOTE, to a "movement." The gay rights movement began before Stonewall, and there have always been several, sometimes openly conflicting, organizations working to end discrimination against gays and lesbians. Though his measures of success are appropriate (popular support, alliances with third parties, alteration in conventional attitudes, and convincing policymakers to decriminalize activities declared "deviant"), his comparison was poorly constructed.

Social movement theory provides a more useful framework for analyzing the achievements of the sex workers' movement.

47. Booth, "New Tricks."

48. Jenness, *Making It Work*, 53.

49. James et al., *Politics of Prostitution*, 24.

50. Jenness, *Making It Work*, 52; William N. Eskridge Jr., "Some Effects of Identity-Based Social Movements on Constitutional Law in the Twentieth Century," *Michigan Law Review* 100 (August 2001): 2062–407; Rosenbleet and Pariente, "Prostitution of Criminal Law."

51. Madeline S. Caughey, "The Principle of Harm and Its Application to Laws Criminalizing Prostitution," *Denver Law Journal* 51 (1974): 236; Jenness, *Making It Work*, 174; Karen DeCrow, "Being a Feminist Means You Are Against Sexism, Not Against Sex," *New York Law School Law Review* 38 (1993): 359.

52. NOW's 1980 resolution, "Delineation of Lesbian Rights," condemned sadomasochism, pederasty, and pornography as issues unrelated to "affectional/sexual preference/orientation"; Liz Highleyman, "NOW Members Seek S/M Policy Reform," *Sojourner: The Women's Forum*, June 1998.

53. Brownmiller, *Against Our Will*, 391.

54. Gloria Lockett, "Leaving the Streets," in *Sex Work*, 96–97; "Gloria Lockett's Story, Working the Streets," interview by Siobhan Brooks, http://www.scapa-lv.org/Resources/aboutsexwork/people/glorialockett.htm.

55. Carmen and Moody, *Working Women*, 24–25.

56. Brooks, "Gloria Lockett's Story."

57. Jenness, *Making It Work*, 49–50.

58. Ibid.

59. Haft, "Hustling for Rights," 9.

60. James et al., *Politics of Prostitution*; Jenness, *Making It Work*, 51.

61. St. James testimony; Haft, "Hustling for Rights," 8–26; Boston Women's Health Book Collective, *Our Bodies, Ourselves* (New York: Simon and Schuster, 1973), 103–5, 260.

62. "Loose Women," *off our backs*, May 31, 1973, 21.

63. M. Anne Jennings, "The Victim as Criminal: A Consideration of California's Prostitution Law," *California Law Review* 64 (1976): 1235–84, citing Riemer v. Jensen, Alameda County Superior Court, February 26, 1975; Kathleen Hendrix, "Prostitution: Part II: The Law vs. a Changing Moral Climate Unequal Application of Penal Code Charged," *Los Angeles Times*, February 9, 1976.

64. Argersinger v. Hamlin, 407 US 25 (1972).

65. Piven and Cloward, *Poor Peoples' Movements*.

66. Robin Clark, "Legal Prostitution as a Last Resort; Beleaguered San Francisco Seeks Answer to Age-Old Problem," *Philadelphia Inquirer*, January 24, 1994; "S.F. Hookers Cheer DA's Soft Stand on Arrests," *Los Angeles Times*, January 7, 1976; author's conversation with Robyn Few, July 27, 2010, Desiree Alliance Conference, Las Vegas.

67. William Endicott, "S.F. Moves to Curb Rise in Prostitution: But Police Deny It's a Crackdown, Say It Would Imply Past Force 'Laxity,'" *Los Angeles Times*, January 5, 1977.

68. Jenness, *Making It Work*, 5.

69. "Judge Gets Hook," *off our backs*, December 31, 1975, 6; Hendrix, "Prostitution: Part II."

70. "Notes on People," *New York Times*, October 25, 1975.

71. "Judge Gets Hook."

72. Jenness, *Making It Work*, 58; Hendrix, "Prostitution: Part II"; Sward, "Former D.A. Joseph Freitas Jr."; "Notes on People," *New York Times*, October 25, 1975; Diana D. Solberg v. Superior Court of San Francisco (1976), 56 Cal. 3d 422 [128 Cal. Rptr. 502; 1976, 1366].

73. AP, "Public Shifting Slowly on Prostitution," *Hartford Courant*, February 15, 1976; Jim Stingley, "Issues Raised by Decriminalization," *Los Angeles Times*, February 9, 1976.

74. Jennings, "The Victim as Criminal"; People v. Superior Court 19 Cal.3d 338, 348 (1977); Norma Jean Almodovar, *From Cop to Call Girl: Why I Left the LAPD to Make an Honest Living as a Beverly Hills Prostitute* (New York: Simon and Schuster, 1993).

75. Pat Miller, "Assailant Nailed," *off our backs*, April 30, 1978, 2.

76. "The State: Governor Brown Signs Law to Protect Rape Victims," *Los Angeles Times*, September 12, 1980.

77. Jenness, *Making It Work*, 52, 42.

78. Booth, "New Tricks."

79. Jim Stingley, "Prostitution: Part III, Life On and Off the Street," *Los Angeles Times*, February 10, 1976.

80. Ibid.

81. Leigh, *Unrepentant Whore*.

82. The welfare rights movement and the prisoners' rights movement also "failed." Piven and Cloward, *Poor Peoples' Movements;* Eric Cummins, *The Rise and Fall of California's Radical Prison Movement* (Stanford, CA: Stanford University Press, 1994).

83. "People Are Talking About . . . ," *Jet*, October 9, 1975, 26; Florynce Kennedy, "Most People Are Not Taught to Understand That the Two O'Clock Orgasm Leads to the Three O'Clock Feed," in *Color Me Flo: My Hard Life and Good Times* (Englewood Cliffs, NJ: Prentice-Hall, 1976), 97–99; Krassner, "The COYOTE Convention."

84. Leslie Fishbein, "COYOTE," paper in author's possession.

85. Kathy Burke, "Hookers at S.F. Convention; This Time It Was Their Own," *Los Angeles Times*, July, 1, 1974; Janine Bertram, "Hookers Convention," *off our backs*, September 30, 1974, 12.

86. Sides, *Erotic City*, 64; "Hookers Huddle in S.F.: Seek Legal Protection," *Jet*, July 18, 1974, 22.

87. Bertram, "Hookers Convention."

88. "Call Me Madam," *Newsweek*, July 8, 1974, 65.

89. Burke, "Hookers at S.F. Convention"; ibid.

90. Booth, "New Tricks"; "Fund Raiser for Bail Bonds."

91. "Stage S.F. Dance: Prostitutes End Strike," *Los Angeles Times*, June 23, 1975; "The World: The Unhappy Hookers," *Time*, June 16, 1975; "France: The Unhappy Hookers," *Newsweek*, February 12, 1973, 43.

92. Stingley, "Prostitution: Part III."

CHAPTER 4

1. Wofsy, "Isolation of AIDS-Associated Retrovirus," 527–29; Constance B. Wofsy, "Human Immunodeficiency Virus Infection in Women," *Journal of the American Medical Association* 257, no. 15 (1987): 2074–76.

2. Corea, *Invisible Epidemic*; Treichler, Cartwright, and Penley, *Visible Woman*, 233.

3. Centers for Disease Control, "HIV Surveillance—United States, 1981–2008," *Morbidity and Mortality Weekly Report* 60, no. 21 (2011): 689–93.

4. Robert R. Redfield et al., "Heterosexually Acquired HTLV-III/LAV Disease (AIDS-Related Complex and AIDS): Epidemiologic Evidence for Female-to-Male Transmission," *Journal of the American Medical Association* 15 (1985): 2094–96; Cohen, Alexander, and Wofsy, "Prostitutes and AIDS," 16–22.

5. Redfield et al., "Heterosexually Acquired HTLV-III/LAV," letters, *Journal of the American Medical Association* 255, no. 13 (April 4, 1986): 1702–6; Lawrence K. Altman, "Heterosexuals and AIDS: New Data Examined," *New York Times*, January 22, 1985.

6. Wofsy, "Isolation of AIDS-Associated Retrovirus."

7. Gerald Oppenheimer, "In the Eye of the Storm," in Fee and Fox, *AIDS*, 286.

8. Randy Shilts, "S.F. Hookers Who Made AIDS History," *San Francisco Chronicle*, August 27, 1987; Debi Brock, "Prostitutes Are Scapegoats in the AIDS Panic," *Resources for Feminist Research* 18, no. 2 (1989): 13–17; Randy Shilts, *And the Band Played On: Politics, People, and the AIDS Epidemic* (New York: St. Martin's Press, 1987), 508–16.

9. Gayle Rubin, "Sexual Politics, the New Right, and the Sexual Fringe," in *What Color Is Your Handkerchief? A Lesbian S/M Sexuality Reader* (Berkeley: SAMOIS, 1979).

10. *What Color* predated "Play Fair!" (Sisters of Perpetual Indulgence, 1982); Richard Berkowitz, "How to Have Sex in an Epidemic" (n.p., May 1983); Carol Leigh, "Further Violations of Our Rights," *AIDS: Cultural Analysis/Cultural Activism*, ed. Douglas Crimp and Leo Bersani (Cambridge, MA: MIT Press, 1987), 177–81.

11. Judith R. Walkowitz, *Prostitution and Victorian Society: Women, Class, and the State* (New York: Cambridge University Press, 1980).

12. Alexander, "A Chronology of Sorts," 169.

13. Maxine Wolfe, "People, People, You Have to Listen," ACT UP Oral History Project, Interview #043, February 19, 2004, 26, http://www.actuporalhistory.org/interviews/images/wolfe.pdf; Dorothy J. Samuels, "A Coming Threat to Constitutional Values," *New York Times*, November 23, 1980.

14. Gayle Rubin, "Thinking Sex: Notes for a Radical Theory of the Politics of Sexuality," in *Pleasure and Danger: Exploring Female Sexuality*, ed. Carol Vance (New York: Routledge and Kegan Paul, 1984), 267–319; Gayle Rubin, "Blood under the Bridge: Reflections on 'Thinking Sex,'" *GLQ: A Journal of Lesbian and Gay Studies* 17, no. 1 (2010): 15–48.

15. Ibid.

16. John Emi, "Ambiguous Elements: Rethinking the Gender/Sexuality Matrix in an Epidemic," in Roth and Hogan, *Gendered Epidemic*, xvii; Thomas A. Peterman and James W. Curran, "Special Communication: Sexual Transmission of Human Immunodeficiency Virus," *Journal of the American Medical Association* 256, no. 16 (1986): 2222–26.

17. Oppenheimer, "In the Eye of the Storm," 279; Constance B. Wofsy, "Women and the Acquired Immunodeficiency Syndrome: An Interview," *Western Journal of Medicine* 149, no. 6 (December 1988): 687–90; Barbara Grizzuti Harrison, "It's Okay to Be Angry about AIDS," *Mademoiselle* (February 1986), quoted in Treichler and Warren, "Maybe Next Year," 124; Ralph Bolton, "AIDS and Promiscuity: Muddles in the Models of HIV Prevention," *Medical Anthropology: Cross-Cultural Studies in Health and Illness* 14, no. 2 (1992): 145–223.

18. C. Everett Koop, *Surgeon General's Report on Acquired Immune Deficiency Syndrome* (Rockville, MD: US Public Health Service, 1986); William N. Eskridge Jr., "No Promo Homo: The Sedimentation of Anti-Gay Discourse and the Channeling Effect of the Judicial Review," *New York University Law Review* 75 (2000): 1358.

19. Julia A. Ericksen and Sally A. Steffen, *Kiss and Tell: Surveying Sex in the Twentieth Century* (Cambridge, MA: Harvard University Press, 1999).

20. Ron Goldberg, "Conference Call: When PWAs First Sat at the High Table," *POZ*, July 1998, http://www.actupny.org/documents/montreal.html.

21. Paula Treichler, *How to Have Theory in an Epidemic: Cultural Chronicles of AIDS* (Durham, NC: Duke University Press, 1999), 328.

22. Sean Strub, "Medical Ethics and the Rights of People with HIV under Assault," *POZ*, April 28, 2010, http://blogs.poz.com.

23. Kaiser Family Foundation, *HIV/AIDS at 30*.

24. Centers for Disease Control, "*Pneumocystis* Pneumonia—Los Angeles," *Morbidity and Mortality Weekly Report* 30, no. 21 (1981): 1–3.

25. David Huminer, Joseph B. Rosenfeld, and Silvio D. Pitlik, "AIDS in the Pre-AIDS Era," *Clinical Infectious Disease* 9, no. 6 (1987): 1102–8.

26. Oppenheimer, "In the Eye of the Storm," 267–300.

27. Ibid.

28. Corea, *Invisible Epidemic*, 1–6.

29. Ibid., 9, 14; Richie, "AIDS: In Living Color," 182; Steven Epstein, *Impure Science: AIDS, Activism, and the Politics of Knowledge* (Berkeley: University of California Press, 1996), 49–50.

30. Women of the ACE Program of the Bedford Hills Correctional Facility, *Breaking the Walls of Silence: AIDS and Women in a New York State Maximum-Security Prison* (Woodstock, NY: Overlook Press, 1998), 10.

31. Richie, "AIDS in Living Color," 184; Cathy J. Cohen, *Boundaries of Blackness: AIDS and the Breakdown of Black Politics* (Chicago: University of Chicago Press, 1999).

32. Philip Boffey, "Army Reports Heterosexual Link in AIDS Cases," *New York Times*, October 18, 1985.

33. Erik Eckholm, "Women and AIDS: Assessing the Risks," *New York Times*, October 28, 1985; Centers for Disease Control, "Perspectives in Disease Prevention," 509–15; Centers for Disease Control, "HIV Surveillance, United States, 1981–2008," *Morbidity and Mortality Weekly Report* 60, no. 21 (2011): 689–93.

34. Bill Keller, "Pentagon to Test All New Recruits for Possible Signs of AIDS Virus," *New York Times*, August 31, 1985.

35. Constance Wofsy, "The AIDS Epidemic in San Francisco: The Medical Response, 1981–1984," in *The San Francisco AIDS Oral History Series, 1981–1984*, vol. 3 (Berkeley: Bancroft Library, University of California, 1997), http://www.bancroft .berkeley.edu/ROHO.

36. W. Robert Lange et al., "HIV Infection in Baltimore: Antibody Seroprevalence Rates among Parental Drug Abusers and Prostitutes," *Maryland Medical Journal* 36, no. 9 (1987): 757–61.

37. French, *Working*, 240.

38. Ibid., 239.

39. St. James Infirmary, *Occupational Health and Safety Handbook*, 3rd ed. (San Francisco: St. James Infirmary, 2010), 21; John C. Cutler, "Current Concepts of Prophylaxis," *Bulletin of the New York Academy of Medicine* 52, no. 8 (October 1976): 887.

40. ASSES flyer excerpt, Gayle Rubin, "The Miracle Mile: South of Market and Gay Male Leather, 1962–1997," in *Reclaiming San Francisco: History, Politics, Culture*, ed. James Brook, Cris Carlsson, and Nancy J. Peters (San Francisco: City Lights, 1998); http://foundsf.org/index.php?title=Sex_Panic_Closes_Bathhouses; Laura Perkins, "D.A. Files Charges Against House of Ecstasy," March 29, 2002 (repost of March 30 [1977]), http://www.sfgate.com.

41. Sylvia Rubin, "COYOTE's New Leadership—An Ex-Teacher and an Ex-Hooker Will Be at the Helm of the Advocacy Group," *San Francisco Chronicle*, February 25, 1986.

42. Radeloff, Brents, and Futrell, "Sex Panics"; French, *Working*.

43. Alexa Albert et al. "Condom Use among Female Commercial Sex Workers in Nevada's Legal Brothels," *American Journal of Public Health* 85, no. 11 (1995): 1514–20.

44. Radeloff, Brents, and Futrell, "Sex Panics," 10–11.

45. French, *Working*, 239.

46. AP, "Man Who Got AIDS on Job to Get Benefits," *San Francisco Chronicle*, March 5, 1987.

47. "Council Attacks Anti-AIDS Program for Prostitutes," *AIDS Weekly*, July 17, 1995, 16, http://www.NewsRx.com.

48. "Hooker on City Task Force in Atlanta Angers Residents," *Jet*, March 18, 1985, 17.

49. Chet Fuller, "Sweeping Hooker Problem off the Street," *Atlanta Journal and Constitution*, March 5, 1986.

50. Sam Hopkins, "State Task Force Urges AIDS Test for Prostitutes," *Atlanta Journal and Constitution*, February 22, 1986.

51. Stoller, *Lessons from the Damned*, 114.

52. Bill Dobbs, ACT UP Oral History interview, 17.

53. Randy Shilts, "N.Y.'s Gamble on Hookers Carrying AIDS," *San Francisco Chronicle*, February 18, 1985.

54. Judith Miller, "Prostitutes Make Appeal for AIDS Prevention," *New York Times*, October 5, 1986.

55. Corea, *Invisible Epidemic*, 124; Maxine Wolfe, ACT UP Oral History, 62.

56. Suzanne Loebl, *The Mothers' Group: Of Love, Loss, and AIDS* (New York: ASJA Press, 2007), 50.

57. Randy Shilts, "N.Y.'s Gamble on Hookers Carrying AIDS," *San Francisco Chronicle*, February 18, 1985.

58. Centers for Disease Control, "Diagnoses of HIV Infection and AIDS in the United States and Dependent Areas, 2009," *HIV Surveillance Report* 21 (2011).

59. Roth and Hogan, *Gendered Epidemic*; Patton, *Sex and Germs*, 85; Watney, *Policing Desire*.

60. Centers for Disease Control, "Perspectives in Disease Prevention," 509–15.

61. Center for HIV Law and Policy, *Ending and Defending against HIV Criminalization: State and Federal Laws and Prosecutions*, vol. 1 (2010), http://www.hivlawandpolicy.org.

62. Center for HIV Law and Policy, *Prosecutions and Arrests for HIV Exposure in the United States, 2008–2012* (2012), http://www.hivlawandpolicy.org.

63. Stephen Hunt, "HIV Positive Prostitute Sent to Prison," *Salt Lake Tribune*, September 17, 2010.

64. "UNAIDS Terminology Guidelines," rev. version (Geneva: UNAIDS, October 2011).

65. Corea, *Invisible Epidemic*, 31–32.

66. Gloria Lockett, "CAL-PEP: The Struggle to Survive," in *Women Resisting AIDS*, 209.

67. Lockett, "CAL-PEP"; Stoller, *Lessons from the Damned*, 81–96.

68. California Prostitutes' Education Project, "About Us," http://www.calpep.org; Stoller, *Lessons from the Damned*, 3.

69. Katy Butler, "Hundreds of Hookers Sought for AIDS Study," *San Francisco Chronicle*, January 3, 1986.

70. Corea, *Invisible Epidemic*, 44.

71. Cohen, "Prostitutes and AIDS," 21.

72. Randy Shilts, "Laws on Prostitution Don't Help," *San Francisco Chronicle*, August 28, 1989.

73. Only the Sex Workers Project of the Urban Justice Center is dedicated to representing sex workers. The ACLU's Privacy Project shifted focus in the 1980s; the Center for Constitutional Rights and the Center for HIV Law and Policy have recently represented sex workers' constitutional interests.

74. Patton, *Sex and Germs*, 85.

75. James L. Fletcher, "Homosexuality: Kick and Kickback," *Southern Medical Journal* 77, no. 2 (1984): 149–50.

76. "Arrest in Man's Home Began Test of Georgia Law," *New York Times*, July 1, 1986; Kaiser Family Foundation, *HIV/AIDS at 30*, 2.

77. Debra Murphree interview in Art Harris and Jason Berry, "Jimmy Swaggart's Secret Sex Life," *Penthouse*, July 1988.

78. Wayne King, "Swaggart Says He Has Sinned, Will Step Down," *New York Times*, February 22, 1988; "Swaggart Is Barred from Pulpit for One Year," *New York Times*, March 20, 1988.

79. *US Attorney General's Commission on Pornography.*

80. Ronald Weitzer, "The Social Construction of Sex Trafficking: Ideology and Institutionalization of a Moral Crusade," *Politics & Society* 35 (2007): 447–75.

81. Carol Anne Douglas, "Pornography: Liberation or Oppression?" *off our backs*, May 1983, 14; Michael S. Kimmel, *Men Confront Pornography* (New York: Crown, 1990).

82. Carolyn Bronstein, *Battling Pornography: The American Feminist Anti-Pornography Movement, 1976–1986* (Cambridge, UK: Cambridge University Press, 2011), 166–68; letters, US Prostitutes Collective to WAVPM, 1983, Women Against Violence in Pornography and the Media Records, 1977–1983, GLBT Historical Society, San Francisco.

83. Alexander, "A Chronology of Sorts."

84. Ronald Bayer, "AIDS, Public Health, and Civil Liberties: Consensus and Conflict in Public Policy," in *AIDS and Ethics*, ed. Frederic G. Reamer (New York: Columbia University Press, 1991), 26–49.

85. Jenness, *Making It Work*, 89.

86. Cohen and Alexander, "Female Sex Workers," 195–219; Ann O'Leary and Loretta S. Jemmott. *Women at Risk: Issues in the Primary Prevention of AIDS* (New York: Plenum, 1995).

87. *Report of the Presidential Commission on the Human Immunodeficiency Virus Epidemic,* June 24, 1988, 130, http://archive.org/details/reportofpresiden00pres; Karen Everett, "State Bills Outrage Prosts," *San Francisco Sentinel*, 1988; Leigh, "Further Violations of Our Rights."

88. James Richardson, *Willie Brown: A Biography* (Berkeley: University of California Press, 1998), 311, 333–47.

89. "The Unhappy Hookers," *Sacramento Bee*, November 14, 1992.

90. Julie Graham, "HIV Testing Law Upheld; A California Court Okays Legislation That Requires HIV Testing of People Convicted of Prostitution," *Gay Community News* (Boston), 1991; George Markell, "Court Upholds AIDS Testing for Prostitutes; 11 S.F. Hookers Sought to Block State Law," *San Francisco Chronicle*, January 1, 1991.

91. Centers for Disease Control, "Perspectives in Disease Prevention," 743.

92. Joe Rollins, *AIDS and the Sexuality of Law: Ironic Jurisprudence* (New York: Palgrave Macmillan, 2004), 91–92.

93. "Prostitute with AIDS Pleads No Contest," *San Francisco Chronicle*, March 21, 1992; "Court Approves Felony Charge For L.A. Hustler With AIDS," *San Francisco Chronicle*, May 24, 1991; "2nd Soliciting Arrest of HIV-Positive Man," *San Francisco Chronicle*, October 26, 1991; "3rd Prostitution Charge For HIV-Positive Man," *San Francisco Chronicle*, February 3, 1993.

94. Gail Pheterson, "The Category 'Prostitute' in Scientific Inquiry," *Journal of Sex Research* 27 (1990): 397–407.

95. James Kinsella, *Covering the Plague: AIDS and the American Media* (New Brunswick, NJ: Rutgers University Press, 1989).

96. Delacoste and Alexander, eds., *Sex Work*.

97. Dorie J. Gilbert and Ednita M. Wright, *African American Women and HIV/AIDS: Critical Responses* (Westport, CT: Praeger, 2003).

98. Priscilla Alexander, "Prostitutes Are People Too," reply to Melissa Farley, *off our backs*, October 1994, 26–28.

99. CAL-PEP, "About Us."

100. Lutnick, "St. James Infirmary," 57.

101. Ibid., 58.

102. St. James Infirmary, "Who We Are," http://www.stjamesinfirmary.org; CAL-PEP, "About Us," http://calpep.org; HIPS, "About," http://www.hips.org.

103. United Nations, *The Universal Declaration of Human Rights*, 1948, http://www.un.org/en/documents/udhr.

104. Best Practices Policy Project et al., *Report on the United States of America*.

105. Centers for Disease Control, "Update: Mortality Attributable to HIV Infection Among Persons Aged 25–44 Years—United States, 1991 and 1992," *Morbidity and Mortality Weekly Report* 42, no. 45 (1993): 869–72; Centers for Disease Control, "HIV Surveillance—United States, 1981–2008," *Morbidity and Mortality Weekly Report* 60, no. 21 (2001): 689–93.

106. Simon Watney, *Policing Desire: Pornography, AIDS and the Media* (New York: Continuum International Publishing Group, 1997); Treichler, Cartwright, and Penley, *Visible Woman*, 108; Treichler and Warren, "Maybe Next Year," 132.

107. Bowers v. Hardwick 478 U.S. 186 (1986); Lawrence v. Texas 539 U.S. 558 (2003).

108. Sol Gordon, "Values-Based Sexuality Education: Confronting Extremists to Get the Message Across," *SIECUS Report* 20, no. 6 (1992): 1–4.

109. Leora Tanenbaum, *Slut! Growing Up Female with a Bad Reputation* (New York: HarperCollins, 2000), 215; Douglas Jehl, "Surgeon General Forced to Resign by White House," *New York Times*, December 10, 1994.

110. Leigh, *Unrepentant Whore*, 128; Kellee Terrell, "Wanted: Feminist Warriors to Fight HIV/AIDS; While AIDS Is Killing Women of Color in the U.S., the Women's Movement Appears to Be M.I.A.," The Body, August 16, 2010, http://www.thebody.com.

111. Anna Forbes, e-mail message to author, June 25, 2011.

CHAPTER 5

1. Guy Gonzales, "Peep: A Times Square Veteran Remembers All Too Well How Dirty Sex Could Get," *New Yorker*, September 28, 2008.

2. bell hooks, *Reel to Real: Race, Sex, and Class at the Movies* (New York: Routledge, 1996).

3. Michael Helquist and Rick Osmon, "Sex and the Baths: A Not-So-Secret Report," *Journal of Homosexuality* 44, nos. 3/4 (2003): 153–75; Michael Helquist and Rick

Osmon, "Beyond the Baths: The Other Sex Businesses," *Journal of Homosexuality* 44, nos. 3/4 (2003): 177–201.

4. Jayme Waxman, "On Helping Debunk the Pervert Myth," in *Naked Ambition: Women Who Are Changing Pornography*, ed. Carly Milne (New York: Carroll & Graf, 2005), 44.

5. Marilyn Adler Papayanis, "Sex and the Revanchist City: Zoning Out Pornography in New York," *Environment and Planning: Society and Space* 18 (2000) 3: 341–54.

6. Shelly Feuer Domash, "Drinking Age Rises to 21 Amid Debate," *New York Times*, December 1, 1985.

7. Susan Gunelius, *Building Brand Value the Playboy Way* (New York: Palgrave Macmillan, 2009), 107.

8. Sheila McClear, "Times Square's Lost 'McDonald's of Porn,'" *Gawker*, April 29, 2008, http://gawker.com/385190/the-life-of-times-squares-mcdonalds-of-porn.

9. Samuel R. Delany, *Times Square Red, Times Square Blue* (New York: New York University Press, 1999).

10. Graney, Grossman, Colosimo, and Associates, *Erie County Demographic Study* (Grove City, PA: privately published, 2003), 34–36.

11. Audacia Ray, "7 Key American Sex Worker Activist Projects," http://www.wakingvixen.com/blog/2009/07/29/7-key-american-sex-worker-activist-projects/.

12. Kate Hausbeck et al., "Sex Industry and Sex Workers in Nevada," in *Social Health of Nevada: Leading Indicators and Quality of Life in the Silver State*, ed. Kate Hausbeck, Barbara Brents, and Crystal Jackson (University of Nevada at Las Vegas: CDC Publications, 2006), http://cdclv.unlv.edu/healthnv/sexindustry.html.

13. Labor Policy Issues, San Francisco Task Force on Prostitution, *The San Francisco Task Force on Prostitution: Final Report* (1996), http://www.bayswan.org/8labor.html.

14. Jessica Weisberg, "'Fifty Shades of Grey': The How-To Class," *New Yorker*, May 22, 2012.

15. Jonathan Coopersmith, "Pornography, Technology and Progress," *ICON* 4 (1998): 97–125.

16. Barrows, *Mayflower Madam*, 45.

17. Michael Fleeman, "Love for Sale Dot Com: Surfing for Prostitutes on the Internet," Associated Press, July 20, 1996.

18. Associated Press, "Want to Block Those 976 Calls? Pacific Bell Will Do It," *Los Angeles Times*, January 21, 1988.

19. Will Sommer, "D.C.'s Oldest Living Smut Kingpin Tells All," *Washington City Paper*, September 17, 2010.

20. Holman W. Jenkins Jr., "Pornography, Main Street to Wall Street," *Policy Review*, February 1, 2001, http://www.hoover.org/publications/policy-review/article/7065.

21. Linda Williams, *Hard Core Power, Pleasure, and the "Frenzy of the Visible"* (Berkeley: University of California Press, 1989), 63.

22. Candida Royalle, "What's a Nice Girl Like You," in Taormino et al., *Feminist Porn Book*, 63.

23. "MOSex Hosts Reunion of World's 1st Porn Star Support Group; The Club 90 Girls Are Back in New York!" *Adult Video News*, May 31, 2012.

24. Jill Nagle, "First Ladies of Feminist Porn: A Conversation with Candida Royalle and Debi Sundahl," in Nagle, *Whores and Other Feminists*, 158.

25. "Ms. Naughty," "My Decadent Decade: Ten Years of Making and Debating Porn for Women," in Taormino et al., *Feminist Porn Book*, 74.

26. Bright, *Big Sex, Little Death*, location 3005.

27. Annalee Newitz, "Obscene Feminists: Why Women Are Leading the Battle against Censorship," *San Francisco Bay Guardian*, May 8, 2002.

28. Danni Ashe, "On Learning How to Launch the Most Popular Adult Web Site from Working at Strip Club," in Milne, *Naked Ambition*, 221–31; Frederick S. Lane, *Obscene Profits: The Entrepreneurs of Pornography in the Cyber Age* (New York: Routledge, 2000), 221.

29. Theresa M. Senft, *Camgirls: Celebrity and Community in the Age of Social Networks* (New York: Lang, 2008), 81.

30. Audacia Ray, *Naked on the Internet: Hookups, Downloads, and Cashing In on Internet Sexploration* (Emeryville, CA: Seal Press, 2007), 136.

31. Naomi Akers interviews Melissa Gira Grant, "Episode 1: Pandering for Our Health," July 9, 2008, RenegadeCast, http://renegadecast.wordpress.com/2008/07/09/hello-world/.

32. Melissa Gira Grant, "She Was A Camera," *Rhizome*, October 26, 2011.

33. "The Alt-Porn Issue," *$pread*, Summer 2009.

34. Annie Tomlin, "Sex, Dreads, and Rock 'n' Roll," *Bitch*, December 2002.

35. Timothy Egan, "Erotica Inc. A Special Report; Technology Sent Wall Street Into Market for Pornography," *New York Times*, October 23, 2000.

36. Stacy Reed, "All Stripped Off," in Nagle, *Whores and Other Feminists*, 183–85; Theresa Flynt, "On Helping Restructure the Hustler Empire," in *Naked Ambition*, 255–62; Eva Pendleton, "Domesticating Partnerships," in Colter and Glenn, *Policing Public Sex*, 373–93.

37. Judith Lynne Hanna, *Naked Truth: Strip Clubs, Democracy, and a Christian Right* (Austin: University of Texas Press, 2012).

38. City of Erie v. Pap's A.M. TDBA "Kandyland," 529 US 277 (2000).

39. Jenness, *Making It Work*, 57.

40. Josh Sides, "Excavating the Postwar Sex District in San Francisco," *Journal of Urban History* 26, no. 32 (2006): 355.

41. Gayle Rubin, "Elegy for the Valley of the Kings: AIDS and the Leather Community in San Francisco, 1981–1996," in *In Changing Times: Gay Men and Lesbians Encounter HIV/AIDS*, ed. Martin P. Levine, Peter M. Nardi, and John H. Gagnon (Chicago: University of Chicago Press, 1997), 101–44; Sides, *Erotic City*.

42. Richard Meislin, "Metro Matters; Filtering the Dirt from the Energy of Times Square," *New York Times*, August 31, 1987.

43. Dylan Ryan, "Fucking Feminism," in Taormino et al., *Feminist Porn Book*, 123–24.

44. Judy Goldberg Dey and Catherine Hill, "Behind the Pay Gap" (Washington, DC: AAUW, 2007), 20, http://www.WageProject.org.

45. Jo Weldon, "Show Me the Money: A Sex Worker Reflects on Research into the Sex Industry," in *Sex Work Matters: Exploring Money, Power, and Intimacy in the Sex Industry*, ed. Melissa Ditmore et al. (London: Zed Books, 2010), 147–48.

46. Miss Mary Ann, "Labor Organizing in the Skin Trade: Tales of a Peepshow Prole," Exotic Dancers Union, http://web.archive.org/web/20050313084238/http://www.eda-sf.org/pages/EDUarticle.html.

47. Reverend Jen, *Live Nude Elf: The Sexperiments of Reverend Jen* (Brooklyn, NY: Soft Skull Press, 2009).

48. Jill Brenneman, "Donna M. Hughes, Censoring Craigslist, the Street," *Sex Workers Without Borders*, November 2, 2010, http://sexworkerswithoutborders.org /donna-m-hughes-censoring-craigslist-the-street/.

49. Rosie Campbell and Maggie O'Neill, *Sex Work Now* (Cullompton, UK: Willan, 2006), xi–xxi; Eileen McLeod, *Women Working: Prostitution Now* (London: Croom Helm, 1982).

50. Wendy Chapkis, *Live Sex Acts: Women Performing Erotic Labor* (New York: Routledge, 1997).

51. Jennifer Schuessler, "Game Theory: Jane Austen Had It First," *New York Times*, April 22, 2013.

52. Julia Query, John Montoya, and Vicky Funari, dir., *Live Nude Girls Unite!* (Brooklyn, NY: First Run/Icarus Films, 2001).

53. Leigh, *Unrepentant Whore*, 25.

54. Siobhan Brooks, "Solid Gold Dancer: An Interview with Gina Gold," *Bitch*, Winter 2000.

55. Maia, *Transnational Desires*, 9.

56. Ibid., 63.

57. Elizabeth Bernstein, "Buying and Selling the 'Girlfriend Experience': The Social and Subjective Contours of Market Intimacy," in *Love and Globalization: Transformations of Intimacy in the Contemporary World*, ed. Mark B. Padilla, Jennifer S. Hirsch, Miguel Munoz-Laboy, and Robert Sember (Nashville, TN: Vanderbilt University Press, 2007), 186–202.

58. Ibid., 192.

59. Anna Holmes, "The Disposable Woman," *New York Times*, March 3, 2011.

60. Clarisse Thorn, "Portrait of a Sugar Baby," *Role/Reboot*, January 5, 2012, http://www.rolereboot.org/sex-and-relationshipsdetails/2012-01-portrait-of-a -sugar-baby.

61. Bryce, "The Daisy Chain."

62. Kerwin Kay, "Naked but Unseen: Sex and Labor Conflict in San Francisco's Adult Entertainment Theaters," *Sexuality and Culture* 3 (1999): 52.

63. Cobble, "More Intimate Unions," in Boris and Parreñas, *Intimate Labors*, 283.

64. Ann Bartow, "*Jespersen v. Harrah's:* Firing of Woman Who Refused to Wear Make-Up Is Upheld," *Feminist Law Professors*, April 14, 2006, http://www .feministlawprofessors.com.

65. Dianne Avery and Marion Crain, "Branded: Corporate Image, Sexual Stereotyping, and The New Face of Capitalism," *Duke Journal of Law, Gender and Policy* 14 (2007): 87; Bernstein, *Temporarily Yours*, 79.

66. Miss Mary Ann, "Labor Organizing."

67. Cobble, "More Intimate Unions," 290.

68. Dorothy Sue Cobble, *Dishing It Out* (Urbana: University of Illinois Press, 1991), 127–29.

69. Kathryn L. Scott, *The Bunny Years* (Los Angeles: Pomegranate Press, 1998).

70. Lyndall MacCowan, "Organizing in the Massage Parlor: An Interview with Denise Turner," in Nagle, *Whores and Other Feminists*, 233.

71. Gayle Rubin with Judith Butler, "Interview: Sex Traffic," *Differences: A Journal of Feminist Cultural Studies* 6 (1994): 73–75.

72. Ibid., 75.

73. MacCowan, "Organizing in the Massage Parlor," in Nagle, *Whores and Other Feminists*.

74. Ai-jen Poo and E. Tammy Kim, "Advocacy Note: Organizing to Transform Ourselves and Our Laws: The New York Domestic Workers Bill of Rights Campaign," *Journal of Poverty Law and Policy* (March–April 2011).

75. Vicky Funari, "Naked, Naughty, Nasty: Peep Show Reflections," 19–35; Eva Pendleton, "Love for Sale: Queering Heterosexuality," 73–82; Tawnya Dudas, "Peepshow Feminism," 98–118; Nina Hartley, "In the Flesh: A Porn Star's Journey," 57–65; Carol Queen, "Sex Radical Politics: Sex-Positive Feminist Thought and Whore Stigma," 125–35; Veronica Monet, "Sedition," 217–22; Siobhan Brooks, "Dancing toward Freedom," 252–55, all in Nagle, *Whores and Other Feminists.*

76. Lori Leibovich, "Happy Hooker on the Hustings: An Only-in-San-Francisco Story That Could Have Legs," Salon.com, November 4, 1996.

77. Paulina Borsook, "How the Internet Ruined San Francisco," Salon.com, October 28, 1999.

78. David Steinberg, "Lap Dancing in San Francisco and the Evolving Face of Sex Work in America," Comes Naturally column, *San Francisco Spectator*, September 16, 2004.

79. Kay, "Naked but Unseen," 39.

80. Michael Jonas, "Lone Rangers," *Commonwealth* (Summer 2005): 62.

81. McCumber, *X-Rated*, 132.

82. Kay, "Naked but Unseen," 51.

83. McCumber, *X-Rated*, 133.

84. Kay, "Naked but Unseen," 41.

85. "Ask Fanny," from *On Our Backs* (May/June 1990), in McCumber, *X-Rated*, 136.

86. Ibid., 139.

87. Kamala Kempadoo, "The Exotic Dancers Alliance: An Interview with Dawn Passar and Johanna Breyer," in *Global Sex Workers: Rights, Resistance, and Redefinition*, ed. Kamala Kempadoo and Jo Doezema (New York: Routledge, 1998), 182–91.

88. Ibid.

89. Exotic Dancers' Alliance, "Interview with Dawn Passar by Siobhan Brooks," FoundSF, August 17, 2009, http://www.foundsf.org.

90. Kempadoo, "The Exotic Dancers Alliance," 188.

91. Steinberg, "Lap Dancing in San Francisco."

92. Bryce, "The Daisy Chain"; Ellen Vickery v. Cinema Seven, Inc. (Cal. App. 1 Dist.), 1996; Lily Burana, *Strip City: A Stripper's Farewell Journey across America* (New York: Hyperion, 2001).

93. Steinberg, "Lap Dancing in San Francisco."

94. David Johnston, "All Talk—No Sex: Studio Operator Accused of Cheating His Clients," *Los Angeles Times*, October 28, 1977.

95. Agence France-Presse, "San Francisco Sex Workers Demand Legal Protection," December 21, 2003.

96. "Interview with Dawn Passar."

97. Siobhan Brooks, "Exotic Dancing and Unionizing: The Challenges of Feminist and Antiracist Organizing at the Lusty Lady Theater," in *Feminism and Antiracism: International Struggles for Justice*, ed. Kathleen Blee and France Twine (New York: New York University Press, 2001), 59–71; Heidi M. Kooy, "Trollops and Tribades: Queers Organizing in the Sex Business," in *Out at Work: Building a Gay-Labor Alliance*, ed. Kitty Krupat and Patrick McCreery (Minneapolis: University of Minnesota Press, 2001), 133; Bernstein, *Temporarily Yours.*

98. Funari et al., *Live Nude Girls Unite!*; Vicky Funari, "Naked, Naughty, Nasty: Peep Show Reflections," in Nagle, *Whores and Other Feminists*; Tawnya Dudas,

"Peepshow Feminism," in Nagle, *Whores and Other Feminists*; Siobhan Brooks, "Dancing Toward Freedom," in Nagle, *Whores and Other Feminists*; Carol Queen, *Real Live Nude Girl: Chronicles of Sex-Positive Culture* (Pittsburgh: Cleis Press, 1997); Siobhan Brooks, *Unequal Desires: Race and Erotic Capital in the Stripping Industry* (Albany: State University of New York Press, 2010); Elisabeth Eaves, *Bare: On Women, Dancing, Sex, and Power* (New York: Alfred A. Knopf, 2002); Erika Langley, *The Lusty Lady* (Zurich: Scalo, 1997).

99. John Koopman, "Lusty Lady Becomes First Worker-Owned Strip Club; From Boas and High Heels to Boardrooms and High Finance," *San Francisco Chronicle*, June 26, 2003; Tad Friend, "Letter From California: Naked Profits," *New Yorker*, July 12, 2004, 56–61; Agreement Between Multivue, Inc. dba The Lusty Lady and the Local 1021, SEIU, June 15, 2011–February 28, 2013.

100. Cyprian Guild, http://web.archive.org/web/19981206220725/http://qadisha.com/guild.html.

101. Califia, "When Sex Is a Job," 54–56.

102. Final Report, "San Francisco Task Force on Prostitution"; Bernstein, *Temporarily Yours*, 37–39.

CHAPTER 6

1. INCITE! Women of Color Against Violence, *Law Enforcement Violence Against Women of Color & Trans People of Color: A Critical Intersection of Gender Violence and State Violence: An Organizer's Resource and Tool Kit* (Redmond, WA: INCITE! Women of Color Against Violence, n.d.), 25.

2. Joann Stevens, "The Boy-Whore World: Male Prostitutes Work D.C. Street Corners," *Washington Post*, October 7, 1980; Franklin Kameny, "Vive Nude Dancing," *Washington Post*, February 12, 1994.

3. Al Kamen, "Woman Gets Year in Jail as City Presses Anti-Prostitution Drive," *Washington Post*, August 13, 1981.

4. B. Drummond Ayres, "Prostitutes Walk the Streets, to Virginia," *New York Times*, July 27, 1989.

5. Scott Bowles, "D.C. Police Probe Link in 20 Deaths," *Washington Post*, September 5, 1995.

6. Ron Shaffer, "Prostitutes on Prowl," *Washington Post*, August 9, 1977.

7. Ylan Mui, "Family's Love Couldn't Save Her," *Washington Post*, August 2, 2002.

8. Bowles, "D.C. Police Probe Link."

9. Brian Mooar, "Vigil Marks Prostitution's Grim Toll; 22 Slain Streetwalkers Are Remembered at D.C. Candlelight Service," *Washington Post*, May 31, 1997.

10. Michael Colton, "A Street Walk for Prostitutes' Safety," *Washington Post*, June 1, 1998.

11. Peter Slevin, "D.C. Jury Sides with Prostitutes in Trial," *Washington Post*, November 20, 1998.

12. Ibid.; Stephanie Mencimer, "On Booty: A Rash of Sexual Misconduct Convictions Shows That D.C. Cops Are Flashing More Than Their Badges These Days," *Washington City Paper*, September 24, 1999.

13. Theola Labb-DeBose, "Sex Workers Criticize Law Enforcement," *Washington Post*, December 18, 2009.

14. Best Practices Policy Project et al., *Report on the United States of America*.

15. YWEP, *Denied Help*, 8; Jan Jordan, "What Would MacGyver Do? The Meaning(s) of Resistance and Survival," *Violence Against Women* 11 (2005): 531–59.

16. Miller, "'Your Life Is on the Line Every Night.'"

17. Catherine, "Army of Me: Sex Worker Self Defense," *Tits & Sass*, May 10, 2011, http://titsandsass.com/army-of-me-sex-worker-self-defense/.

18. "Seattle Grrrl Army Stands with Sex Workers," *Seattle Grrrl Army*, October 12, 2012, http://tmblr.co/Z5MTRuV9hfRd.

19. Miller, "'Your Life Is on the Line Every Night,'" 422.

20. Gayatri Chakravorty Spivak, "Can the Subaltern Speak?" in *Colonial Discourse and Postcolonial Theory: A Reader*, ed. Patrick Williams and Laura Chrisman (New York: Columbia University Press, 1994), 66–111.

21. Lawrence Friedman, *A History of American Law* (New York: Simon and Schuster, 1985), 585.

22. INCITE!, "Policing Sex Work," 25.

23. Jody Miller and Martin D. Schwartz, "Rape Myths and Violence against Street Prostitutes," *Deviant Behavior: An Interdisciplinary Journal* 16 (1995): 1–23.

24. Ibid., 10.

25. Angela Y. Davis, "Dialectics of Rape," in *Angela Y. Davis Reader*, 158.

26. Brownmiller, *Against Our Will*, 365–66.

27. Pheterson, "The Whore Stigma," 39–64.

28. Brownmiller, *Against Our Will*, 366.

29. Jane Gross, "203 Rape Cases Reopened in Oakland as the Police Chief Admits Mistakes," *New York Times*, September 20, 1990.

30. Wayne King, "Focus of Slaying Trial Had Humble Origins: Joan Little," *New York Times*, July 29, 1975; Genna Rae McNeil, "The Body, Sexuality, and Self-Defense in State vs. Joan Little, 1974-75," *Journal of African American History* 93 (2008): 235-61.

31. Davis, "Joanne Little: Dialectics of Rape," *Ms.*, May 1975, reprint: http://www.msmagazine.com/spring2002/davis.asp; Angela Davis, *Women, Race and Class* (New York: Random House, 1982), 152.

32. Mogul, Ritchie, and Whitlock, *Queer (In)Justice*.

33. Wayne King, "Joan Little's Attorney Scorns Legal System and Says He 'Bought' Her Acquittal," *New York Times*, October 20, 1975.

34. Ibid.

35. Angela Y. Davis, "Black Women in the Academy," in *Angela Y. Davis Reader*, 224–25.

36. Sears, "Introduction," 2.

37. Tyrone Kirchengast, *The Victim in Criminal Law and Justice* (Houndmills, Basingstoke, UK: Palgrave Macmillan, 2006), 73.

38. Fairstein, *Sexual Violence*, 172–73.

39. Andy Izenson, "Radicalizing Consent: Towards Implementing an Affirmative Consent Model in New York's Rape Law," *Yes Means Yes!*, June 12, 2012, http://yesmeansyesblog.wordpress.com.

40. Ibid.

41. Merle Hoffman Summer, "A Discussion with Liz Holtzman and Alice Vachss," *On the Issues*, Summer 1994, http://www.ontheissuesmagazine.com/.

42. Fairstein, *Sexual Violence*, 172–73.

43. Mogul, Ritchie, and Whitlock, *Queer (In)Justice*, 42–43.

44. Jason Gratl, "'Wouldn't Piss on Them If They Were On Fire': How Discrimination Against Sex Workers, Drug Users, and Aboriginal Women Enabled a Serial Killer," *Report of Independent Counsel to the Commissioner of the Missing Women Commission of Inquiry*, June 25, 2012, http://www.scribd.com/doc/103641727/Independent-Counsel-Report-to-Commissioner-of-Inquiry-August-16-2012.

45. Eugene Robinson, "Prostitutes Return Despite Sentence: Prostitutes Return to Logan Circle Despite One-Year Sentence," *Washington Post*, August 14, 1981.

46. Brian Mooar, "Prostitutes Fan Out as D.C. Police Crack Down on L Street Business," *Washington Post*, June 17, 1991; Joan Biskupic, "Court Upholds Criminal Forfeiture Law; States Can Seize Belongings Used in Offenses—Even If Owner Is Innocent," *Washington Post*, March 5, 1996.

47. Martin Weil, "Subject of Washington Post Series Dies," *Washington Post*, July 8, 1995; Leon Dash, *Rosa Lee: A Mother and Her Family in Urban America* (New York: Basic Books, 1996).

48. *Paula Zahn Now*, interview with Nick Broomfield, CNN transcripts, February 26, 2004, http://transcripts.cnn.com/TRANSCRIPTS/0402/26/pzn.01.html.

49. Aileen Carol Wuornos v. State of Florida, May 9, 1996, per curium at 2.

50. "There Are Women Political Prisoners in the USA," *Out of Control*, n.d., http://freedomarchives.org/Documents/Finder/DOC39_scans/39.what.is.pp.ooc.pdf.

51. Crossroad Support Network, "The Story of Aileen Wuornos," *Crossroad* 6, no. 3 (n.d.), http://web.archive.org/web/20010531222058/http://www.prisonactivist.org/pubs/crossroad/6.3/.

52. Aileen Wuornos, *Dear Dawn: Aileen Wuornos in Her Own Words*, ed. Lisa Kester and Daphne Gottlieb (Berkeley, CA: Soft Skull Press, 2012).

53. Chesler, "Sexual Violence Against Women."

54. Abbe Smith, "The 'Monster' in All of Us: When Victims Become Perpetrators," *Suffolk University Law Review* 38 (2005): 367, 378.

55. Phyllis Chesler, "Foreword," Wuornos, *Dear Dawn*, 5.

56. Chesler, "Sexual Violence Against Women."

57. Katheryn Russell-Brown, *Underground Codes: Race, Crime, and Related Fires* (New York: New York University Press, 2004), 37.

58. Quinet, "Prostitutes as Victims," 74–110.

59. Fairstein, *Sexual Violence*, 171.

60. Estate of Konerak Sinthasomphone v. Milwaukee, 785 F.Supp. 1343 USDC, E.D. Wisc. (1992).

61. Will Rockwell, "'No Humans Involved': Ending Violence Against Queer and Transgender Sex Workers," *Gay City News* (New York), January 5, 2011.

62. *Sinthasomphone v. Milwaukee*.

63. Mark Fuhrman, *Murder in Spokane: Catching a Serial Killer* (New York: Cliff Street Books, 2001).

64. Tomas Guillen, *Serial Killers: Issues Explored Through the Green River Murders* (Upper Saddle River, NJ: Pearson Prentice Hall, 2007).

65. Rule, *Green River, Running Red*, 36.

66. Ibid., 10.

67. King County [Washington] Sheriff's Department, Green River Homicides Investigation, http://www.kingcounty.gov/safety/sheriff/Enforcement/Investigations/GreenRiver.aspx, updated December 26, 2007.

68. Marilyn Bardsley, "Reckoning," *Crime Library*, http://www.trutv.com/library/crime/serial_killers/predators/greenriver/8.html.

69. Alan Feuer, "Guardians on the Streets of Despair; New Jersey Task Force Focuses on Crimes Against Prostitutes," *New York Times*, July 28, 1998.

70. Dawn S. Onley, "Sex-Assault Suspect Faces 79 Charges—Man Also Accused of Kidnapping, Theft," *Star-Ledger* (Newark, NJ), March 19, 1999.

71. Kate Zen, "The Merseyside Model, Part I: Can Sex Worker Activists Partner with the Police and a Conservative London Politician?" *Tits & Sass*, April 23, 2013, http://titsandsass.com/the-merseyside-model-part-i-can-sex-worker-activists-partner-with-the-police-and-a-conservative-london-politician/.

72. Ibid.

73. Jaclyn Gallucci, "Lost Girls: When Women Go Missing on LI Some Matter, Prostitutes Don't," *Long Island News*, October 21, 2010; Jaclyn Gallucci, "Without a Serial Killer, Dead Prostitutes Just Don't Matter," *Long Island News*, January 27, 2011.

74. Audacia Ray, "Protect, Don't Prosecute," http://www.redumbrellaproject.org/advocate/protect-dont-prosecute/.

75. Zen, "The Merseyside Model."

76. Robbie Brown, "Murder of Transgender Woman Revives Scrutiny," *New York Times*, November 17, 2008; Rockwell, "'No Humans Involved.'"

77. Alan Pittman, "Whitewash: Victims' Attorneys Blast City Report on Officer Sex Scandal," *Eugene (OR) Weekly*, March 29, 2007, http://www.eugeneweekly.com/2005/10/27/coverstory.

78. Alan Pittman, "New Chief Ignored Magaña Complaint," *Eugene Weekly*, October 9, 2008, http://www.eugeneweekly.com/2008/10/09/news.

79. Alan Pittman, "Top Cop Tarnished: Victim Alleged Kerns Ignored Cop Rape Complaint," *Eugene Weekly*, September 9, 2009, http://www.eugeneweekly.com/2009/09/03/news1.html.

80. David A. Fahrenthold, "Transgender Teens Killed on D.C. Street," *Washington Post*, August 13, 2002; Petula Dvorak, "Transgender Teens, Slain Last Year, Mourned at D.C. Vigil," *Washington Post*, September 18, 2002; Libby Copeland, "Mean Streets," *Washington Post*, August 14, 2002; Ylan Mui, "Vigil Marks Loss of Two Teens," *Washington Post*, August 14, 2002; Bob Moser, "Violence Engulfs Transgendered Population in D.C.," *Intelligence Report* (Southern Poverty Law Center), no. 112 (Winter 2003), http://www.splcenter.org.

81. Katie Urbaszewski, "NOPD Officer Found Guilty of Attempted Rape and Kidnapping," *New Orleans Times-Picayune*, February 15, 2011.

82. Katie Urbaszewski, "Trial Begins for New Orleans Police Officer Accused of Rape," *New Orleans Times-Picayune*, February 9, 2011.

83. Ibid.

84. Leonard N. Moore, *Black Rage in New Orleans: Police Brutality and African American Activism from World War II to Hurricane Katrina* (Baton Rouge: Louisiana State University Press, 2010), 39–40.

85. Civil Rights Division, US Department of Justice, "Investigation of the New Orleans Police Department," March 16, 2011, http://www.justice.gov/crt/about/spl/nopd_report.pdf.

86. Ibid., 45–46.

87. Sears, "Introduction," 1–6.

88. Amnesty International USA, *Stonewalled*, 40.

89. Dissent of Commissioner Russell Redenbaugh, US Commission on Civil Rights, *Revisiting Who Is Guarding the Guardians? A Report on Police Practices and Civil Rights in America* (Washington, DC: November 2000), 144.

90. Amnesty International USA, *Stonewalled*, 40.

91. GiGi Thomas testimony, February 23, 2006, in Alliance for a Safe & Diverse Washington, *Move Along*, 10.

92. Anna North, "In NYPD Custody, Trans People Get Chained to Fences and Poles," Jezebel.com, February 2, 2012.

93. The PROS Network and Sex Workers' Project, *Public Health Crisis: The Impact of Using Condoms as Evidence of Prostitution in New York City* (New York: PROS Network, April 2012), 11–12.

94. Califia, "When Sex Is a Job," 54, 56; Seth Hemmelgarn, "DA Agrees to New Condoms Policy," *Bay Area Reporter*, April 11, 2013.

95. PROS Network, *Public Health Crisis*, 11–12.

96. Megan McLemore, *Sex Workers at Risk: Condoms as Evidence of Prostitution in Four US Cities* (Washington, DC: Human Rights Watch, July 2012).

97. No Condoms as Evidence Coalition, http://www.nocondomsasevidence.org; PROS Network, *Public Health Crisis*, 21.

98. Open Society Institute, *Criminalizing Condoms: How Policing Practices Put Sex Workers and HIV Services at Risk in Kenya, Namibia, Russia, South Africa, the United States, and Zimbabwe* (New York: OSI Foundation, July 2012).

99. Heather Doyle, "Sex Workers and HIV: When Morality Trumps Science," June 7, 2011, http://www.soros.org/voices/sex-workers-and-hiv-when-morality-trumps-science.

100. Barbara A. Rockell, *Women Street Hustlers: Who They Are and How They Survive* (Washington, DC: American Psychological Association, 2008); Miller, "'Your Life Is on the Line Every Night.'"

101. Andrea Smith, "Beyond Restorative Justice: Radical Organizing Against Violence," in *Restorative Justice and Violence Against Women*, ed. James Ptacek (New York: Oxford University Press, 2010), 258.

102. YWEP, *Girls Do What They Have to Do*, 15.

103. Gail Garfield, *Knowing What We Know: African American Women's Experiences of Violence and Violation* (New Brunswick, NJ: Rutgers University Press, 2005), 13.

104. Audrey Doe et al. v. Bobby Jindal, US D.C. Eastern District of Louisiana, February 15, 2011, 14–15.

105. Miller, "'Your Life Is on the Line Every Night.'"

106. Ronald Weitzer, "Flawed Theory and Method in Studies of Prostitution," *Violence Against Women* 11, no. 7 (July 2005): 934–49.

107. Ibid., 942.

108. Sea Ling Cheng, "Commentary on Hughes, Chon, Ellerman," *Violence Against Women* 14, no. 3 (2008): 359–63; Donna M. Hughes, Katherine Y. Chon, and Derek P. Ellerman, "Modern-Day Comfort Women: The US Military, Transnational Crime, and the Trafficking of Women," *Violence Against Women* 13, no. 9 (September 2007): 901–22.

109. YWEP, *Denied Help*, 7.

110. YWEP, *Girls Do What They Have to Do*, 20.

111. Gail Garfield, *Knowing What We Know*, 13.

112. YWEP, *Girls Do What They Have to Do*, 15.

113. Ibid., 36.

114. YWEP, *Denied Help*, 11.

115. Ibid., 31.

116. Smith, "Beyond Restorative Justice," 269.

117. Jennifer Moore, "Vea Cleary YWEP Ally from the Broadway Youth Center in Chicago," YouTube, June 24, 2010, http://www.youtube.com/watch?v=YyQK9dGUsRM.

118. YWEP, *Girls Do What They Have to Do*, 12.

119. Smith, "Beyond Restorative Justice," 256.

120. Center for Constitutional Rights, "Louisiana's Crime Against Nature Law: A Modern-Day Scarlet Letter," 2011, http://ccrjustice.org/scarletletter.

121. "Prostitution Law Breakthrough Overturned," *off our backs*, December 31, 1974, 5.

122. *Doe v. Jindal*, 14–15.

123. Pamela Coyle, "400 Sex Offenders in Region; Web Site Lists Many in N.O.; 44% Probably Prostitutes," *New Orleans Times-Picayune*, May 2, 2000.

124. Jordan Flaherty, "Her Crime? Sex Work in New Orleans," *Colorlines*, January 13, 2010, http://www.colorlines.com; Jordan Flaherty, "Federal Civil Rights Suit Challenges Louisiana's Felony Sex Work Law," *Colorlines*, March 17, 2011.

125. *Doe v. Jindal*, 5.

126. Jacqueline Lewis, "Shifting the Focus: Restorative Justice and Sex Work," *Canadian Journal of Criminology and Criminal Justice* 52 (June 2010): 285–301.

127. *Doe v. Jindal*, 5.

128. "POM Offender Locator," by GoVision20/20.com, a division of ThinAirWireless .com, Version 3.0.

129. Ibid.

130. NO Justice, *"Just a Talking Crime": A Policy Brief in Support of the Repeal of Louisiana's Solicitation of a Crime Against Nature (SCAN) Statute* (New Orleans: Women With A Vision, February 2011).

131. "SCAN Victory in the Louisiana House!!," Women With A Vision, June 6, 2011, http://wwav-no.org/june-6th-victory-in-the-house.

132. "New Orleans Groups Applaud Change in 'Scarlet Letter' Law," Women With A Vision, June 29, 2011, http://wwav-no.org/new-orleans-groups-applaud-change-in -"scarlet-letter"-law.

133. "Groups Ask Court to Remove Individuals Convicted of Crime Against Nature by Solicitation from Sex Offender Registry," news release, Women With A Vision, August 10, 2011, http://wwav-no.org.

134. Center for Constitutional Rights, "Louisiana Must 'Cease and Desist,'" news release, April 12, 2012, http://ccrjustice.org.

135. "OUR WIN: Letter from Executive Director Deon Haywood," Women With A Vision, March 30, 2012, http://wwav-no.org/our-win-letter-from-executive-director -deon-haywood.

CHAPTER 7

1. Favianna Rodriguez, "Take ur conservative laws and go F*** yourself! 3 New Posters for the Woman Bashing Year," Favianna.com, http://favianna.typepad.com /faviannacom_art_activism/2012/03/take-ur-conservative-laws-and-go-f-yourself-3-new-posters-for-the-woman-bashing-year.html; Erin Gloria Ryan, "President Calls Sandra Fluke, Tells Her That Her Parents Should Be Proud," Jezebel.com, March 2, 2012.

2. Bright, *Big Sex, Little Death*, location 3144.

3. Ibid., 3400–3401.

4. Annette Insdorf, "A 'Working Girls' Boswell," *Los Angeles Times*, April 7, 1987.

5. Monica Shores, "The Best Movies About Sex Work," Alternet, February 17, 2009, http://www.alternet.org/story/127421/the_best_movies_about_sex_work.

6. Mark O'Brien, *Reimaging America: The Arts of Social Change* (Philadelphia: New Society Publishers, 1990), 1–8, 306.

7. "International: The Unhappy Hookers," *Newsweek*, February 12, 1973; "The World: The Unhappy Hookers," *Time*, June 16, 1975.

8. Frederique Delacoste, "Les Putes Sont En Grèves . . ." in Delacoste and Alexander, *Sex Work*, 12.

9. Jennifer Gilley, "Writings of the Third Wave: Young Feminists in Conversation," *Reference & User Services Quarterly* 44, no. 3 (Spring 2005): 187–98.

10. Kate Ellis, Barbara O'Dair, and Abby Tallmer, "Introduction," in *Caught Looking: Feminism, Pornography & Censorship*, ed. Caught Looking, Inc. (Seattle: Real Comet Press, 1988), 6.

11. Bright, *Big Sex, Little Death*, location 3281.

12. Ibid., 3522–23.

13. Joan Kennedy Taylor, "Feminists for Free Expression," in Nagle, *Whores and Other Feminists*, 256–58; Feminists for Free Expression, "Prostitution," August 31, 2012, http://ffeusa.livejournal.com/42420.html.

14. Angela Johnson, "Start a Fucking Riot: Riot Grrrrl D.C.," *off our backs*, May 1993, 6.

15. London SlutWalk, "Who We Are," *Slut Means Speak Up*, http://slutmeansspeakup .org.uk/about.

16. "17-Year-Old Girl," SlutWalk Toronto, October 14, 2011, http://www .slutwalktoronto.com/im-not-trying-to-persuade-people-to-call-themselves-sluts.

17. Olive Seraphim, "How to Be a Feminist Ally to Sex Workers," April 2013, http:// oliveseraphim.wordpress.com/articles/how-to-be-a-feminist-ally-to-sex-workers/.

18. "About," http://www.feminisnt.com/.

19. Kathleen Barry, *Female Sexual Slavery* (Englewood Cliffs, NJ: Prentice-Hall, 1979).

20. Gail Pheterson, *A Vindication of the Right of Whores* (Seattle: Seal Press, 1989).

21. Gayle Rubin, "Anti-Porn Laws and Women's Liberation: Censored," *Gay Community News* (Boston), December 22, 1984.

22. Evelina Giobbe and B. Julie Johnson, letter to the editor, *Women's Review of Books* 7 (July 1990): 10–11.

23. Ruth Rosen and Sue Davidson, eds., *The Maimie Papers* (Old Westbury, NY: Feminist Press, 1977); Sheila Rothman, "The Limits of Sisterhood," *Reviews in American History* 7, no. 1 (March 1979): 92–97.

24. William A. Henkin, "Review of *A Vindication of the Rights of Whores*," Sexuality.org, 1989, reposted http://www.sexuality.org/authors/henkin/whvindic.html.

25. Edward DeGrazia, *Girls Lean Back Everywhere: The Law of Obscenity and the Assault on Genius* (New York: Random House, 1992), 594–95.

26. *US Attorney General's Commission on Pornography*, 886.

27. Pheterson, "Whore Stigma," 60.

28. International Network of Sex Work Projects, "History," http://www.nswp.org /page/history.

29. "UNAIDS Terminology Guidelines," revised (Geneva: USAIDS, October 2011), 26.

30. Wendy Babcock, "Girls," *Lover Magazine*, August 4, 2011, http://lovermagazine .ca/2011/08/girls.

31. Melissa Gira Grant, "The War on Sex Workers," *Reason*, January 21, 2013, http:// reason.com/archives/2013/01/21/the-war-on-sex-workers.

32. Tiffany Williams, "The Dual Mandate: Immigration Enforcement and Human Trafficking," Break the Chains Campaign, Institute for Policy Studies, January 10, 2013.

33. Lori Adorable, "What Antis Can Do to Help, Part One: Aiding Those Still in the Industry," *Tits & Sass*, March 19, 2013, http://titsandsass.com/what-antis-can-do -to-help-part-one-aiding-those-still-in-the-industry.

34. Maggie McNeill, *The Honest Courtesan* (blog), reposted, http://slutwalkseattle .com/post/24834383235/the-claim-that-sex-workers-sell-our-bodies-is.

35. Melissa Farley, "The Opposition's Opening Remarks," *Economist*, September 6, 2010, http://www.economist.com/debate/days/view/572; EmpowerThailand, comment, posted September 12, 2010, https://www.economist.com/user/3834142/comments.

36. Shannon Bell et al., *Bad Attitude on Trial: Pornography, Feminism, and the Butler Decision* (Toronto: University of Toronto Press, 1997).

37. Catharine MacKinnon, "Prostitution and Civil Rights Symposium: From Academia to Activism," *Michigan Journal of Gender and Law* 1 (1993) 13–32; Patricia Williams, closing address, "Speech, Equality, and Harm: Feminist Legal Perspectives on Pornography and Hate Propaganda," reported in *off our backs*, May 1993, 5.

38. Jacobsen, "Fighting for Visibility," 135–41.

39. Ibid., 137; S.3063, "Pornography Victims Protection Act of 1984," sponsored by Sen. Arlen Specter.

40. "Carol Leigh's Response," *Prostitution in Film*, WMST-L discussion, March 1995, http://userpages.umbc.edu/fflkorenman/wmst/sexwork_film.html.

41. Tamar Levin, "Furor on Exhibit at Law School Splits Feminists," *New York Times*, November 13, 1992.

42. Anonymous, "A Narrative by a Former 'Call Girl,'" *Michigan Journal of Gender and Law* 1 (1993): 105–6.

43. Evelina Giobbe, "An Analysis of Individual, Institutional, and Cultural Pimp- ing," *Michigan Journal of Gender and Law* 1 (1993): 33–57.

44. "Carol Leigh's Response."

45. Jacobsen, "Fighting for Visibility," 140.

46. *P.C. Casualties* (Spring 1991), cited in S. Brun Austin with Pam Gregg, "A Freak Among Freaks: The 'Zine Scene," in *Sisters, Sexperts, Queers: Beyond The Lesbian Na- tion*, ed. Arlene Stein (New York: Plume, 1993), 87.

47. Lisa Duggan, "Queering the State," in *Sex Wars: Sexual Dissent and Political Culture*, ed. Lisa Duggan and Nan D. Hunter (New York: Routledge, 2006), 175.

48. Elena Kagan, "Regulation of Hate Speech and Pornography after R.A.V.," *Uni- versity of Chicago Law Review* 60, nos. 3/4 (Summer-Autumn 1993): 873–902.

49. Williams, "Speech, Equality and Harm."

50. Ibid.

51. Lee Bey, "Prostitutes Protest at U. of C. Law Conference," *Chicago Sun-Times*, March 7, 1993.

52. Williams, "Speech, Equality, and Harm," 5; Catharine MacKinnon, "Speech, Equality, and Harm: The Case Against Pornography," in *The Price We Pay: The Case Against Racist Speech, Hate Propaganda, and Pornography*, ed. Laura Lederer and Rich- ard Delgado (New York: Hill and Wang, 1995).

53. Patricia J. Williams, *Alchemy of Race and Rights* (Cambridge, MA: Harvard University Press, 1991), 73.

54. Kris Kovik, "What Is Women's Music? Whine, Women-Only and Song," *Hot Wire* 9, no. 1 (January 1993): 44.

55. Jennifer Baumgardner, "Kathleen Hanna's Eye of Le Tigre," *Rockrgrl* 36 (November/December 2000): 25–28.

56. Mark Andersen and Mark Jenkins, *Dance of Days: Two Decades of Punk in the Nation's Capital* (New York: Akashic Books, 2003), 308.

57. Ibid., 317.

58. Michelle Tea, "Good Intentions, Mixed Results at Olympia's Sex Workers' Art Show," *Stranger*, February 20–26, 2003, http://web.archive.org/petabox/20061112110246 /http://www.mercyzine.com/workers.cfm.

59. Ibid.

60. Chris Kraus, "Sex Workers' Art Show," February 7, 2008, *Reality Sandwich*, http://www.realitysandwich.com.

61. David Henry Sterry, "Sexual Free-For-All Lets It All Hang Out," *San Francisco Chronicle*, January 11, 2004, http://www.sfgate.com/.

62. Lotta Tess, "The Sex Worker's Art Show Takes It on the Road," *Media Cake* (on-line magazine) 1 (2007), http://www.mediacakemagazine.com/cake_spring_07_002.htm.

63. Tara Perkins, "Sex Workers' Art Show Tour Reunion!" December 2012, http:// www.indiegogo.com/projects/sex-workers-art-show-tour-reunion.

64. Toni Bentley, "Meet, Pay, Love," *New York Times*, August 23, 2009.

65. Caty Simons, "Activist Spotlight: Audacia Ray, on Telling Stories and the Tricky Politics of Inclusion," *Tits & Sass*, March 20, 2013. http://titsandsass.com/activist-spotlight-audacia-ray-on-the-red-umbrella-project-telling-stories-teaching-advocacy-and-the-tricky-politics-of-inclusion/.

66. Audacia Ray, "Progress! A Report on No Condoms as Evidence Lobby Day in Albany," news release, April 24, 2013; Red Umbrella Project, "Stories of Condom Confis-cation and Police Harassment," http://www.redumbrellaproject.org/nycondom.

67. Richard Meyer, *Outlaw Representation: Censorship & Homosexuality in Twentieth-Century American Art* (New York: Oxford University Press, 2002), 234–37; Prostitutes of New York (PONY) collaborated with Gran Fury of ACT UP on "Love for Sale . . . Free Condoms Inside," Spring 1991, http://archive.newmuseum.org; Melissa Ditmore, "Oscar Buzz: How to Survive a Plague, and the History of Sex Workers with ACT UP," January 25, 2013, http://blogs.poz.com/melissaditmore/.

68. Furry Girl, "SWAAY's Pro-Sex Worker Billboard Rejected by All Major Ad Companies, but Launching Soon!" October 13, 2011, http://www.Feminisnt.com.

69. Shared Hope International, "Do You Know Lacy? National Billboard Cam-paign," http://sharedhope.org/what-we-do/prevent/awareness/.

70. Elena Jeffreys et al., "Listen To Sex Workers: Support Decriminalisation and Anti-Discrimination Protections," *Interface: A Journal for and about Social Movements*, Strategy Contribution, 3, no. 2 (November 2011): 271–87; Marlise Richter, "Sex Work as a Test Case for African Feminism," *BUWA! A Journal of African Women's Experiences* (October 2012): 62–69.

71. Renegade Evolution, "Sex Work Activism: Topic One, Harm Reduction," *Feministe*, August 19, 2008, http://www.feministe.us/blog/archives/2008/08/19 /sex-work-activism-topic-one-harm-reduction/.

72. "What Is Hook?" HOOK Online, http://www.hookonline.org/home /whatishook.HTM.

73. Janet R. Jakobsen and Elizabeth Lapovsky Kennedy, "Sex and Freedom," in *Regulating Sex: The Politics of Intimacy and Identity*, ed. Elizabeth Bernstein and Laurie Schaffner (New York: Routledge, 2005), 253.

74. Catherine Stimpson, "Dirty Minds, Dirty Bodies, Clean Speech," in *Unfettered Expression: Freedom in American Intellectual Life*, ed. Peggie J. Hollingsworth (Ann Arbor: University of Michigan Press, 2000).

75. Scott Dagostino, "Splitsville: Queers Launch Alternatives to Official Pride Toronto Events," *Xtra*, June 3, 2010, http://www.xtra.ca/public/National/Splitsville _Queers_launch_alternatives_to_official_Pride_Toronto_events-8740.aspx; Kate Zieman, "The Dyke March—Looking Back," *Queeries*, June 30, 2011, http://queeriesmag .com/index.php/2011/06/30/the-dyke-march-looking-back/; "Take Back the Dyke Takes over Toronto Streets," *Xtra*, July 5, 2010, http://www.xtra.ca/public/National /Take_Back_the_Dyke_takes_over_Toronto_streets-8880.aspx.

76. Tracy Clark-Flory, "How Technology Is Actually Changing Sex Work; Prostitutes Call Foul on a Recent Report That Facebook Is the 'New Craigslist,'" February 12, 2011, *Salon*, http://www.salon.com/2011/02/12/facebook_prostitution/.

77. Jaime Woo, "At SlutWalkTO, Sisters Are Doin' It for Themselves," *Torontoist*, April 4, 2011, http://torontoist.com/.

78. Ibid.

79. Colleen Westendorf and Heather Jarvis, "SWTO," speech, 2012 National Sexual Assault Conference in Chicago, http://www.slutwalktoronto.com/slutwalk-toronto-speech-from-the-2012-national-sexual-assault-conference-in-chicago-nsac2012.

80. Lauren Michelle McNicol, "'SlutWalk Is 'Kind of Like Feminism': A Critical Reading of Canadian Mainstream News Coverage of SlutWalk," master's thesis, Queen's University, Ontario, Canada, 2012, 91.

81. Stoya™, "I'm a Porn Star, and If You Harass Me I Will Punch You in the Balls," *Jezebel*, September 10, 2012, http://jezebel.com/5941068/im-a-porn-star-and-if-you-harass -me-i-will-punch-you-in-the-balls.

82. Ginia Bellafante, "Arrests by the Fashion Police," *New York Times*, April 5, 2013; Wendy Ruderman, "For Women in Street Stops, Deeper Humiliation," *New York Times*, August 6, 2012.

83. Rachel Aimee, author interview, July 24, 2011, Brooklyn, NY.

84. Hugo Schwyzer, "Feminism, Porn, and SlutWalk: Part One of a Conversation with Meghan Murphy," June 13, 2011, http://www.hugoschwyzer.net/2011/06/13 /feminism-porn-and-slutwalk-part-one-of-a-conversation-with-meghan-murphy/.

85. PACE (Vancouver, BC), "SlutWalk," *Newsletter* 2 (Summer 2011): 3, http://www .pace-society.org/library/pace-newsletter/summer-2011.pdf.

86. Shira Tarrant in Melanie Klein, "To Reclaim Slut or Not To Reclaim Slut: Is That the Question?" May 20, 2011, *Ms.* magazine blog, http://msmagazine.com/blog /2011/05/20/to-reclaim-slut-or-not-to-reclaim-slut-is-that-the-question; Gail Dines and Wendy J. Murphy, "SlutWalk Is Not Sexual Liberation," *Guardian* (UK), May 8, 2011.

87. "SlutWalks v. Ho Strolls," Crunk Feminist Collective, May 23, 2011, http://www .crunkfeministcollective.com/2011/05/23/slutwalks-v-ho-strolls.

88. Yasmin Nair, "Is Slutwalk the End of Feminism?," http://www.yasminnair.net /content/slutwalk-end-feminism.

89. Andrea Smith, "Heteropatriarchy and Three Pillars of White Supremacy," in *The Color of Violence: The INCITE! Anthology* (Cambridge, MA: South End Press, 2006), 66–73; Heather Jarvis, "Racism and Anti-Racism: Why They Matter to SlutWalks," SlutWalk Toronto, October 31, 2011, http://www.slutwalktoronto.com/racism-and -anti-racism.

90. "Maggie's Responds to Death of Kera Freeland," Maggie's, March 24, 2011, http://maggiestoronto.ca/.

91. Native Women's Association of Canada, Sisters in Spirit, *What Their Stories Tell Us: Research Findings from the Sisters In Spirit Initiative* (Ohsweken, Ontario: Native Women's Association of Canada, 2010), 31.

92. Stella (Montreal), "The Basics: Decriminalization of Sex Work 101," April 2013, http://www.chezstella.org/docs/StellaInfoSheetTheBasic.pdf.

93. Doug Hempstead, "Ottawa Sex-Worker Advocates Applaud Ruling," *Ottawa Sun*, September 28, 2010.

94. "Ontario Court Leaves Most Vulnerable Sex Workers Unprotected," Maggie's, news release, March 26, 2012, http://maggiestoronto.ca/press-releases?news_id=49.

SELECTED BIBLIOGRAPHY

Alexander, Priscilla. "A Chronology of Sorts." In Rieder and Ruppelt, *AIDS*.

Alliance for a Safe and Diverse Washington, DC. *Move Along: Policing Sex Work in Washington, DC*. Washington, DC: Different Avenues, 2008.

Allyn, David. *Make Love, Not War: The Sexual Revolution, an Unfettered History*. New York: Little, Brown, 2000.

Almodovar, Norma Jean. "For Their Own Good: The Results of Prostitution Laws as Enforced by Cops, Politicians and Judges." *Hastings Women's Law Journal* 10 (1999).

Amnesty International USA. *Stonewalled: Police Abuse and Misconduct Against Lesbian, Gay, Bisexual and Transgender People in the US*. New York: Amnesty International USA, 2005.

Armstrong, Elizabeth. *Forging Gay Identities: Organizing Sexuality in San Francisco, 1950–1994*. Chicago: University of Chicago Press, 2003.

Armstrong, Elizabeth, and Suzanna Crage. "Movements and Memory: The Making of the Stonewall Myth." *American Sociological Review* 71 (2006): 7241–7251.

Barrows, Sydney Biddle. *Mayflower Madam: The Secret Life of Sydney Biddle Barrows*. New York: Ivy Books, 1987.

Benjamin, Harry. *The Transsexual Phenomenon*. New York: Julian, 1966.

Bernstein, Elizabeth. *Temporarily Yours: Intimacy, Authenticity, and the Commerce of Sex*. Chicago: University of Chicago Press, 2007.

Best Practices Policy Project et al. *Report on the United States of America, 9th Round of the Universal Periodic Review, November 2010*. March 30, 2010, http://www.bestpracticespolicy.org/resources/reports/.

Boris, Eileen, and Rhacel Salazar Parreñas. *Intimate Labors: Cultures, Technologies, and the Politics of Care*. Stanford, CA: Stanford Social Sciences, 2010.

Boyd, Nan Alamilla. *Wide-Open Town: A History of Queer San Francisco to 1965*. Berkeley: University of California Press, 2005.

Bright, Susie. *Big Sex, Little Death*. Berkeley, CA: Seal Press, 2011. Kindle edition, Santa Cruz, CA: Bright Stuff.

Brownmiller, Susan. *Against Our Will: Men, Women, and Rape*. New York: Simon and Schuster, 1975.

Bryce, Jennifer. "The Daisy Chain: Autobiography of an Activist." http://www.eda-sf.org/submissions/activist.html.

Califia, Pat. *Public Sex: The Culture of Radical Sex*. Pittsburgh: Cleis, 1994.

———. "When Sex Is a Job." *Out*, April 1999.

Cannato, Vincent. *The Ungovernable City: John Lindsay and His Struggle to Save New York*. New York: Basic Books, 2001.

Carmen, Arlene, and Howard Moody. *Working Women: The Subterranean World of Street Prostitution*. New York: Harper & Row, 1985.

Centers for Disease Control. "Perspectives in Disease Prevention and Health Promotion Public Health Service Guidelines for Counseling and Antibody Testing to Prevent HIV Infection and AIDS." *Morbidity and Mortality Weekly Report* 36, no. 31 (1987): 509–15.

Chesler, Phyllis. "Sexual Violence Against Women and a Woman's Right to Self-Defense: The Case of Aileen Carol Wuornos." *Criminal Practice Law Report*, October 1993. http://www.phyllis-chesler.com/114/sexual-violence-against-women-self-defense -wuornos.

Cobble, Dorothy Sue. "More Intimate Unions." In Boris and Parreñas, *Intimate Labors*.

Cohen, Judith B., Priscilla Alexander, and Constance B. Wofsy. "Prostitutes and AIDS: Public Policy Issues." *AIDS and Public Policy Journal* 3, no. 2 (1988): 16–22.

Cohen, Judith Blackfield, and Priscilla Alexander. "Female Sex Workers: Scapegoats in the AIDS Epidemic." In O'Leary and Sweet-Johnson, *Women and AIDS*.

Colter, Dan, and Ephen Glenn. *Policing Public Sex: Queer Politics and the Future of AIDS Activism*. Boston: South End Press, 1996.

Corea, Gena. *Invisible Epidemic: The Story of Women and AIDS*. New York: Perennial, 1993.

Davis, Angela Y. *The Angela Y. Davis Reader*. Malden, MA: Blackwell, 1998.

Delacoste, Frederique, and Priscilla Alexander, editors. *Sex Work: Writings by Women in the Sex Industry*. San Francisco: Cleis Press, 1987, 1998.

Dewey, Susan, and Patty Kelly. *Policing Pleasure: Sex Work, Policy, and the State in Global Perspective*. New York: New York University Press, 2011.

Duberman, Martin. *Stonewall*. New York: Plume, 1994.

Fairstein, Linda A. *Sexual Violence: Our War Against Rape*. New York: William Morrow, 1993.

Fee, Elizabeth, and Daniel M. Fox, editors. *AIDS: The Burden of History*. Berkeley: University of California Press, 1988.

French, Dolores. *Working: My Life as a Prostitute*. London: Victor Gollancz, 1997.

Friedan, Betty. *The Feminine Mystique*. New York: W. W. Norton, 1963.

Gall, Gregory. *Sex Worker Union Organizing: An International Study*. New York: Palgrave Macmillan, 2006.

Haft, Marilyn. "Hustling for Rights." *Civil Liberties Review* 2 (1974).

Hegarty, Marilyn E. *Victory Girls, Khaki-Wackies, and Patriotutes: The Regulation of Female Sexuality During World War II*. New York: New York University Press, 2008.

Hobson, Barbara Meil. *Uneasy Virtue: The Politics of Prostitution and the American Reform Tradition*. Chicago: University of Chicago Press, 1990.

Jacobsen, Carol. "Fighting for Visibility: Notes on the Censorship Battle of 'Porn' Imagery: Picturing Prostitutes." *Social Text* 37 (Winter 1993): 135–41.

James, Jennifer, Jean Withers, Marilyn G. Haft, and Sara Theiss. *Politics of Prostitution: Resources for Legal Change*. Seattle: Social Research Associates, 1977.

Jay, Karla, and Allen Young, editors. *Out of the Closets: Voices of Gay Liberation*. New York: New York University Press, 1992.

Jenness, Valerie. *Making It Work: The Prostitutes' Rights Movement in Perspective*. New York: Aldine de Gruyter, 1993.

Kaiser Family Foundation. *HIV/AIDS at 30: A Public Opinion Perspective*. Washington, DC: Kaiser Family Foundation, 2011.

Kay, Kerwin. "Naked but Unseen: Sex and Labor Conflict in San Francisco's Adult Entertainment Theaters." Special issue. *Sexuality and Culture* 3 (1999).

Kitsuse, John I. "Coming Out All Over: Deviants and the Politics of Social Problems." *Social Problems* 28 (1980): 1–13.

Leff, Walli F., and Marilyn G. Haft. *Time Without Work: People Who Are Not Working Tell Their Stories, How They Feel, What They Do, How They Survive*. Boston: South End Press, 1983.

Leigh, Carol. *Unrepentant Whore: The Collected Works of Scarlot Harlot*. San Francisco: Last Gasp, 2004.

Lockhart, William B., and Frederick H. Wagman. *The Report of the Commission on Obscenity and Pornography*. Washington, DC: US Government Printing Office, 1970.

Lutnick, Alexandra. "The St. James Infirmary: A History." *Sexuality & Culture* 10, no. 2 (Spring 2006): 56–75.

Maia, Suzana. *Transnational Desires: Brazilian Erotic Dancers in New York*. Nashville, TN: Vanderbilt University Press, 2012.

Masters, William H., and Virginia E. Johnson. *Human Sexual Response*. New York: Bantam Books, 1966.

McCumber, David. *X-Rated: The Mitchell Brothers; a True Story of Sex, Money, and Death*. New York: Simon & Schuster, 1992.

Meyerowitz, Joanne. *How Sex Changed: A History of Transsexuality in the United States*. Cambridge, MA: Harvard University Press, 2002.

Miller, Jody. "'Your Life Is on the Line Every Night You're on the Streets': Victimization and the Resistance among Street Prostitutes." *Humanity & Society* 17, no. 4 (1993): 422–46.

Millett, Kate. *The Prostitution Papers: A Candid Dialogue*. New York: Avon Books, 1973.

Milne, Carly, editor. *Naked Ambition: Women Who Are Changing Pornography*. New York: Carroll & Graf, 2005.

Mogul, Joey L., Andrea J. Ritchie, and Kay Whitlock. *Queer (In)Justice: The Criminalization of LGBT People in the United States*. Boston: Beacon Press, 2011.

Morgan, Bill. *North Beach Leathers: Tailors to the Stars*. San Mateo, CA: William Morgan Publishing, 2010.

Nagle, Jill, editor. *Whores and Other Feminists*. New York: Routledge, 1997.

National Coalition for LGBT Health and the Sexuality Information and Education Council of the United States (SIECUS). *Report on the United States of America, 9th Round of the Universal Periodic Review, November 2010*. Washington, DC: National Coalition for LGBT Health and the Sexuality Information and Education Council of the United States, 2010.

Nestle, Joan. "Lesbians and Prostitutes: A Historical Sisterhood." In Delacoste and Alexander, *Sex Work*.

O'Leary, A., and L. Sweet-Johnson. *Women and AIDS: The Emerging Epidemic*. New York: Plenum Publishing, 1995.

Oppenheimer, Gerald M. "In the Eye of the Storm: The Epidemiological Construction of AIDS." In Fee and Fox, *AIDS*.

Patton, Cindy. *Sex and Germs: The Politics of AIDS*. Montreal: Black Rose Books, 1986.

Pheterson, Gail. "Whore Stigma: Female Dishonor and Male Unworthiness." *Social Text* 37 (1993).

Piven, Frances Fox, and Richard A. Cloward. *Poor Peoples' Movements: Why They Succeed, How They Fail*. New York: Vintage, 1979.

Quinet, Kenna. "Prostitutes as Victims of Serial Homicide: Trends and Case Characteristics, 1970–2009." *Homicide Studies* 15 (2011): 74–100.

Radeloff, Cheryl, et al. "Sex Panics and the Regulation of Prostitution in Late Capitalism: The Origins of Nevada's HIV Policies for Prostitutes." Paper for the American Sociological Association, August 12, 2005.

Richie, Beth. "AIDS: In Living Color." In White, *Black Women's Health Book*.

Rieder, Ines, and Patricia Ruppelt. *AIDS: The Women*. San Francisco: Cleis Press, 1988.

Roby, Pamela, and Virginia Kerr. "The Politics of Prostitution." *Nation*. April 10, 1972, 463–66.

Rosenbleet, Charles, and Barbara J. Pariente. "The Prostitution of Criminal Law." *American Criminal Law Review* 11 (1973): 374.

Roth, Nancy L., and Katie Hogan, editors. *Gendered Epidemic: Representations of Women in the Age of AIDS*. New York: Routledge, 1998.

Rule, Ann. *Green River, Running Red: The Real Story of the Green River Killer, America's Deadliest Serial Murderer*. New York: Free Press, 2004.

Sears, Clare. "Introduction: Sexuality, Criminalization, and Social Control." *Social Justice* 37, no. 1 (2010–11): 1–6.

Schneider, Beth E., and Nancy E. Stoller, editors. *Women Resisting AIDS: Strategies of Empowerment*. Philadelphia: Temple University Press, 1995.

Sheehy, Gail. "Wide Open City/Part I: The New Breed." *New York Magazine*, July 1974.

Sides, Josh. *Erotic City: Sexual Revolutions and the Making of Modern San Francisco*. New York: Oxford University Press, 2009.

Stoller, Nancy E. *Lessons from the Damned: Queers, Whores, and Junkies Respond to AIDS*. New York: Routledge, 1998.

Taormino, Tristan, Celine Parreñas Shimizu, Constance Penley, and Mireille Miller-Young, editors. *The Feminist Porn Book: The Politics of Producing Pleasure*. New York: Feminist Press at the City University of New York, 2013.

Tiefer, Leonore. *Sex Is Not a Natural Act and Other Essays*. Boulder, CO: Westview Press, 1995.

Treichler, Paula, and Catherine Warren. "Maybe Next Year: Feminist Silence and the AIDS Epidemic." In Roth and Hogan, *Gendered Epidemic*.

Treichler, Paula A., Lisa Cartwright, and Constance Penley. *The Visible Woman: Imaging Technologies, Gender, and Science*. New York: New York University Press, 1998.

US Attorney General's Commission on Pornography: Final Report. Washington, DC: US Department of Justice, 1986.

Ward, Jane. *Respectably Queer: Diversity Culture in LGBT Activist Organizations*. Nashville, TN: Vanderbilt University Press, 2008.

Watney, Simon. *Policing Desire: Pornography, AIDS and the Media*. New York: Continuum International, 1997.

Weeks, Jeffrey. *Sexuality and Its Discontents: Meanings, Myths & Modern Sexualities*. Boston: Routledge, 1985.

Weitzer, Ronald. "Prostitutes' Rights in the United States: The Failure of a Movement." *Sociological Quarterly* 32, no. 1 (Spring 1991): 23–41.

White, Evelyn C., editor. *Black Women's Health Book: Speaking for Ourselves*. Seattle: Seal Press, 1990.

Wofsy, Constance B., et al. "Isolation of AIDS-Associated Retrovirus from Genital Secretions of Women with Antibodies to the Virus." *Lancet* 327, no. 8480 (1986).

Wuornos, Aileen. *Dear Dawn: Aileen Wuornos in Her Own Words*. Lisa Kester and Daphne Gottlieb, editors. Berkeley, CA: Soft Skull Press, 2012.

Young Women's Empowerment Project. *Denied Help! How Youth in the Sex Trade and Street Economy Are Turned Away from Systems Meant to Help Us*. Chicago: YWEP, July 2012.

———. *Girls Do What They Have to Do to Survive*. Chicago: YWEP, 2009.

INDEX

ACE (AIDS Counseling and Education), 93

ACE (Association of Club Executives), 129

ACLU, 61, 62, 63, 70, 129, 180

ACT UP (AIDS Coalition to Unleash Power), 15, 87, 99

Adorable, Lori, 194

Adult Industry Medical clinic, 98

Adult Video Association (AVN), 125

African Americans: in activist organizations, 19, 23, 184, 208; disproportionate arresting of in New Orleans, 180–81; evidence of AIDS among, 92; HIV education aimed at, 112; prejudices against in society and the courts, 160–61; stigmatizing of black women, 99–100. *See also* women of color

ageist sex discrimination, 139–40

AIDS Coalition to Unleash Power (ACT UP), 15, 87, 99

AIDS Counseling and Education (ACE), 93

AIDS crisis: activists' partnerships with public health officials, 112–13, 114; assumption that an infected woman is a prostitute, 84, 86, 103; CDC's focus on frequency of exposure, 89; CDC's labeling of the disease, 92–93; congressional-level disagreements about survey methodologies, 90; COYOTE's response to AIDS among sex workers, 86–87, 101–2; cultural interventions used as tools against, 115; current public health policy, 116; current state of knowledge about AIDS and HIV, 91; employment discrimination fight, 97–98; federal governments' moral basis for prevention advice, 101, 116; feminist efforts to create a women's health care industry, 109–10; feminist research project on disease transmission, 102–3; fight

to include women as victims of the disease, 99–100; health consequences of the identity framing of the virus, 110; human rights principles invoked regarding, 14–15, 16–17, 114; impact of connecting HIV/AIDS with promiscuity, 94–95; intravenous drug use and, 85, 103; introduction of identity politics into scientific discourse, 90–91, 92–93; legislation criminalizing HIV status and AIDS transmission, 101, 103, 106–9; marginalization of sex workers by white gay male activists, 87; marginalization of women and minorities in sex and medical research, 83–84, 109; occupational and class biases against condom use, 96; officials' focus on risk groups rather than high-risk behaviors, 85, 86, 89; officials' response to the public sex panic, 15, 96–97; persistence of myths about modes of transmission, 92, 103; political climate in the 1980s, 87, 100–101; "Prostitute Study" and, 83, 85; prostitutes' willingness to practice safe sex, 95–96; science's slow response to understanding the disease, 84–85, 89, 103; shift in activists' focus to harm reduction, 112–13; start of the St. James Infirmary, 113–14; state governments' responses to, 98–99; state of the disease in early 1990s, 115

Akers, Naomi, 114

Alexander, Priscilla, 59, 60, 98, 101, 102, 110, 113, 192

Alinsky, Saul, 58

Alligood, Clarence, 159

Almodovar, Norma Jean, 72, 188

American Bar Association, 71

American Law Institute, 72

American Massage Parlor (Ann Arbor, Michigan), 141

Child Protection and Safety Act (2006),
128
Ching, Tamara, 9
Christian Right, 82, 104–5
Christman, Fran, 35
civil rights: "deviant" label invoked to
deny, 54–56; exclusion of sex workers
from the LGBT rights movement, 9,
10–11; framing of anti-prostitution
laws as unconstitutional, 63–65, 69;
labeling of HIV as a status offense
and, 101, 103; link between sex-gender
conformity and a moral right to civil
rights, 11; marginalization of sex workers by white gay male activists, 87;
political power of gay rights activists,
72–73; protests by various groups, 69;
stigmatizing of black women and,
99–100. See also human rights and
harm reduction
Clay, Cyndee, 154, 201
CLC (California Labor Commission),
146, 147
Clear Channel, 204
Cleary, Vea, 179
Clinton, Bill, 115
Cloward, Richard, 69
Coalition Against Trafficking in Women
(CATW), 194
Coalition of Labor Union Women, 23
Cobble, Dorothy Sue, 139
Cockerline, Danny, 15
Cockettes, 81
Cohen, Judith, 102
COINTELPRO (Counter-Intelligence
Program, FBI), 77
Collins, Toni, 173
Combahee River Collective, 24
Combs, Ryhannah, 174
Comfort, Alex, 44
commercial sex industry: changes due to
technology and distribution means,
123–25; corporate investment in,
128–29; court fights against zoning
and merchandising regulations,
129–30; customer relations skills re-
quired, 134–35; diversity of businesses,
122–24; diversity of performances
within transactional relationships,

135–37; entrepreneurial opportunities,
126–27; entry onto the web, 125–27;
factors impacting the growth in the
1980s and 1990s, 119–20, 122; federal
legislation limiting online activity,
127–28; game theory's applicability to
transactions, 134–35; labor conditions
in, 131–32; market for sex-positive
films and alt porn, 125; nature of the
work and environment, 132–34; occupations and venues in, 122–23; profitability of, 128; question of commercial
sex as a capitalist enterprise, 41–42;
workers' advocacy (see organizing the
sex market); zoning laws used to close
businesses and benefit developers, 130
Commission on Obscenity and Pornography (1971), 30
Compton's Cafeteria, San Francisco, 8–9,
10
condoms: campaign against possession
arrests, 174–76, 204; endorsed as part
of a safe-sex strategy, 103; social biases
against use, 96, 97
Condor Club, 55
Conference on Prostitution (1971): debate
about sexual freedom during, 40–41;
disruptive presence of feminist prostitutes, 36; feminists' attitudes towards
prostitution, 34, 37–39; participating
organizations, 33–34; prostitutes'
refusal to be categorized as victims,
45–46; prostitutes' view of straight
feminists, 37, 38; results of outreach to
prostitutes, 34; sex workers' distrust
of decriminalization, 39–40; topics
discussed, 34–35
Conrad, Paula, 35
Conti, Sam, 146–47
Coppola, Francis Ford, 81
Cosmopolitan, 99
Counter-Intelligence Program, FBI
(COINTELPRO), 77
COYOTE (Call Off Your Old Tired Ethics): advocacy of decriminalization of
prostitution, 61–62, 64; approach to
organizing, 58–59; attempts to reframe
the debate on AIDS and sex workers, 101–2; campaign against selective